Listen to the Word

Commentaries on selected Opening Prayers of Sundays and Feasts with Sample Homilies

by Daniel McCarthy OSB

Project

APPRECIATING THE LITURGY

Project moderator

EPHREM CARR OSB

Project directors

JAMES G. LEACHMAN OSB
DANIEL P. MCCARTHY OSB

« DREI »

Publications

DOCUMENTA RERUM
ECCLESIASTICARUM INSTAURATA

VARIA

Endorsed by

THE PRESIDENT'S COUNCIL
THE PONTIFICAL INSTITUTE OF LITURGY
SANT'ANSELMO, ROME

Listen to the Word

Commentaries on Selected Opening Prayers
of Sundays and Feasts with Sample Homilies

Revised from articles that appeared in
The Tablet
18 March 2006 – 15 September 2007
augmented with five Homilies

by
Daniel P. McCarthy OSB

with two Homilies by
James G. Leachman OSB

Published by

The Tablet Publishing Company Limited
London

Nihil obstat
Fr Anton Cowan, Censor
Archdiocese of Westminster

Imprimatur
Rt Rev. Barnabas Senecal OSB, Abbot
St Benedict's Abbey, Atchison, Kansas

Rt Rev. Alan Hopes, VG,
Auxiliary Bishop of Westminster

Westminster, 6th January 2009, Solemnity of the Epiphany

The Nihil obstat *and* Imprimatur *are a declaration that a book or pamplet is considered
to be free from doctrinal or moral error. It is not implied that those who have granted
the* Nihil obstat *and* Imprimatur *agree with the contents,
opinions or statements expressed.*

Superiorum permissu
Rt Rev. Barnabas Senecal OSB, Abbot
St Benedict's Abbey, Atchison
Rt Rev. Martin Shipperlee OSB, Abbot
St Benedict's Abbey, Ealing

Cover photo
Aurelio e Francesca Amendola, in *La Cappella Redemptoris Mater*,
© Libreria Editrice Vaticana, Mosaic by Marco Ivan Rupnik SJ

Interior photos
Daniel P. McCarthy OSB

Acknowledgement
Excerpts from the English translation of the
Opening Prayers in *The Roman Missal* © 1973,
International Committee on English in the Liturgy, Inc. All rights reserved.

Published by The Tablet Publishing Company Limited
1 King Street Cloisters, Clifton Walk,
London, W6 0QZ, United Kingdom
E-mail: publisher@thetablet.co.uk

Publisher: Ignatius Kusiak
Designer: James Chasteauneuf

Printer: T J International Ltd,
Trecerus Industrial Estate, Padstow, Cornwall PL28 8R

R E G I N A L D O
E R U D I T O R I
G R A T I A R U M
I L L I C A U S A
N U T R I T O R I
A G E N D A R U M
L A T I N O R U M
D E D I C A T A E
O R A T I O N E S

Monumental stones of the ambo in the basilica of Santa Sabina, Rome.

The difference between a lectern and an ambo is that a lectern is but a book-holder while an ambo is the garden of the empty tomb from which the Angel proclaimed the good news of the resurrection to the myrrh bearing women and then sent them out to tell the good news to the disciples (Matthew 28:1-10). Every proclamation of the good news of Jesus Christ may be interpreted in light of this command of the angel from the empty tomb. Accordingly, the photos internal to this volume are from the marble balustrade that forms the garden with its monument to the empty tomb from which the Gospel is still proclaimed in the fourth-century basilica of Santa Sabina on the Aventine, Rome.

An Icon of the Empty Tomb. The divine-human exchange is presented as an icon of the empty tomb. The outer circle evokes the perfection of God without beginning or end. The square inscribed within and proportionate to the circle evokes humanity formed in the image and likeness of God yet broken and delineated. From the outer circle in four places there is a flux, composed of two entwined strands, that passes through the square into its centre. This flux first evokes the incarnation whereby the eternally begotten Word assumed our mortal humanity in Christ, fully human, fully divine. The incarnation elicits our divinization, our coming to share in the divine life, which is evoked then by the flux passing to encircle the eight-pointed star in the centre. Sunday is not only the first day of creation and thus of history, but also the day after the seven days of the week and of history, thus, the eighth day when Christ arose unto eternal life, as expressed by the eight-pointed star. Our sharing in the divine life, then, is both healing and prompts us to mission. This is evoked by the four fleur-de-lis patterns that point to the four broken angles of the square, indicating that divinisation heals our brokenness and sends us out to proclaim the divine-human exchange to the four corners of the world. This monumental stone is set under the loggia from which the Gospel is proclaimed.

Contents

Feast of the Lord in Ordinary Time

Appendix

John Flack

Preface

My first encounter with Daniel McCarthy was through his regular articles in *The Tablet*. "Listen to the Word" - a series of weekly articles on the Latin version of the Sunday collects - became mandatory reading as soon as *The Tablet* was delivered to my door. As the series came to an end with the liturgical year, I began to realise how much I would miss Daniel's wisdom and erudition. But I need not have worried, because the work on the collects was followed by a second series on the prayers over the gifts and now a series on the prayers after communion.

Here at last is a liturgist who is also a Latinist and who understands how language communicates. Daniel McCarthy shows us that translation is not just a matter of finding the equivalent English words, but of listening to the syntax, the grammar and the rhythm of the prayers. The prayers are written to be spoken aloud in the Eucharistic assembly, and they have to gather up the prayers of the assembly into a form which enables worshippers to participate with understanding. Latin can do this if we understand its layers of meaning which take us to greater depths. This becomes obvious as you read Daniel McCarthy's commentaries. You will find many places in these articles where he writes a whole paragraph in English to unpack one Latin word!

Some may question the need for this collection of articles because they feel that Latin belongs to the past. Others might think that this book is part of a campaign to re-introduce Latin liturgy at parish level. Neither is true. This scholarly study of public prayers is to help us all appreciate the liturgy, to know where we have come from and to where we are going as worshipping Christians. In the western Church the Latin language was the sole vehicle for the transmission of Christian doctrine and worship for well over a thousand years. It is time to study and evaluate what that great tradition can give us today. Those whose task it is to lead and shape the church's liturgical renewal today will find this study invaluable.

I write as an Anglican Bishop. I find myself required to preach a homily on most Sundays in the year. For the last two years I have returned time and again to Daniel McCarthy's scholarship, piercing the mystery of Christ in word and sacrament and learning how to communicate to others the treasures I have found for myself. Readers can see for themselves how this can be achieved by turning to the sample homilies at the end of this collection.

Daniel McCarthy is steeped in the Benedictine tradition of monasticism. In that tradition, the vow of *conversatio morum* is the commitment to continual and never-ending transformation. It is my prayer that all who study this collection of articles will know themselves to be moving forward on that path of transformation.

+ *Right Reverend John Flack*

Director of the Anglican Centre in Rome 2003 - 2008
Assistant Bishop of Peterborough from 2008   ☐

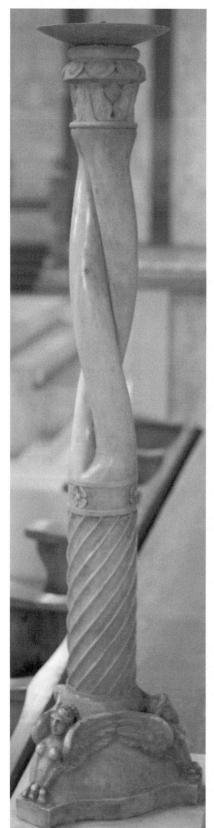

Icon of the Easter Proclamation.

The *Exsultet* is proclaimed from the loggia of the empty tomb to the Easter Candle standing in this candle holder, which narrates in stone the history of salvation proclaimed in song. The candle holder is read from the bottom to the top.

Christ the light of the world in his glorious incarnation, fully human, fully divine (double helix), in his death and resurrection (acanthus leaf), in his self-offering (bowl).

By the waters of the red sea (spiral) God delivers Israel and brings her to the promised land flowing with milk and honey (flower on band). From this people God raises Christ the messiah, fully divine, fully human (double helix).

The narration begins as God delivers Israel from slavery in Egypt, the land of abundance.

Alan Griffiths

Foreword

The prayers of the Roman Mass are one of the great spiritual resources of the Catholic Church. During Mass the celebrant prays three short prayers known as the collect, prayer over the offerings and prayer after communion. These prayers envision the Eucharistic act as coloured by the feasts and seasons of the Church's year. The Roman Missal contains over 1500 of them.

The prayers tell us what the Church thinks it is doing as it approaches the altar to offer the sacrifice of the Mass. They speak of how that liturgical act will express itself in the lives of those who participate in it and encourage them on their pilgrimage to the Kingdom of God. They approach the divine presence with due modesty, but also with a boldness formed by the sure persuasion that God is always in charge, that God's creative energy is ever fresh, that the Lord will never abandon those he has called to his service.

These texts represent the creative genius of the Roman Church over many centuries. The oldest of them go back to the Fathers, the most recent echo the teachings and texts of the Second Vatican Council. Some show great similarities with the writings of known authors such as popes Leo the Great and Gregory the Great.

In their Latin form, they represent a flowering of Latin speech which took place long after the classical period had ended. As pieces of literature they have been neglected by Latinists, a pity, because the best of them possess an elegance and an economy that makes them highly memorable.

Over the last four years, Father Daniel McCarthy OSB has interpreted these prayers for readers in *The Tablet*. He has done this against the background of a revived interest in translating these texts, an interest which will soon bear fruit in a new English version of the Roman Missal.

Fr Daniel draws on recent scholarly work which has provided a means of interpreting these texts. In each case he offers a brief explanation of the sources and background of the prayer and a phrase by phrase exposition of the sense. He shows how the syntax and structure of the text is as important in determining its meaning as is the sense of the words themselves. He relates all this skilfully to the teaching of Scripture, and demonstrates how these prayers represent, in different mode, the same spirit which inspires the Psalms and other scriptural prayers.

In comparing this interpretation with the existing translations, Fr Daniel demonstrates how the English prayers we use at present offer only a limited taste of the rich Latin prayer tradition, both in meaning and form. It is to be hoped that the new English version will represent a much closer approach to both.

Grateful thanks are due both to Fr Daniel himself and to the editors of *The Tablet*. This collection will benefit not only bishops responsible for translating the liturgy and their scholarly collaborators, but also those who teach, study and reflect upon the liturgy; that is anyone who understands that intelligent liturgical participation is the foundation for solid Catholic spirituality.

Alan Griffiths
December 29th 2008
□

Valuing the Opening Prayer

A choice fruit of the liturgical renewal mandated by the Second Vatican Council was the restoration and enlargement of the liturgy of the Word to provide a richer fare at the table of the Word and to promote the active participation of the assembly. It is easy to forget that before the Council there were only two readings: the epistle and the Gospel. Not only was a reading added to the Roman liturgy, but other elements of the liturgy of the Word were restored to their ancient practice, while yet others were further developed: the entrance rites were reorganized, the responsorial psalm was restored, the selection of readings was expanded to a two and three year cycle, the homily promoted, the prayers of the faithful reintegrated, the use of the vernacular was expanded and the minister turned toward the assembly.

As a result, today, we hear the word of God in our own language and respond in prayer and lives of service motivated by the Word that has entered our hearts, taken root and produces abundant fruit.

One development of the liturgy of the word, however, has received little notice, although the scholarship behind it is as solid as its tradition is broad and profound: the opening prayer. Often called the 'collect', the opening prayer concludes the introductory rites of the Mass, and comes right before the first reading.

In all the attention given to the renewed liturgy of the word, I believe the opening prayer largely has been overlooked, because, however brief, these prayers are synthetic, complex and demand the time and attention that their effective proclamation requires.

The opening prayer beguiles with brevity and apparent simplicity, and we too easily shy away from the rewarding harvest of encountering them in their mature abundance and gleaning the fruit in their proclamation.

The prayer of the assembly furthermore requires a gentle unfolding of these prayers so that *in the hearing* the assembly can make the prayer its own. A simple example suffices to drive this point home. The length of an average opening prayer is merely four short lines. It can be recited in about 10 seconds, but if we want the assembly to join in the prayer itself, then more time and attention must be given to its effective proclamation. I have found that understanding the literary structure of the prayer is helpful, because part of the task of proclamation is to unfold the prayer according to its literary structure, in such a way that the assembly can make the prayer its own in the hearing.

I invite you to reflect with me on the literary structure of the opening prayer, a structure well honed over more than 1,400 years of our written prayer tradition. By appreciating the structure of these prayers, we can begin to unfold their complexity, appreciate their synthesis and prepare ourselves to make the prayer our own in the hearing. So I invite you to join with me as we meditate together on the opening prayer of the Mass.

Writing these commentaries on the opening prayers has provided a journey of prayer and reflection. As I wrote the commentaries, my writing style and depth of reflection upon the opening prayer genre matured. For the purposes of this little collection of prayer commentaries, I have significantly revised the articles and invite

the reader to journey with me as we both develop in understanding and sharing in these prayers of the church.

The methods employed in writing these commentaries are a combination of several sources. To Reginald Foster, to whom this book is gratefully dedicated, I owe my understanding of the Latin Language. To Renato De Zan, professor of liturgy at the Pontifical Institute of Liturgy, I owe my understanding of the hermeneutics of the opening prayer. I offer the gratitude of friendship to Dom James Leachman, who initially prompted me to inquire into writing this column in *The Talbet*, and then coaxed out some of my deeper sentiments expressed in the commentaries. To Catherine Pepinster, Editor, and the staff of *The Tablet*, I owe the debt of gratitude for fostering this column. To long time friends Owen Purcell, Peggy Stanton and Robert Aaron, and to a new colleague, John Stapleton, I am grateful for their inspiration and help in developing my writing style. To the participants in a course on intensive Latin held 4-8 September, 2006, at the Benedictine Study and Arts Centre, Ealing, London, I am grateful for our shared discoveries in the theology of these prayers, which enriched my writing thereafter. Finally, I owe the debt of gratitude to the copy editor James Chasteauneuf, whose patient diligence brought this book to its mature form, to Ignatius Kusiak, publisher of *The Tablet*, whose zeal brought this volume to ready publication, and to The Tablet Trust, who made this volume possible. For the support and freedom to pursue this research, I am grateful to St Benedict's Abbey.

Daniel McCarthy OSB
Epiphany 2009   □

Illustrations

Front cover:

Our sharing in divine life on the day of Pentecost.

Mary, image of the church at prayer, stands in honour of the resurrection with her hands raised in prayer, as the Spirit descends upon the church. Mosaic by M.I. Rupnik SJ is located in the *Redemptoris mater* chapel of the Apostolic palace, Vatican City.

Internal photos:

Monumental stones of the ambo in the basilica of Santa Sabina, Rome.

The rest of the monumental stones pictured within this volume are parts of the balustrade that form the garden. Through the garden motif the lapidary has created images that are fundamentally ecclesiological, expressing the unity of Christians.

xiii: The pillars of the earth and the vault of heaven, the sun and moon frame this life giving tree, the cross of Christ. Its braided strands express both the triune life and the union of divinity and humanity in Christ. This life, this union gives life to all living creatures. When one cross appears alone, it refers to the cross of Christ. When numerous crosses appear together, they refer to those signed with the cross of Christ.

119: This geometric interlocking of elements seems to form individual circles, which are really parts of one another. This is a fuller image of that pictured in detail on page 120.

120: This is a detail of the image pictured on page 119.

128: Top and Bottom: This is a variant on the vine and branches motif presented more clearly on page 134. Here each tendril of the vine encircles a cross in the form of a light-giving star. These crosses are in motion, rotating, and life-giving. Above is a detail of the fuller image below.

132: The leaves and the birds in the trees decorate the panels of this monumental stone evoking the image of the mustard seed that grows into a mighty bush where the birds of the heavens make their homes (Matthew 13:31-32). From this parable we get not only the image of mustard-seed faith, but of the church as a vibrant bush welcoming all types of birds in its branches. Above is a detail of a bird eating from a fruit in the garden. The detail is taken from the top left pannel of the larger stone pictured below.

134: Jesus is the vine and we are the branches drawing life from a common source (John 15:5). Multiple crosses here indicate those who are signed with the cross of Christ: Christians. The cross is life giving because it comes from the vine.

138: A geometric abstraction of the crosses and circles that make up Christian community, the Church.

Literary genre of an opening prayer

To help the reader understand the grammatical structure of many of these prayers, I include the following chart developed from the course on the hermeneutics of euchological texts taught by Renato De Zan at the Pontifical Institute of Liturgy, Sant'Anselmo, Rome.

In the course of writing these prayers, I have also come to include participial phrases within the purpose clause as motive clauses, and I have termed the adjective *propitius*, used as an adverb, as a type of one word motive clause.

Type of clause:	Latin grammatical construction.
Invocation:	simple: one noun. complex: a noun and one or more adjectives.
Amplification:	a noun or noun and adjectives placed in apposition. a relative clause.
Petition:	imperative. exhortative subjunctive.
Purpose:	*ut* + subjunctive (classical). *ad* + gerund (or: infinitive, less classical). *ad* + gerundive.
Motive:	*quia* + subjunctive (classical). relative clause in purpose clause. Participial phrase in purpose clause.

Premise:
(especially in
Prayers after
Communion)
	ablative absolute.
	    (ex. *sumptis divinis mysteries*,
	    which is translated temporally:
	    "after the divine mysteries have been taken up".)

The Performative Stages of an Opening Prayer

It is to be noted that the collect has four parts:

1. Invitation to pray: *Oremus*, "Let us pray",

2. Silent prayer of the community,

3. The opening prayer or collect given by the presider, which the rest of the assembly makes their own in the hearing,

4. And the ratification of the assembly's "Amen".

Between two comings

In our prayer for the first Sunday of Advent we prepare to welcome Christ. Bringing our good works to him as he approaches, we think not only of his birth, but also of being called to his side when he returns

---

the opening prayer
1st Sunday of Advent

All-powerful God, increase our strength of will for doing good that Christ may find an eager welcome at his coming and call us to his side in the kingdom of heaven. (*The Roman Missal*, Collins, London, 1974)	Da, quaesumus, omnipotens Deus, hanc tuis fidelibus voluntatem, ut, Christo tuo venienti iustis operibus occurrentes, eius dexterae sociati, regnum mereantur possidere caeleste. (*Missale Romanum*, Città del Vaticano, 2002)

The opening prayers for the four Sundays of Advent replace those given in the 1962 *Missale*, giving insight into the mind of the liturgical renewal.

Source. The current prayer replaces one now assigned to Friday of the first week of Advent, which includes the following purpose clause: "that, as you are protecting, we may be worthy to be snatched from the imminent perils of our sins; as you are liberating, to be saved". Its focus on our impending demise has been replaced with an ancient prayer found both in the Gelasian (628-715, Rome) and Gallican (seventh century, Gaul) Sacramentaries, and their eighth-century adaptations, when the Latin was corrected and made more classical and its theology renewed.

Analysis of the literary form

Petition: The prayer begins with the imperative petition *Da, quaesumus ... hanc tuis fidelibus voluntatem*, "Grant, we ask, this intention to your faithful", which is omitted in translation. The meaning of *voluntatem* ("free will, desire, inclination") is perhaps best gleaned from the Lord's Prayer where we pray *fiat voluntas tua*, "may your will be done". The current text

clarifies the ancient manuscripts by substituting *tuis fidelibus*, "to your faithful", for the ambiguous *cunctae familiae tuae*, which can mean "[give] to your whole family" or "[grant the desire] of your whole family".

Invocation: Preserving the original text *omnipotens Deus*, the complex invocation is translated literally as "All-powerful God".

Purpose: The meaning of *hanc voluntatem*, "this will", is explained in the purpose clause constructed classically by *ut*, "that", followed by the subjunctive *mereantur*, "they may be worthy": *ut ... regnum mereantur possidere caeleste*, "that they may be worthy to take possession of the heavenly reign", from which comes the English "in the kingdom of heaven".

The Gallican Sacramentary spelled correctly *caeleste*, "heavenly", modifying the neuter noun *regnum*, "reign", but the Roman Gelasian introduced the misspelling *caelesti*, which was widely diffused in its eighth-century adaptations. The Gallican also correctly used the word *ut*, "in order that", to establish the purpose clause calling for the subjunctive verb *mereantur*, "they may merit"; in its place the Roman Gelasian had *et*, "and", which error continued in many of the eighth-century manuscripts. Furthermore, while the plural verb *mereantur*, "may they be worthy", is maintained from the original, in the modern text it refers to the plural noun *fidelibus*, "to the faithful", improving the ancient manuscripts, which used the singular *familiae*, "to/of the family".

First motive: God is supplied two motives for granting that the faithful be made worthy to possess heaven, both given as prepositional phrases within the purpose clause. First, *Christo tuo venienti iustis operibus occurrentes* means "[they] running with good works to meet your Christ, the one coming", is rendered by the imperative petition, "increase our strength of will for doing good", and the first of two purpose clauses, "that Christ may find an eager welcome at his coming".

In the ancient texts this clause is placed outside the purpose clause as an object sentence describing the will of the family. The Gelasian text reads: *in Christo filio tuo domino nostro uenienti in operibus iustis aptos occurrere*, "[that] in just works they may appear worthy in Christ, your son, our coming lord". The phrase is structured as an accusative *nos*, "we", implied in *aptos*, "worthy", followed by the infinitive *occurrere*, "to run up to, to meet", or in a transferred sense, "to appear", which substitutes for the subjunctive *occurrant*, "they may appear". The Gallican introduces the misspelling *aptus*. By drawing the phrase into the purpose clause, the prayer gets more densely interrelated.

The modern text uses *occurrentes* according to its root meaning, "people running to meet"; its dative object *Christo tuo venienti*, "your Christ, the one coming", replaces the weaker prepositional phrase *in Christo* ... "in Christ ...". The current text uses the ablative of instrument *iustis operibus*,

to say that we are running "by just works", replacing the weaker prepositional phrase *in iustis operibus*, "in just works". In the current text *venienti* is correctly used as a dative contemporaneous participle, "to the one coming", whereas the ancient texts include a scribal error that makes *veniente* the ablative participle, meaning "[in] the one coming".

Second motive: Constant in all texts, the second motive for God's saving action is the anterior participial phrase *eius dexterae sociati*, "[they] having been joined to the right of him", which is translated by a second purpose clause, "and [that Christ may] call us to his side".

Summary. The improved theology, I suggest, is due to the times of the verbal elements. The independent verb is the imperative petition *da*, "grant!, give!". Relative to *da*, the subjunctive verb *mereantur*, "they may be worthy", is incomplete, unfinished, ongoing, eternal, future, contemporaneous. Thus, we ask that God grant that we may be worthy not only now, even if incompletely so, but also at the end of time and eternally. An allusion to the two comings of Christ is expressed by one antecedent and two contemporaneous participles. The two participles *occurrentes*, "[the faithful] running to meet", and *venienti*, "to the one coming", are contemporaneous with one another. The action of the antecedent participle *sociati*, "[the faithful] having been joined", would seem to precedes that of *mereantur*; but must be understood here as a future perfect meaning "once the faithful will have been joined". Thus the sequence of our prayer is that we are running out to meet Christ the one coming, then once we have been joined to his side, we may merit to possess the heavenly reign. Yet we are in Christ by baptism and so enjoy the reward along the way to its fullness, as we live between the two comings of Christ. ∎

From **earth** and from **heaven**

On the Second Sunday of Advent, we ask for the wisdom of Christ, so that we may be reborn in baptism, and take on his divine nature as he became a human being like us

The voice of John the Baptist, foretold by Isaiah (40:3), crying out: "Prepare the way of the Lord", resounds perennially in this Sunday's gospel (Matthew 3:1-12, Mark 1:1-8, Luke 3:1-6). In the 1962 *Missale* the opening prayer this Sunday echoed his voice: "Rouse up, O Lord, our hearts unto preparing the ways of your only-begotten", but was followed by a different Gospel (Matthew 11:2-10). After the Second Vatican Council the Gospel is the Baptist's call, but its corresponding prayer has been transferred to the following Thursday. The new prayer does not echo the Baptist's voice, but resists any histori-cising tendency, for, while founded in history, the liturgy does not celebrate the Nativity primarily as the anniversary of a historical event, but through the rites and prayers of the liturgy the mystery of the incar-nation ever encounters us anew. Thus, the opening prayer this Sunday is the Church's response to God's ever present self-gift.

Source. Both prayers first appeared among those assigned to Advent in the Gelasian Sacramentary, composed between 627 and 715 for use in the presbyteral liturgy in the titular churches of Rome, but, whereas the 1962 prayer was included in the Hadrianum, the papal Sacramentary given by Hadrian I to Charlemagne in 785-786, and thus pre-served and widely diffused, the current prayer was not so included, not even in its supplement, and thus fell into disuse until after the Second Vatican Council, when the lectionary and daily proper prayers were developed.

Analysis of the literary form
Invocation: The prayer begins with the complex invocation *Omnipotens et*

> ### *the opening prayer*
> ### 2nd Sunday of Advent
> God of power and mercy, open our hearts in welcome. Remove the things that hinder us from receiving Christ with joy, so that we may share his wisdom and become one with him when he comes in glory.
> (*The Roman Missal*, Collins, London, 1974)
>
> Omnipotens et misericors Deus, in tui occursum Filii festinantes nulla opera terreni actus impediant, sed sapientiae caelestis eruditio nos faciat eius esse consortes.
> (*Missale Romanum*, Città del Vaticano, 2002)

misericors Deus, "All-powerful and tender-hearted God", translated as, "God of power and mercy".

Motive: Preceding the first petition, its object, the contemporaneous participle *festinantes*, supplies God's motive for acting on our behalf, *in tui occursum Filii festinantes*, "people hastening towards meeting your Son", which informs two English phrases, "from receiving Christ with joy", and "when he comes in glory". While *occursum*, "meeting, a falling-in with", takes the genitive *tui Filii*, "of your Son", God's Son comes to encounter us, hence we hasten "towards the meeting of your Son".

The current prayer rephrases its ancient source, which began: *Festinantes, omnipotens Deus, in occursum Filii tui domini nostri*, "People hastening, all-powerful God, towards meeting your Son our Lord". The first word in the ancient text, *festinantes*, "ones hastening", emphasises our response, whereas its current reworking places the invocation of God first in an expanded invocation, then states our goal as meeting God's Son, postponing the reference to our hastening, *festinantes*, but upon which the preceding prepositional phrase *in tui occursum*, "unto meeting your Son", depends grammatically. Thus reworked, the prayer emphasises that God is origin (*omnipotens*), enabling (*misericors*) and goal (*in occursum*), to which the prayer subordinates our cooperation (*festinantes*) necessary to attain the goal. The current word order of this phrase is found in two ancient sacramentaries and in the Rotulus of Ravenna, a fifth- to sixth-century compilation of prayers.

First petition: The above motive clause is the object of the first petition expressed as an exhortative subjunctive, *nulla opera terreni actus impediant*, "may no works of earthly activity impede [people hastening]", which is rendered by the imperative petition, "remove the things that hinder us". An extra imperative petition is added to the English: "open our hearts in welcome".

Second petition: The second exhortative petition, *sed sapientiae caelestis eruditio… faciat*, "but may the instruction of heavenly wisdom make … ", is rendered as, "so that we may share his wisdom". *Eruditio* refers to the learning we have obtained by the Son's instruction.

The current prayer reworks the word order of its ancient source, which included the phrase *opera actus terrini, sed caelestis sapienciae erudicio*; the three misspellings have been corrected (*terreni, sapientiae, eruditio*). Moreover, there is a *chiasmus* or inverted correlation of *opera* (work) with *erudicio* (instruction), *actus* (of activity) with *sapienciae* (of wisdom)

and *terrini* (of terrestrial) with *caelestis* (of heavenly). The reworking maintains the *chiasm*, but, by placing *terreni* (of earthly) and *caelestis* (of heavenly) in the middle of their respective phrases, they become its hinge-pins.

Result: What we want the instruction of heavenly wisdom to bring about is expressed by an object sentence composed of the accusative *nos*, "us" and the infinitive *esse*, "to be", which substitutes for the result clause *ut… simus*, "that … we are": *nos [faciat] eius esse consortes*, "[make] us to be partners of the Son (wisdom)", which is rendered, "and become one with him when he comes in glory". Relative to *faciat*, "may it bring about", our being made partners (*ut simus consortes*) is incomplete, unfinished, ongoing, eternal, future, contemporaneous. Thus by co-operating with divine initiative we become partners, now and later, however incompletely, definitively at the final meeting of God's Son and forever.

Summary. The hinge-pins *terreni* and *caelestis* are an allusion to 1 Corinthians: "The first man was from the earth, a man of dust [*terrenus*]; the second man is from heaven [*caelestis*]. As was the man of dust [*terrenus*], so are those who are of the dust [*terreni*]; and as is the man of heaven [*caelestis*], so are those who are of heaven [*caelestes*]. Just as we have borne the image of the man of dust [*terreni*], we will also bear the image of the man of heaven [*caelestis*] (15:47-49; NRSV, Vulgate). Thus were we born of Adam, who are reborn in baptism, and follow wisdom's instruction, who took on our earthly nature to join us to the divine: O, wondrous divine-human exchange.

The opening prayer concludes the entrance procession of Mass and, thus, our hastening to the encounter of God's wisdom proclaimed; our cooperation's fruition is our participation in the divine communion. ∎

Give us the grace for joy

As the prayers for the third and fourth Sundays of Advent and for Christmas Day show, our preparation to welcome the Incarnation of God requires the grace of the Word made flesh. This gift that allows us, at our Lord's Nativity, to express outwardly in joyful celebration what has already been received inwardly

"Rejoice [*Gaudete*] in the Lord always, again I say, rejoice [*gaudete*]. Indeed, the Lord is near" (Entrance Antiphon; cf. Philippians 4:4 ff.). Before the Second Vatican Council, that reading and antiphon corresponded to this Sunday's relaxation of ascetical practices, for Advent was a penitential season parallel to Lent. Since the Council, the whole season is now characterised by expectant hope, anticipated rejoicing.

Source. Faced with the task of developing proper prayers for every day of Advent, those responsible for the renewal of the liturgical books after the Second Vatican Council turned to the fruit of scholarly research on the ancient sources of the Roman liturgy and found in the *Rotulus* of Ravenna, a fifth- to sixth-century compilation of prayers for the Advent/Christmas cycle, a source for at least 12 prayers for Advent and one for Christmas. Of these, only the present one was assigned to a Sunday until the revision of the *Missale* in 2002, when two more prayers from the *Rotulus* were added to the Christmas cycle. The Ambrosian Missal was similarly renewed, borrowing from 23 prayers of the *Rotulus*, including the present one. Thus most of the *Rotulus*, long forgotten until its publication in 1883, is now incorporated into the Church's prayer.

Analysis of the literary form

Invocation: The simple invocation *Deus*, "God", is rendered complex, "Lord God".

Amplification: The invocation is amplified by the relative clause, *qui conspicis*, "you who see", which is not translated.

---

the opening prayer
3rd Sunday in Advent

Lord God, may we, your people, who look forward to the birthday of Christ, experience the joy of salvation and celebrate that feast with love and thanksgiving.
(*The Roman Missal*,
Collins, London, 1974)

Deus, qui conspicis populum tuum nativitatis dominicae festivitatem fideliter exspectare, praesta, quaesumus, ut valeamus ad tantae salutis gaudia pervenire, et ea votis sollemnibus alacri semper laetitia celebrare.
(*Missale Romanum*,
Città del Vaticano, 2002)

Premise: What God sees is expressed by the entire sentence with the accusative subject *populum tuum*, "your people", and the infinitive verb *exspectare*, "to look out for", gives the premise presmued by the prayer, *popu-lum tuum nativitatis dominicae festivi-tatem fideliter exspectare*, "that your people faithfully longs for the feast of the Lord's nativity", rendered as a subjunctive petition: "may we, your people, who look forward to the birthday of Christ".

The liturgy, more than a birthday party, is the mystery of the Incarnation (*incarnationis*) encountering us, in our expectation (*exspectant*) of its transformative power. The current phrase *nativitatis dominicae festivitatem*, "the feast of the Lord's Nativity", is an elaboration of the original prayer, which had only *incarnationem dominicam*, "the Lord's Incarnation". The same prayer is similarly adapted in the Ambrosian Sacramentary which says *natalis dominici festivitatem*, "the festival of the Lord's birth". By making the object of our hope not the birth of the Lord, a historical event, but the feast of the Nativity, the prayer centres on the divine-human exchange in its sacramental celebration.

Petitions: The imperative praesta, "grant, guarantee", is not translated. *Quaesumus* is expressed as, "we ask this", in the doxology.

First purpose: The core of the purpose clause is composed classically by *ut*, followed by the subjunctive *valeamus*. While one may argue that *ut valeamus* is a result clause meaning "[guarantee] that we are strong", translating it as a purpose clause subtly reinforces both God's gift and our cooperation "[grant] that we may be able to...". This core has two compliments, both contemporaneous infinitives. The first, *ad tantae salutis gaudia pervenire*, "[that we may be able] to attain to the inner joys of so great a salvation", is rendered as "may we ... experience the joy of salvation".

Second purpose: The second *et ea votis sollemnibus alacri semper laetitia celebrare*, "and [that we may be able] always to celebrate them by solemn prayers with eager rejoicing", is rendered as, "... and celebrate that feast with love and thanksgiving". A second adaptation made to the original text is the insertion of the word *ea*, "the joys", which makes the second purpose build logically upon the first, for first we arrive at inner joys, then we celebrate *ea*, "the joys" outwardly; in both cases God's gift of grace makes us able. In the Ambrosian Sacramentary, however, the word *eam* is inserted, which refers either to *festivitatem*, "the feast", or to *tantae salutis*, "of such great salvation".

To pray that we are able to come to the joys of such great salvation and then to celebrate the salvation, emphasises that our feast is more than an anniversary celebration of a birth long ago, but indeed a saving encounter with the mystery we celebrate.

Summary. The two purpose clauses contrast our attaining inner joys (*gaudia*) with our expressing them outwardly (*laetitia*) by celebrating. God's grace for which we pray makes us able to come to the joys and to celebrate them. This prayer does not suggest that we celebrate the feast in order to get the grace. Rather, we petition God to pour grace into our hearts in order that we may be able to come to the joys of salvation and then celebrate either the joys of salvation (Roman) or the salvation (Ambrosian) outwardly in the feast.

Our current prayer replaces one assigned to this Sunday in the 1962 *Missale*, which prayer was also included in both the Hadrianum and the Paduense, but is no longer found in the *Missale Romanum*. Its second half states: ... *et mentis nostrae tenebras, gratia tuae visitationis illustra*, "and illumine the darknesses of our mind/heart by the grace of your visitation". Here, human cooperation with the divine gift is limited to our yielding to divine visitation within the darkness of our very selves.

The current prayer, conversely, assigns a far greater role to human cooperation with divine gift, for by grace we are made able (*valeamus*) to act. Such action, moreover, by grace brings us to the inner joys of salvation itself; human cooperation with divine gift then leads us to express by outward actions and celebrations the inner joy of salvation encountered in this feast. □

---

the opening prayer
4th Sunday of Advent

Lord, fill our hearts with your love, and as you revealed to us by an angel the coming of your Son as man, so lead us through his suffering and death to the glory of his Resurrection. (*The Roman Missal*, Collins, London, 1974)	Gratiam tuam, quaesumus, Domine, mentibus nostris infunde, ut qui, Angelo nuntiante, Christi Filii tui incarnationem cognovimus, per passionem eius et crucem ad resurrectionis gloriam perducamur. (*Missale Romanum*, Città del Vaticano, 2002)

This prayer is familiar for its use in the *Angelus*, where it is traditionally translated: "Pour forth we beseech you, O Lord, your grace into our hearts..." Its history and theology, moreover, reveal much about the origins of Christmas.

Source. This prayer first appears in the Hadrianum, the papal sacramentary given by Pope Hadrian I to Charlemagne in 785-786, in which it served as a post-Communion prayer of a Mass formulary titled *VIII kalendas apriles id est XXV die mensis martii Adnuntiatio sanctae Mariae*, "The eighth day before the calends of April, that is the twenty-fifth day of the month of March, the Annunciation to Holy Mary". The prayer also appears in a later redaction of an earlier source, the Paduense, an adaptation of the papal sacramentary compiled around 670-680 for presbyteral use for pilgrims to St Peter's, in which it served as the opening prayer of a Mass formulary titled *VIII kalendas aprilis Adnuntiatio sanctae Dei genitricis et passio eiusdem Domini*, "The eighth day before the calends of April, the Annunciation of the holy mother of God and the Passion of the same Lord". The phrase *eiusdem Domini*, "of the same Lord", agrees with *Dei*, "of God", and refers to the Passion of our Lord, born of Mary. Using this prayer on the Sunday before Christmas warrants fuller explanation according to the currently most developed theory of Thomas Talley, who refutes

the attribution of Christmas as a Christianisation of the pagan feast of the unconquered sun (*sol invictus*).

The original Christian feast is Sunday, the Lord's day, on which we celebrate the entire mystery of salvation. By the end of the first century an annual celebration of the Passion was celebrated on 14 Nisan, the day in the Jewish lunar calendar on which Christ died according to John (but not Matthew, Mark and Luke). By the beginning of the second century the nascent Christian community could no longer look to the Jewish leaders to determine when to add an extra month to their lunar calendar to keep it synchronised with the solar calendar, so they decided to calculate back to the year of our Lord's Passion to reckon its exact date according to the solar calendar. In Rome they decided that this fell on 25 March, but in Asia Minor the same day was reckoned as 6 April, because their respective calendars were 12 days off.

Now, this annual feast celebrated in one day the whole mystery of the Lord's dying and rising, to which *passio* in the Paduense refers. Furthermore, the idea was then current that a holy person's birth was to be celebrated on the day of the person's death so that the life makes a unity. Thus the Incarnation was added to the celebration of the Passion. This accounts for the title in the Paduense, which unites the Annunciation to the Passion. As the mystery of the Incarnation was apportioned different feasts, the Annunciation remains to this very day on 25 March, and the Nativity was assigned to 25 December – nine months later. Similarly, nine months after 6 April is 6 January, the feast of the Epiphany, thus creating the 12 days of Christmas. As Easter has since been transferred to Sunday, so has the Epiphany (and most recently the Ascension, in some regions); of these, only the Annunciation and Christmas remain on fixed dates. Thus, the genius of offering the prayer of the Annunciation and Passion on the Sunday, the fundamental Christian feast, before the particular feast of the Nativity.

Analysis of the literary form

Petition: The prayer begins with the imperative petition, *Gratiam tuam, quaesumus ... mentibus nostris infunde*, "pour forth your grace, we ask, into our hearts", which is translated as, "fill our hearts with your love". *Mentibus* refers to the internal life and thus the mind, heart, conscience, intention.

Invocation: The simple invocation *Domine* is translated literally as "Lord".

Purpose: Constructed classically by *ut* followed by the subjunctive *perducamur*, the purpose for which we pray is *ut ... per passionem eius et crucem ad resurrectionis gloriam perducamur*, "that we may be led through his Passion and Cross unto the glory of the Resurrection", which is translated as, "so lead us through his suffering and death to the glory of his Resurrection".

Motive: God's motive for bringing us through is given classically by a relative clause nestled within the purpose clause, *qui ... Christi Filii tui incarnationem*

cognovimus, "we who have come to know the Incarnation of Christ your Son", which is translated by, "as you revealed to us ... the coming of your Son as man". The form *cognovimus* literally means, "we have come to know", thus, "we know".

Premise: An ablative absolute is nestled within the motive clause, *Angelo nuntiante*, "as the angel announces", which is translated as an ablative of instrument, "once through the message an angel". The participle *nuntiante* is contemporaneous with *cognovimus*, for, although the Angel's annunciation to Mary is set in history, its proclamation in the liturgy has ever brought us to understanding.

Summary. The prayer synthesises that early Christian feast which combined the Incarnation in its complex mystery of the Annunciation and Incarnation, with the Passion, in its complexity as Christ's Passover from this life to eternal glory. Indeed, as the Scriptures tell it, this child was born to die, as the swaddling clothes imitate the burial wrappings, the manger is an image of the sepulchre, the incense and myrrh foreshadow those used in burial. So, too, the opening prayer takes the angel's greeting to Mary in the Annunciation as the premise for our contemplation of the mystery of the Incarnation, which contemplation is God's motive for leading us through the Passion to glory. ☐

the opening prayer
Christmas: Mass during the day

Lord God, we praise you for creating man, and still more for restoring him in Christ. Your Son shared our weakness: may we share his glory.
(*The Roman Missal*, Collins, London, 1974)

Deus, qui humanae substantiae dignitatem et mirabiliter condidisti, et mirabilius reformasti, da, quaesumus, nobis eius divinitatis esse consortes, qui humanitatis nostrae fieri dignatus est particeps.
(*Missale Romanum*, Città del Vaticano, 2002)

Christmas has four Mass formularies, restoring the Gelasian pattern: a vigil Mass (restored after the Second Vatican Council); a Mass during the night (*Ad Missam in nocte*, translated as "Midnight Mass"); Mass at dawn; and Mass during the day. The theological heavyweight is the Mass during the day with its proclamation of the Prologue of the Gospel of John (1:1-18); the Church's response to the Prologue is given in the opening prayer, an eloquent model of the Church's *lectio divina*.

Source. The current prayer replaces one found in both the ancient presbyteral tradition (Gelasian, 628-715) and the papal tradition (Hadrianum, 785-786; *the* Sacramentary of Padua, 670-680). That prayer, now assigned to 30 December, includes the following purpose clause: *ut nos Unigeniti tui nova per carnem Nativitas liberet; quos sub peccati iugo vetusta servitus tenet*, "that the Nativity of your Only-begotten, singular in the flesh, may free us, whom age-old slavery holds bound under the yoke of sin". The word *tenet*, striking for its present tense, indicates that even after baptism "[slavery] holds [us] in its power".

The new prayer, by contrast, speaks of the dignity of human nature fashioned and restored by God. It is found in two versions; one with the more corrupt Latin appears in the Verona Sacramentary, a compilation of Mass booklets compiled between 600 and 625, and in several Ambrosian sources. The other one is found in both the Gelasian and Hadrianum as well as in other manuscripts.

Analysis of the literary form

Invocation: The simple invocation *Deus*, "God", is rendered complex as "Lord God". The single word expresses the divine simplicity, for "in the beginning was the Word, and the Word was with God, and the Word was God" (NRSV except where noted; John, 1:1), which is then developed according to creation and redemption, and the prayer ends with the Trinitarian, "for he lives and reigns with you and the Holy Spirit, one God, for ever and ever".

Amplification: The Latin text amplifies *Deus*, "God", with the relative phrase, *qui humanae substantiae dignitatem et mirabiliter condidisti, et mirabilius reformasti*, "you who both wonderfully fashioned and more wondrously restored the dignity of human nature". The English text subordinates God's creative and restorative power to our double praise of God, "we praise you for creating man, and still more for restoring him in Christ". Concerning creation, "all things came into being through him, and without him not one thing came into being" (John, 1:3); concerning redemption, "He will transform [*reformabit*] the body of our humiliation that it may be conformed to the body of his glory" (Vulgate, throughout; Philippians 3:21).

Petitions: The imperative petition *da*, "grant" is not expressed, but *quaesumus*, "we ask" is, in the doxology as, "we ask this".

Purpose: The purpose clause describes how we are restored. The imperative *da* has as its complement the dative *nobis*, "to us", and the infinitive *esse*, "to be": *eius divinitatis esse consortes*: "to us to be sharers of the divinity of him", which is rendered by the exhortative subjunctive petition, "may we share his glory". This late Latin construction forms a purpose clause which would be expressed classically by *ut*, "that", followed by the subjunctive *simus*, "we may be", as in *da, quaesumus, ut eius divinitatis simus consortes*: "grant, we ask, that we may be sharers of the divinity of him". *Consortes* refers to people sharing in a community of goods, as is in the early Christian community (cf. Acts 4:32), or partaking of something in common, as in Eucharistic Communion. *Consortes* is an allusion to 2 Peter 1:4, "that … you may become sharers of the divine nature [*ut … efficiamini divinae consortes naturae*]" (author's translation), and to John 1:12, "to all who received him, who believed in his name, he gave power to become children of God [*filios Dei fieri*]".

Motive: God's motive for bringing us to share in Christ's divinity is given as a relative clause nestled in the purpose clause. [*Q*]*ui humanitatis nostrae fieri dignatus est particeps*, ""who regarded it worthy to become a partaker of our humanity", is rendered by the indicative sentence, "Your Son shared our weakness". Because such self-emptying love is worthy of the divine communion, God gave us a share not merely of glory, but in God's self-emptying love itself.

Summary. The divine–human exchange,

whereby divinity becomes human that we may share in the divine, happens in Christ's very self, for in Christ is humanity wed to divinity. In terms of the canticle, Christ "emptied himself, taking the form of a slave, being born in human likeness" (NRSV; Philippians 2:7). This exchange happens, I suggest, not so much in successive moments, whereby God's self-emptying love is followed by our sharing in divine glory; rather, in Christ our humanity shares in the very act of God's self-emptying, and thus divine, love.

There is no better commentary on this feast than the Christmas sermon of Leo the Great given in the year 440, which I translate at length: "For the Son of God in the fullness of time, which the inscrutable depth of the divine plan established, took upon himself reconciling the nature of the human race to its own origin, such that the author of death, the devil, through the very nature by which he had prevailed, was vanquished … Acknowledge, O Christian, your dignity [*dignitatem*], and, having been made a sharer [*consors*] of the divine nature, don't return unto former baseness by unworthy conduct. Remember of whose head and of whose body you are a member. Be mindful that, having been snatched from the power of darkness, you have been brought into the light and reign of God. Through the Sacrament of baptism you have been made a temple of the Holy Spirit." ∎

The illustrations used in the preceding three articles (on this page, page 8 and page 6), are of roof bosses originally in Utrecht Cathedral. These three images are also reproduced in Netherlandish Sculpture, 1450-1550 by Paul Williamson (V&A Publications, £25).

In your house

The opening prayer for the feast of the Holy Family shows that, through domestic virtues and acts of charity, we can shape our lives more closely to those of Jesus, Mary and Joseph. And as we do we can experience something of our eternal home

As an idea feast, the Holy Family is not centred on a particular saving mystery in the life of Christ, and, thus, is, regrettably, susceptible to being interpreted according to our own experiences and needs, for example as a modern nuclear family. In contrast, for example, the Church of the Annunciation in Nazareth commemorates the Holy Family's home, a cave typical of the poor of their time and place. To avoid manipulating this feast according to prevailing felt needs, let us turn to the opening prayer to discover its theology.

Source. The feast of the Holy Family, instituted by Pope Leo XIII in 1893, was made a universal feast by Pope Benedict XV in 1921. Before the Second Vatican Council this feast was assigned to the first Sunday after Epiphany, whereas to this Sunday between Christmas and New Year's Day was assigned the second half of the Gospel of the presentation of the Lord in the temple (Luke 2:33-40). The liturgical reform mandated by the Second Vatican Council transferred the Feast of the Baptism of the Lord from 13 January to the Sunday (sometimes Monday) after Epiphany and the feast of the Holy Family to this Sunday (sometimes 30 December), then assigned the entire Gospel of the presentation in the temple to 2 February, recasting the feast of the Purification of Mary as the Feast of the Presentation of the Lord.

The former opening prayer this Sunday was atypically addressed to *Domine Iesu Christe*, "O Lord Jesus Christ, who, having been subjected to Mary and Joseph, consecrated the domestic family by ineffable

> *the opening prayer*
> **Holy Family:**
> **Jesus, Mary and Joseph**
>
> Father, help us to live as the holy family,
> united in respect and love.
> Bring us to the joy and peace
> of your eternal home.
> (*The Roman Missal*,
> Collins, London, 1974)
>
> Deus, qui praeclara nobis sanctae
> Familiae dignatus es exempla
> praebere, concede propitius, ut,
> domesticis virtutibus caritatisque
> vinculis illam sectantes, in laetitia
> domus tuae praemiis fruamur aeternis.
> (*Missale Romanum*,
> Città del Vaticano, 2002)

virtues ...", from which the new prayer, composed for the 1970 *Missale Romanum*, borrows only two words: *domesticam*, "domestic", and *virtutibus*, "by virtues".

Analysis of the literary form

Invocation: The simple invocation *Deus*, "God", is rendered as "Father". Even here the Latin text resists the temptation to apply the family as a metaphor for the Trinity, which translating *Deus* as "Father" may suggest.

Amplification: The invocation is amplified by the relative phrase, *qui praeclara nobis sanctae Familiae dignatus es exempla praebere*, "you who have deemed it worthy to offer the wonderful examples of the Holy Family to us", which is not expressed in the English. Were *dignatus es* followed by the accusative with the ablative, for example *praeclaro sanctam familiam dignatus es exemplo*, it would mean "you deemed the Holy Family worthy by example", but the contrary is true here, where *dignatus es* is followed by the infinitive *praebere*, to mean "you regarded it as worthy of yourself to offer to us the beautiful examples of the Holy Family".

Petition: The imperative petition *concede*, "grant", is also absent in translation.

First motive: As an adjective, *propitius* means "merciful one", but is one of several adjectives used as an adverb to mean "mercifully". Our petition, "mercifully grant", also means "grant, merciful God", thereby reminding God, in the very act of petitioning, of God's own mercy as a motive for granting our request.

Purpose: Expressed classically by *ut*, "that", followed by the subjunctive *fruamur*, "we may enjoy", the purpose clause *ut ... in laetitia domus tuae praemiis fruamur aeternis*, "that we may enjoy eternal rewards in the happiness of your home", is rendered as an independent sentence with an imperative petition, "Bring us to the joy and peace of your eternal home". *Fruamur* is one of Latin's five deponent verbs, whose complement is an ablative of instrument. Thus, *praemiis fruamur aeternis* means literally, "may we derive enjoyment from eternal rewards". *Domus tuae* is ambiguous as it can go with *laetitia*, "the joys of your house", or with *praemiis*, "the rewards of your house".

Motive: God's motive for granting that we enjoy eternal rewards is expressed by the contemporaneous participial phrase *domesticis virtutibus caritatisque vinculis illam sectantes*, "we, immitating that family with domestic virtues and bonds of love". The translation recasts the motive as the first of two imperative petitions, "help us to live as the Holy Family, united

in respect and love". As *sectantes* we are "people striving after, pursuing". *Illam* can refer simply to "that family" or even "that famous family". *Virtutibus*, "by virtues", and *vinculis*, "by bonds", are both ablatives of instrument stating the means by which we strive after the holy family.

Summary. The former prayer referred to the ineffable virtues, perhaps alluding to the unreported domestic life of the Holy Family. The current prayer speaks of our domestic virtues and bonds of charity as expressive means of imitating the Holy Family.

The prayer recognises that God acts in ways worthy of God's self, whether in offering the examples of the Holy Family or in acting mercifully. Only because offering the examples of the Holy Family is worthy of God, who grants that we may enjoy the eternal rewards of the heavenly home, do we cooperate with so noble an example and merciful a gift by striving after that family by our practice of domestic virtues and bonds of charity; such cooperation, in turn, becomes God's motive for granting that we may enjoy the eternal rewards of God's house. Because *sectantes* is contemporaneous with *fruamur*, by our eagerly following the Holy Family now by concrete practice of the virtues and charity, God grants that we enjoy now the eternal rewards in the joy of God's house.

The divinisation of our humanity is rendered explicit in this prayer in that God considers the examples of the Holy Family worthy of God's self, and that as we cooperate we come to enjoy the eternal rewards, whereas the self-emptying love of the divine-human exchange is implied in the Christ child, son of God and son of Mary, and in the self-emptying love that inspires and sustains the practice of virtues and charity. ∎

Our guided journey

The Magi travelled by the light of faith towards the adoration of the Christ Child in Bethlehem. The prayer for the Epiphany Mass expresses the way the path of our own life, illuminated by divine light, approaches the contemplation of the beauty of God

The pilgrimage of the Magi is a metaphor for our own journey in faith until we shall see God face to face.

Source. Of the entire Advent-Christmas cycle only four opening prayers, which may fall on a Sunday in the current *Missale Romanum*, remain assigned to the same Mass from the 1962 *Missale*: Christmas Masses during the night and at dawn, the octave of Christmas, and this prayer assigned to Epiphany Mass during the day. A new Mass formulary, a complete set of proper prayers and antiphons, has been provided for the vigil Mass of Epiphany in the 2002 edition of the *Missale Romanum*.

Although this feast's opening prayer is not found in the Gelasian (Roman presbyteral) sacramentary of the seventh century, it is found in several of its eighth-century adaptations from Gaul and Germany. It appears, too, in the Hadrianum or papal sacramentary given by Pope Hadrian I to Charlemagne in 785-786, and in the Sacramentary of Padua, a later redaction of a seventh-century papal sacramentary adapted for use with pilgrims to St Peter's.

Analysis of the literary form

Invocation: The simple invocation *Deus*, "God", is rendered as "Father".

Amplification: The invocation is amplified by the relative clause *qui hodierna die Unigenitum tuum gentibus stella duce revelasti*, "you who on the present day revealed your Only-begotten to the nations, a star being the guide", which is translated as, "you revealed your Son to the nations by the guidance of a star".

> ### *the opening prayer*
> ### Epiphany: Mass during the Day
>
> Father, you revealed your Son to the nations by the guidance of a star.
> Lead us to your glory in heaven by the light of faith.
> (*The Roman Missal*,
> Collins, London, 1974)
>
> Deus, qui hodierna die Unigenitum tuum gentibus stella duce revelasti, concede propitius, ut, qui iam te ex fide cognovimus, usque ad contemplandam speciem tuae celsitudinis perducamur.
> (*Missale Romanum*,
> Città del Vaticano, 2002)

Stella duce, literally "star guide", could be an ablative of instrument, "by a guide star", but I have translated it as an ablative absolute with the verb "being" implied.

Petition: The imperative petition *concede*, "grant", is not translated.

First motive: Used as an adverb here to mean "mercifully", *propitius* as an adjective recalls God's motive for granting our petition, because God is "merciful"; it is not translated.

Purpose: Expressed classically by *ut*, "that", followed by the subjunctive *perducamur*, "we may be guided", our purpose for praying is *ut ... usque ad contemplandam speciem tuae celsitudinis perducamur*, "that we may be led all the way to contemplating the vision of your majesty". Although *perducamur*, "may we be guided", is a divine passive expressing our cooperation with divine guidance, the translation has changed the subject to "you-God" by changing the purpose clause to an imperative petition in an independent sentence, "Lead us to your glory in heaven".

The clause alludes to what Gregory the Great (Pope from 590 to 604) says in his sermons on Job: *Usque ad celsitudinem contemplandae intimae lucis ascendat./ Per amorem iam ad contemplandum gloriam regni caelestis elevatur* – "May one ascend all the way unto the highness of contemplating the innermost light./ Through love one is already lifted up unto contemplating the glory of the heavenly reign" (Sermons on Job 27:15).

Second motive: God's motive for granting that we be brought to divine contemplation is expressed in a relative clause included within the purpose clause: *qui iam te ex fide cognovimus*, "we who have come to know you already by faith", which is rendered as "by the light of faith". The prayer alludes to the Second Letter of Paul to the Corinthians: "for we walk by faith, not by sight [*per fidem enim ambulamus et non per speciem*]" (NRSV, Vulgate, 2 Corinthians 5: 7). Similarly, in one of his homilies on Ezekiel, Gregory the Great says: "In becoming acquainted with God omnipotent, however, in the first place, faith (*fides*) is our entrance. Secondly, however, is the sight (*species*) of him, unto whom we arrive by walking through faith (*ad quam per fidem ambulando pervenimus*). In this life, indeed, we engage in this faith, that afterwards we may be led (*perducamur*) unto that sight" (2, 5, 8).

Summary. Because of its grammatical simplicity, Latin has only one subjunctive time (*perducamur* – "may we be led") to express all that is incomplete, unfinished, ongoing, eternal, future or contemporaneous relative to the finite verb *concede*, "grant". This polyvalence of the grammar naturally expresses the inbreaking of

eternity into the present. Thus, the simple purpose clauses of the Sunday collects typically do not distinguish between the final end and its inbreaking into our lives along the journey.

This prayer, however, distinguishes between our being guided in this present life, and our final goal, the direct contemplation of the divine, by the choice of the words *perducamur usque ad*, "may we be conducted all the way unto", and the gerundive *ad contemplandam speciem*, "unto contemplating the sight", which expresses here the final purpose of our being led. Both the journey towards and the contemplation of the Christ Child by the Magi have inspired this prayer to consider our entire life as a journey by faith; at its end is the direct contemplation of the divine. Paul distinguishes between our walking now by faith (*per fidem*) not by sight (*speciem*), in which he does not oppose the visible with the invisible, but the faith of this life as we await the direct experience of God. Yet Christ is already the image of the unseen God (Colossians 1:15); Who has seen Christ has seen the Father (John 14:9). Thus, our journey, like that of the magi, is to find Christ wherever revealed in the world.

The revelation of God's only-begotten is distinguished from the divine contemplation that comes about only after we know God by faith, for even as three Magi saw the star and came to adore the king of the Jews, even so Herod, under the pretence of wishing to adore, enquired from the Magi the time of the star's appearance, leading to the slaughter of the innocents (Matthew 22:16-18). There is an ambivalence associated with natural vision; what is needed is faith. Thus, by our cooperation with the divine gift of faith do we come to know God, who further guides us as we walk by faith in this life that at the end we may arrive at the direct contemplation of God's beauty. ∎

In thought and deed

We are pointed to the Lenten exercises by which we contemplate the mystery of Christ and conduct our daily lives in a way worthy of Him

Our participation in God's gift is drawn forward by the promise of who we are becoming.

Source. The opening prayer this Sunday is assigned to the First Sunday of Lent in the Gelasian Sacramentary, an adaptation of the Papal Sacramentary composed between 628-715 for presbyteral use in the titular churches of Rome. In 1970 it replaced a prayer no longer included in the *Missale Romanum*.

Analysis of the Literary Form
Petition: The prayer begins with the imperative petition *Concede nobis*, "grant to us", which is translated as "help us". All other verbs in the Latin text refer to our actions.

Invocation: The complex invocation *omnipotens Deus*, "all-powerful God", is rendered as "Father". God's omnipotence is manifested in God's self-gift to us in such a way that elicits our response of self-gift to God. God's self-surrender is full, but accords with our mode of understanding and protects our freedom for responding by developmental stages.

First purpose: Our purpose for praying is that God grant that we may act in two ways, as expressed by two purpose clauses. The first is *ut ... et ad intellegendum Christi proficiamus arcanum*, "that we may both make progress towards understanding the mystery of Christ". *Arcanum* means "sacred secrets, secret rites", and refers not only to the mystery of Christ, but also to the rites by which we participate in Christ's mystery. Because *ad* followed by the accusative gerundive *intellegendum*

> *the opening prayer*
> ## First Sunday of Lent
> Father, through our observance of Lent help us to understand the meaning of your Son's death and resurrection, and teach us to reflect it in our lives.
> (*The Roman Missal*, Collins, London, 1974)
>
> Concede nobis, omnipotens Deus ut, per annua quadragesimalis exercitia sacramenti, et ad intellegendum Christi proficiamus arcanum, et effectus eius digna conversatione sectemur.
> (*Missale Romanum*, Città del Vaticano, 2002)

arcanum involves movement towards, the idea here is not as if our understanding were a condition in which we remain while making progress, rather understanding Christ's mystery is a further purpose drawing our progress forward. In this way, God grants that we may participate by advancing, but our every progress is drawn forward by our desired ever-greater appreciation of Christ's mystery.

The translation orientates the first Sunday of Lent towards the paschal mystery by specifying the meaning of *arcanum*: "to understand the meaning of your Son's death and resurrection"; while the paschal mystery is rooted in history, the Latin text locates *Christi arcanum*, "the mystery of Christ", within the gerundive clause, itself a further purpose within the first purpose clause. Thus, as a future understanding to which we are drawn by progressive steps, as the Apostle says: "All of us, with unveiled faces, seeing the glory of the Lord as though reflected in a mirror, are being transformed into the same image from one degree of glory to another" (NRSV throughout, 2 Corinthians 3:18).

Second purpose: The second purpose clause, *ut ... et effectus eius digna conversatione sectemur*, "and that we may eagerly pursue its effects by a way of life worthy of Christ", is translated as "and teach us to reflect it in our lives". *Eius*, "of him, it", referring either to Christ or to *Christi arcanum*, "the mystery of Christ", is ambiguous in that it either goes with *effectus* to mean "his accomplishments", or with *digna*, which takes the genitive to mean, "by a way of life worthy of him". While *effectus sectemur* can be translated with a historical referent, "may we seek to imitate his accomplishments", because the results of Christ's actions in history are revealed in eternity in the Resurrection and in our eschatological future, the phrase could also be translated with a future referent "may we eagerly pursue its effects".

We Benedictines take the vow of *conversatio morum*, in that we profess to live according to a monastic way of life and conduct. In this prayer the means by which we eagerly pursue the effects of the mystery of Christ is *eius digna conversatione*, "by a way of life worthy of Christ".

Motive: God's motive for granting that we may understand and pursue is also the means by which we cooperate with divine grace: *per annua quadragesimalis exercitia sacramenti*, "through the annual exercises of the 40-day mystery", translated as, "through our observance of Lent".

A *sacramentum* in classical Latin is a military oath of allegiance. Tertullian (c. 155-230) used the term to translate the Greek word *mysterion*, referring to hidden things revealed in Christ, as in the passage: God "has made known to us the mys-

tery of his will ...to gather up all things in [Christ], things in heaven and things on earth" (Ephesians 1:9-10). Then *sacramentum* came to mean our liturgical participation in the mysteries of Christ, as the *salutaria sacramenta* are the salvation-bearing eucharistic mysteries, the nuptial bond between God and humanity. In this prayer the annual exercises (*annua exercitia*) are the means (*per*) through which we progress towards an ever-deepening contemplation of authentic living of Christ's mystery.

Summary. By God's gift, we participate in the exercises of the Lenten mysteries, which prompt us both to contemplation as we progress towards understanding the mystery of Christ, and to action as we conduct our daily lives in a way worthy of Christ's mystery. By the process of *lectio divina*, then, the Church's meditation on such contemplation-in-action arising from our cooperation with God's gift finds its voice in this prayer, leading to an even greater appreciation of so great a mystery.

The perplexing problem of how our contemporary liturgical action relates to historical salvific events finds its response in the terse genre of opening prayers by which the Spirit prompts the human heart's intimate crying out to the transcendent God, who already lies hidden in the heart's secret recesses. God's self-gift comes to us through the resurrected one, revealed in the eternal glory of his Crucifixion, ever drawing us according to our way of life and capacity for understanding into the wonderous exchange of mutual self-surrender, the nuptial bond of God and humanity, an icon of the of the reciprocal self-gift in the triune Godhead. ∎

A gift whole and complete

The Word nourishes both when it is proclaimed and when it is celebrated in the Eucharist. Our spiritual understanding is transformed by the Word so that we are led towards the glory of God

Only in Luke's account (read in 2007 and triennially) is prayer given as the purpose for ascending the mountain of the transfiguration; only in Luke's account do the disciples enter trembling into the cloud. As this series of commentaries on the annual cycle of opening prayers concludes, we see the liturgy not only as the school of the Lord's service, but primarily as the privileged encounter in mutual self-surrender between God and humanity mediated by rites, prayers and lives of self-transcending love.

Source. The opening prayer this Sunday is a new composition, which takes inspiration from the preface for Friday of the second week of Lent in the ancient Mozarabic Sacramentary.

Analysis of the Literary Form

Invocation: The simple invocation *Deus*, "God", is rendered complex as, "God our Father".

Amplification: The invocation is amplified in the relative clause *qui nobis dilectum Filium tuum audire praecepisti*, "you who have instructed us to listen to your beloved Son", which is rendered an imperative petition, "help us to hear your Son". The allusion is to the transfiguration of Jesus when the voice from the cloud said: "*hic est Filius meus dilectus* [This is my Son, the Beloved]" (Vulgate, NRSV throughout; Matthew 17:5, Mark 9:6, Luke 9:35), which echoes the voice from the heavens at Jesus' baptism (Matthew 3:16; cf. Mark 1:11, Luke 3:22).

Petition: The exhortative subjunctive petitions, *verbo tuo interius nos pascere*

---

the opening prayer
Second Sunday of Lent

God our Father, help us to hear your Son. Enlighten us with your word, that we may find the way to your glory.
(*The Roman Missal*, Collins, London, 1974)

Deus, qui nobis dilectum Filium tuum audire praecepisti, verbo tuo interius nos pascere digneris, ut, spiritali purificato intuitu, gloriae tuae laetemur aspectu.
(*Missale Romanum*, Città del Vaticano, 2002)

---

digneris, "may you consider it worthy to nourish us more deeply with your Word", is rendered by an imperative petition, "Enlighten us with your Word". The allusion is to the same voice, which continued to speak at Jesus' transfiguration, saying: "*ipsum audite* [Listen to him!]" (Matthew 17:5 and parallels).

The combination of *verbo* and *pascere* is an allusion to the Eucharist, for we are fed on the Word living in its proclamation and we feed on the Word enacted in sacramental celebration. This connection is made in the Mozarabic preface which includes at one point the phrase *de verbo tuo*, "from your word", and at another, *sermo pascebat interitus*, "he was nourishing them intimately with speech", which is then followed by a reference to eating and drinking in the Eucharist, suggesting that we are nourished by the Word, which nourishes both in its liturgical proclamation and sacramental celebration. We, who have listened to Jesus, petition God to nourish us deeply in the living Word proclaimed and enacted in the sacrament, both revealing God's self-emptying love.

While translating *digneris* as "may you deign" is obvious, the more belaboured "may you consider it worthy of yourself" moves beyond God's granting benefits, by pointing to the self-surrendering love proper to the divine Trinity.

Motive: The consequence of our being fed deeply on the Word is expressed by the motive clause, the ablative absolute, *spiritali purificato intuitu*, ,"spiritual insight having been purified", which is not translated. The ablative absolute may also be translated as the ablative it is: "with purified spiritual insight". Alone, *purificato* means "having been purified" and can refer to purifying religious rites. It strikes me, however, that the purification of insight is not limited to removing what is sinful, as in baptism, which forgives sins, but in elevating the insight to what is noble refers to a much broader transformation. Once our spiritual insight is purified, our transformation becomes God's motive for bringing us to rejoice.

Purpose: Expressed classically, the purpose clause expresses our hope that by feeding deeply on God's Word we will be transformed – *ut ... gloriae tuae laetemur aspectu*, "that we may rejoice at the sight of your glory", which corresponds to the English phrase, "that we may find the way to your glory", which is odd for disassociating the way to God's glory from Jesus Christ, the way, truth and life (John 14:6), whose transfiguration revealed the glory of God. The new prayer was inspired by the Mozarabic preface, which says *et illum glorie tue glorificabat adspectus*, "and the countenance of your glory was glorifying him".

Summary. Let us enter with the disciples into the cloud of prayer to rejoice at the sight of God's glory. As Mary rejoiced, who conceived upon hearing the announcement of the Archangel, and bore Jesus, our saviour, fully human, fully God, so may we rejoice, who at God's bidding ask to be nourished intimately by the living Word proclaimed in the assembly and by the enacted Word celebrated in the sacraments. This Word, once received, is effective not only in purifying but in elevating our insight into the divine indwelling so that we too may come to rejoice as Mary did in her *Magnificat*. We rejoice, however, at the sight of God's glory, revealed in the transfiguration of the beloved Son, to whom God bids us to listen, and the prayer's developmental cycle continues.

The transfiguration of Jesus is the prefiguring during his life of the glory of his Crucifixion, revealed in the Resurrection. In Matthew (17:9), Mark (9:9) and Luke (9:44), the transfiguration is followed by a prediction of his Passion and Resurrection. John's gospel makes it clear that Jesus' exultation is his being raised up on the Cross from which he reigns as king, his glory is his life-giving death. In the appearance to Thomas, the glory of the crucified is revealed and we are invited with Thomas to enter into Christ's wounds healed yet ever open, portals to the mystery of God's self-emptying love, and icon of the liturgical encounter. Inviting us within, Christ, whose self-gift to us is whole and complete, gives us to experience his mystery by stages. As we are thereby purified, all substitutes fall away and divisions are healed. We might be ennobled to participate by giving ourselves, by the grace of God, to that which alone satisfies, the divine-human mutual self-surrender. ∎

May we be raised up

This opening prayer of the Mass, a seemingly simple prayer, is one of the most profound and complex of the Church

Following the Second Vatican Council mandate for liturgical renewal, various elements of the Liturgy of the Word were restored to their ancient practice. The opening prayer, or collect, is one of the shortest prayers of the Church, but the scholarship behind it is as solid as its tradition is broad and profound. In all the attention given to the renewed Liturgy of the Word, I believe the opening prayer has largely been overlooked. However brief they are, these prayers are synthetic, complex and demand the time and attention that their effective proclamation requires. The opening prayer beguiles with brevity and apparent simplicity, and we too easily shy away from the rewards of studying and praying them more deeply.

Source. This Sunday, when the Rite of Christian Initiation of Adults is celebrated, the prayers come from the Gelasian Sacramentary, compiled between 628-715, when the preparation for baptism, confirmation and communion at the Easter Vigil provided the structure for Lent. Otherwise, the opening prayers for Mass this and next Sunday are taken from two weekday liturgies in the Gelasian, where today's prayer is found in a slightly altered version and assigned to Saturday of the fourth week of Lent. This Sunday's prayer replaces one from the 1962 Roman Missal, which is originally from the Hadrianum, a sacramentary given by Pope Hadrian I to Charlemagne in 785-786. That prayer has not been maintained in the post-conciliar sacramentary.

Analysis of literary form.
The Invocation: *Deus* means simply "God", which is translated as "Father". The invocation is amplified by two phrases.

the opening prayer
Third Sunday of Lent
Father, you have taught us to overcome our sins by prayer, fasting and works of mercy. When we are discouraged by our weakness, give us confidence in your love. Sacramentary (*The Roman Missal*, Collins, London, 1974)

Deus, Omnium misericordiarum et totius bonitatis auctor, qui peccatorum remedia in ieiuniis, orationibus et eleemosynis demonstrasti, hanc humilitatis nostrae confessionem propitius intuere, ut, qui inclinamur conscientia nostra, tua semper misericordia sublevemur. (*Missale Romanum*, Città del Vaticano, 2002)

The first amplification is set in apposition: *omnium misericordiarum et totius bonitatis auctor*: "source of all works of charity and of all goodness". This first amplification is not represented in the English translation. To call God the "source", *auctor*, is to invoke the originator, promoter and exemplar. Thus, we receive from the originator, we are fostered by the promoter and are drawn to the exemplar. The noun *misericordia* appears twice in the prayer. At the end, it means "by compassion". Here in the plural it has the special meaning "of works of charity". The noun *bonitas* generally means "goodness" whether of character or conduct. Here, by its parallel to "works of charity", conduct such as "kindness" or "benevolence" seems fitting.

The **second amplification** is a relative clause: *qui peccatorum remedia in ieiuniis, orationibus et eleemosynis demonstrasti* – "you who have pointed out the remedies of sins in fasts, prayers and alms". The English translation favours direct address, rather than the relative clause: "you have taught us to overcome our sins by prayer, fasting and works of mercy". The main verb, *demonstrasti*, means "to point out with the finger", although in this prayer its special meaning "to guide by pointing out the way" is an apt reference to Christ, who points out *remedia*, "things which heal again, remedies". Three remedies for sin are specified in this prayer: fasts, prayers and alms, the three classic Lenten practices. Jesus points out the way by his own fasting and prayer for 40 days in the desert.

The **petition** is an imperative: *hanc humilitatis nostrae confessionem … intuere*: "look upon the confession of our humility". The English translation has been reworked in two ways. It introduces a full stop after the second amplification and omits this petition.

The imperative *intuere* literally means "look at …! ", or as a mental activity, "consider, pay attention!". We petition God to pay attention to the *confessionem* or "confession" of our humility. *Confessionem* recalls The Confessions of St Augustine, the account of his life and conversion to God. *Humilitatis* has a positive sense as the opposite of pride, and refers to "lowness, humility". This confession of our lowness also implies a confession of belief in God, the originator of all mercies.

The **motive** for our demanding God's attention is the adjective *propitius*, describing God as gracious or kind. It comes from the adverb *prope*, meaning "near". *Propitius* is omitted in the English text, and with it the motive clause.

The **purpose** for which we petition God to pay attention to our admission is *ut … tua semper misericordia sublevemur*: "that … we may ever be raised up by your compassion". The English text omits the hinge word *ut*, and reworks the purpose clause as a petition: "give us confidence in your love". There is a play between the two meanings of the word *sublevemur*. It has a physical meaning, "may we be raised up", which anticipates the resurrection, and recalls our being raised up from the waters of baptism. It also means "may we be consoled".

Inserted into the purpose clause is the **premise** for raising us up: *qui inclinamur conscientia nostra*: "we who are bent down by our conscience". The English text begins its second sentence with the premise clause: "When we are discouraged by our weakness".

Two meanings are again at play in the Latin text, as *inclinamur* can be taken physically to mean "we are bent down", and thus is contrasted with God raising us up, or it can mean "to turn in favour of" and thus relates to our conversion in lowliness. We are bent down because our conscience is aware of wrongdoing, and we are turned in favour of what our conscience knows to be right.

Summary. The action of God becomes increasingly intimate as this prayer develops in its Latin text. It begins with God as the originator, who then points out the way; the motor of the prayer is God's nearness, then God directly acts to raise us up and console us.

Our human action is confession. It is implied in the sins needing a remedy, then in our confession of humility. Because we are bent down by our conscience and turn to what is right, we hope to be raised up and consoled by God. The prayer turns on the idea of compassion, which is specified by fasts, prayers and alms. God's graciousness is the theme. ∎

Rejoice and hasten

The collect for the fourth Sunday of Lent urges us toward Easter with faith fortified by joy

---

the opening prayer
Fourth Sunday of Lent

Father of peace, we are joyful in your Word, your Son Jesus Christ, who reconciles us to you.
Let us hasten toward Easter with the eagerness of faith and love.
(Sacramentary, Catholic Book, New York, 1985)

Deus, qui per Verbum tuum humani generis reconciliationem mirabiliter operaris, praesta, quaesumus, ut populus christianus prompta devotione et alacri fide ad ventura sollemnia valeat festinare.
(Missale Romanum, Città del Vaticano, 2002)

The opening prayer, or collect, is one of the shortest prayers of the Church, but the scholarship behind it is as solid as its tradition is broad and profound. The opening prayer has largely been overlooked in all the attention given to the renewed Liturgy of the Word. Yet these prayers demand the time and attention that their effective proclamation requires. The opening prayer beguiles with brevity and apparent simplicity, and we too easily shy away from the rewards of studying and praying them more deeply.

Source. The first half of this prayer, comprising the invocation and amplification clauses, comes from a prayer originally assigned to Wednesday of the second week of Lent in the Gelasian Sacramentary, compiled between AD 628 and AD 715. The Gelasian contains a mixture of papal and parochial prayers from Rome with other prayers from Gaul. The second half of our prayer is apparently a new composition and echoes the words of Leo the Great, who says in a sermon "we have been taught that one does not live on bread alone, but on every word of God, let us then undertake the annual fast with

ready devotion and eager faith" (sermon 2.4).

Analysis of the literary form
Invocation. *Deus* means simply "God", which is rendered in English by "Father of peace".

Amplification. *Qui per Verbum tuum humani generis reconciliationem mirabiliter operaris*: the relative clause literally means "you who wonderfully bring about the reconciliation of the human race through your Word". This relative clause is rendered in English by an independent sentence in direct address: "we are joyful in your word, your Son Jesus Christ, who reconciles us to you". The English has changed the subject from "God" to "we". Moreover, in the English text God's Son Jesus Christ reconciles us to the Father, whereas in the Latin text God reconciles us through the Word.

The verb *operor* can mean, "to serve the gods, perform sacred rites", but here, conversely, it refers to God's work on our behalf, as *operaris* means "you work, carry into effect". God's work is *reconciliationem*, which has as its core meaning "re-establishing, restoration, renewal". Here God's reconciliation is not limited to Christians, but is of the human family: *humani generis*. The reconciliation is wrought *per* "by means of, through the instrumentality of", God's Word, *Verbum tuum*.

Petition: *Praesta, quaesumus*. The petition is the simple imperative "grant", followed by the verb "we ask" that softens the effect of using the command form with God. The prayer has been reworked in the English by adding a full stop after the amplification, and rendering the petition in the doxology as, "we ask this".

Purpose: The classical form of the purpose clause is used: *ut* followed by the subjunctive *valeat*: *ut populus christianus prompta devotione et alacri fide ad ventura sollemnia valeat festinare*. We ask God to grant "that the Christian people may be able with ready devotion and eager faith to hasten toward the up-coming solemnities". The English text rewrites the purpose clause as an exhortative petition: "Let us hasten toward Easter with the eagerness of faith and love". This translation simplifies the phrase "unto the coming solemnities" by saying "unto Easter", and changes "the Christian people" to "us".

Valere means, "to be strong, be in a condition to do something". We are made strong by devotion and faith.

Devotio can mean "any form of prayer" as in devotions, and thus alludes to the prayer, fasting and almsgiving characteristic of Lenten practice. Among ancient Christian authors the meaning of this word ranges from "piety", to "devotion" and "zeal". Our devotion is to be *prompta*, which means "brought to light, exposed to view" or even "at hand".

Our manifest devotion is joined to *fide*, often translated as "by faith". *Fide*, however, can have a range of meanings including "by confidence, reliance, belief", but at its core it means "by trust" in a person. To have faith in God is to trust in God, to rely upon or have confidence in God. *Alacri* is an adjective meaning, "eager, happy, ready". Cicero used the same word to express the idea of joyous activity.

Made strong by devotion and faith we hasten to the coming solemnities. *Sollemnia* has at its root the idea of "yearly, annual". The implied reference here is to the annual celebration of the paschal mystery, the reconciliation wrought by the Word.

Summary. This prayer offers a clear example of how the opening prayer, as a literary form, turns on the word *ut*, "in order that", such that what appears before the *ut* correlates with what follows. In this case, the amplification and purpose clauses complement one another. The amplification clause speaks of God's work through the Word, which is then specified in the purpose clause as God's work in us by our prayer and trust in God. Reference to the human family is then specified in the Christian people. The general reference to God's reconciliation is specified as the upcoming solemnities. The reconciliation (restoration, renewal) finds its parallel in the prayer that we may be strong. This prayer highlights the force of the Latin *ut* as a fulcrum upon which the see-saw of the prayer turns.

The force of this prayer is that we Christians are hastening towards the annual celebration of the ongoing reconciliation, of God at work in the human family. Christians name and celebrate God's reconciliation of the human family.

This is *Laetare* Sunday because the first word of the Entrance Antiphon is *laetare*, "rejoice". As our Lenten journey is more than half over, the opening prayer encourages us to hasten to the coming solemnities with faith strengthened with joy. ∎

Ones who walk in love

The collect for the fifth Sunday of Lent speaks of the inspiration of Christ's love, made manifest in his sacrifice

---

the opening prayer
Fifth Sunday of Lent

Father, help us to be like Christ your Son, who loved the world and died for our salvation. Inspire us by his love, guide us by his example.
(*The Roman Missal*,
Collins, London, 1974)

Quaesumus, Domine Deus noster, ut in illa caritate, qua Filius tuus diligens mundum morti se tradidit, inveniamur ipsi, te opitulante, alacriter ambulantes.
(*Missale Romanum*,
Città del Vaticano, 2002)

The opening prayer, or collect, is one of the shortest prayers of the Church, but the scholarship behind it is as solid as its tradition is broad and profound. The opening prayer beguiles with brevity and apparent simplicity, and we too easily shy away from the rewards of studying and praying it more deeply.

Source. The liturgy this Sunday has been restructured since the Second Vatican Council. Before the Council the Sunday was called Passion Sunday, and Palm Sunday followed a week later, according to the arrangement found in the Hadrianum, a papal sacramentary sent by Pope Hadrian I to Charlemagne in 785-786. Since the Second Vatican Council, Passion and Palm Sunday have been combined and are celebrated next week. This restructuring leaves the fifth Sunday of Lent available for the celebration of the third scrutiny of the Rite of Christian Initiation of Adults.

When the scrutiny is not celebrated, the liturgy comes from the fifth Sunday of Lent, where the opening prayer is a post-Vatican II reworking of a prayer from the *Liber Mozarabicus* of the ancient liturgical tradition of Spain. As such, this prayer is an example of how the post-conciliar liturgy draws on prayers from every age, giving greater expression to the catholicity or universality of the Church. The Mozarabic prayer was addressed to *Christe Deus*, "Christ God", whereas our prayer is addressed to the Lord our God. Less than half of the original prayer was used, as only its purpose clause was reworked into that of our prayer. The Mozarabic prayer was said as part of the sign of peace. One word in our opening prayer offers a connection to the sign of peace of the Mozarabic rite: *caritate*. Isidore of Seville says in his treatise On Ecclesiastical Duties: "Introduction is given before the sign of peace, that all, having been reconciled mutually by charity ... " (v. Matthew 5:23-24). In our prayer, however, the charity is reinterpreted as that with which God's Son gave himself up to death.

Analysis of the literary form
Petition: The prayer begins with the petition using a standard classical formula: *quaesumus ... ut* followed by the subjunctive *inveniamur*. "We ask ... that ... we may be found". The petition proper is simply *quaesumus*, "we ask, desire". The rest of the formula *ut inveniamur* is the purpose clause. Thus, this classical formula

unites the prayer. The English translation has provided three petitions, each in the imperative: "help us to be like Christ your Son. ... Inspire us by his love, guide us by his example."

Invocation: Inserted between the petition and the purpose clause is the simple invocation *Domine*: "Lord", which has been translated into English as "Father".

Amplification: The invocation is amplified by the apposition of *Deus noster*: "our God". The amplification is not expressed in the English text.

Purpose: *Ut in illa caritate... inveniamur ipsi ... alacriter ambulantes*: "that we may be found as the very ones walking eagerly in that love". The purpose clause has been rephrased in the English by the three imperative petitions as mentioned above.

Inveniamur means "we may be found out, discovered, ascertained". The passive here is called the divine passive, because God ascertains. We ask to be found as *ipsi*, "the very ones", *ambulantes*, "ones walking, journeying".

This prayer recalls that of last Sunday in two ways. Our journeying echoes our hastening, *festinare*, mentioned in last week's prayer, and our travelling is *alacriter*, "briskly, eagerly". *Alacriter* is the adverb form of the adjective used last week to describe our eager faith, *alacri fide*, by which we hasten to the annual solemnities. The prayer also anticipates by antithesis the disciples walking sadly to Emmaus, when they were discovered by the risen Lord (Luke 24:17), as we pray to be discovered walking eagerly.

We also pray to walk "in love", *in caritate*. Three Latin words are used to express "love". *Amor* means "love", whether high or low. Because *amour* is associated with the lower forms of love, the Vulgate Bible

prefers to use either *caritas* or *dilectio*. *Caritas* first means "dearness, costliness, high price", then comes to mean "esteem, affection, love", whereas *dilectio* comes from the verb *diligo*: "to value, esteem highly, love" (v. *"amo"* in Lewis & Short's *A Latin Dictionary*). In ecclesiastical Latin *ambulare*, "to walk", often has the sense of "to live" as in Paul's Letter to the Ephesians, which recapitulates our purpose clause: "live in love, as Christ loved us and gave himself up for us" (5:2. Cf. Galatians 2:20).

Motive: The motive for asking that God find us travelling eagerly is: *qua Filius tuus diligens mundum morti se tradidit*, literally "with which love your Son, loving the world, gave himself over to death". The motive clause is expressed in English, but in the form of an amplification of the word "Son": "who loved the world and died for our salvation", the force of the clause as a motive for our asking, however, is not translated.

The words *se tradidit* have the specific meaning of "he gave himself up, yielded, surrendered". The motive clause recalls John 3:16: "God so loved the world, as to give up his only begotten son", where the subject is God. The subject in the motive clause, however, is Jesus, who yields to death, as in John's Gospel where Jesus gave up (*tradidit*) the spirit (19:30).

Premise: Lest we think that God finds us walking on our own impetus, *te opitulante* is interjected, meaning "as you are helping", for even our walking is by the grace of God.

Summary. Last week we prayed to hasten unto the coming solemnities. This week, as we approach Holy Week, the solemnities are named more clearly: the Son of God, loving the world, gave himself up to death, that we might live in that love, by the help of God. ∎

Suffering shared

The collect for Palm Sunday begins our Holy Week readings, focusing on Christ's acceptance of the cross

---

the opening prayer
Palm Sunday

Almighty, ever-living God, you have given the human race Jesus Christ our Saviour as a model of humility.
He fulfilled your will by becoming man and giving his life on the cross.
Help us to bear witness to you by following his example of suffering and make us worthy to share in his resurrection..
(*The Roman Missal*, Collins, London, 1974)

Omnipotens sempiterne Deus, qui humano generi, ad imitandum humilitatis exemplum, Salvatorem nostrum carnem sumere, et crucem subire fecisti, concede propitius, ut et patientiae ipsius habere documenta et resurrectionis consortia mereamur.
(*Missale Romanum*, Città del Vaticano, 2002)

The scholarship behind the collect is as solid as its tradition is profound. It beguiles with apparent simplicity, and we too easily shy away from the rewards of studying it more deeply.

Source. An axiom of the historical development of liturgy is that times of heightened religious importance preserve older customs. Because of the importance of this Sunday, marking the beginning of Holy Week, the conservative nature of the liturgy is seen in the constant use of this opening prayer, at least since the Gelasian Sacramentary composed between 628 and 715, where the prayer has but a few variations from current form. The prayer achieved this form in the Hadrianum, a sacramentary given by Pope Hadrian I to Charlemagne in 785-6. This is the same opening prayer as was used on this day in the pre-Second Vatican Council Roman Missal, and it is the only opening prayer for any Sunday of Lent from that Missal in the current Sacramentary. This continuity is also seen in the companion to this prayer, the Canticle of Philippians 2, proclaimed before the Passion in both the pre- and post-conciliar liturgy.

Analysis of the literary form.
Invocation: *Omnipotens sempiterne Deus* is a complex invocation consisting of a noun and two adjectives. It is translated in the English prayer as "Almighty, ever-living God". The power and eternity of God in the invocation are contrasted in the amplification with the incarnation and death of Christ on the cross.

Amplification: Right after the invocation of God's grandeur the relative clause begins: *qui humano generi ... fecisti*, literally "who brought it about on behalf of the human family". This is expressed in English by the implicit dative "[to] the human race". These first six words in the Latin move from an affirmation of God's self, to God for us.

Purpose 1: Inserted into the amplification clause is a type of purpose clause composed of *ad* followed by the gerundive: *imitandum* *humilitatis exemplum* – "for imitating the example of humility". This first purpose clause has been rendered in English as an amplification clause, "as a model of humility", which describes "Jesus Christ our Saviour". The Latin phrase is ambivalent in that it can be applied both to Christ and to us. First, Christ became flesh and mounted the cross that he might give the example of humility, and then we are to resemble in our lives that example. The beauty of the Latin is that it flows so effortlessly from God's glory, to God for us, to Christ's example and then to our imitation of Christ.

Result: What God brought about is stated in the sentence, *Salvatorem nostrum carnem sumere, et crucem subire fecisti*: "that our Saviour took on our flesh and endured the cross", rephrased in two sentences. The first like the Latin phrase, has God as its subject: "you have given the human race Jesus Christ our Saviour", whereas the second changes the subject to Jesus Christ: "he fulfilled your will by becoming man and giving his life on the cross". The controlling verb is *fecisti*: literally "you brought to pass, caused". Two mysteries of Christ on our behalf are mentioned: the incarnation and redemption. Referring to the incarnation, *sumere* has a wide range of meaning including "to assume, put on (a garment), take upon one's self". On our behalf Christ assumed our flesh in the incarnation. In regard to the redemption, *subire* can have a more passive meaning as in "to submit to, endure", as in "he endured the cross", or the more active meaning "to undertake" or even "to mount", as in "he mounted the cross".

Petition: *Concede*: is the simple imperative "grant". The English omits this petition.

Motive: As typical in opening prayers, the adjective *propitius* is used as an adverb "mercifully". However, as an adjective it means "merciful one"; and so offers a type

of motive. God's motive for granting anything is because God is merciful. It is mercy that unites God's glory with God's saving action in Christ. The word is omitted in the English translation.

Purpose 2: *Ut et patientiae ipsius habere documenta et resurrectionis consortia mereamur*: literally, "that we may be worthy to possess both the proofs of the suffering and the fellowship of the resurrection of the very one who lives …".The English prayer reworks the purpose clause as two conjoined independent sentences. The first begins with the imperative, "help us", and continues with the purpose clause, "to bear witness to you by following his example"; the second begins with the imperative "make us worthy", and continues with the purpose clause "to share in his resurrection". In this, the English prayer changes the subject from "we" to the implied "God". The controlling verb *mereamur* means at its root, "to receive one's share" and thus, "to be worthy of a thing". *Documenta patientiae* are "proofs of suffering", perhaps alluding to the saving wounds of Christ, healed yet ever portals to his mystery, and thus to the proffs of our suffering with Christ by daily lives lived patiently. *Consortia* is a neuter plural, "fellowship elements", difficult to render exactly into English, I have suggested the singular, "fellowship".

Summary. This prayer parallels the second reading at Mass today, the canticle of Philippians 2:6-11, which speaks of Christ Jesus who emptied himself to take on our human form, accepting even death upon a cross. Because of this, God raised him and exalted him above all things, that all living beings might praise the glory of Christ's name. We pray to share in the self-emptying of Jesus that we might share in a like resurrection. Now that our Lenten journey and practices have brought us to the beginning of Holy Week, the prayer invites us to unite ourselves with the paschal mystery. ∎

Sacrifice and banquet

Here we explore the collect for Holy Thursday, which evokes the marriage supper of the Lamb, and Christ's eternal sacrifice, offered so that we may draw the fullness of love and life from him, now and at the eternal banquet to which we are invited

The Christian feast is Sunday, the first day of creation, and of our recreation in Christ, the day of the Spirit's descent. By the end of the first century Christians began to celebrate an annual feast at the time of the Passover, which falls in the Jewish lunar calendar on the fourteenth day of Nisan, regardless of the day of the week. Christians eventually transferred the nascent Easter feast to Sunday (like the Ascension), and celebrated in one day the passover of our Lord from death to life, which we celebrate as one feast in three days (*Triduum*): Friday, beginning on Thursday evening, Saturday and Sunday. Thus, they found the tomb empty on the third day.

Source. This prayer is a new composition replacing a prayer in the 1962 Missal, which appears 103 times in the ancient manuscripts in both the presbyteral tradition (Gelasian; Good Friday) and the Papal (Hadrianum; Holy Thursday). That prayer was superseded perhaps because of its focus on Judas: "O God, from whom both Judas received the punishment of his offence and the thief the reward of his confession ..."

Analysis of the literary form

Invocation: Included within the first petition, the simple invocation *Deus*, "God", is expanded to "God our Father".

First petition: The imperative petition, *Sacratissimam ... frequentantibus Cenam ... da nobis* – "grant to us celebrating the most holy Supper" – is translated as "we are gathered here to share in the supper". *Frequentantibus* means either "to ones frequenting" referring to our faithfulness

> *the opening prayer*
> **Holy Thursday:**
> **Mass of the Lord's Supper**
> God our Father, we are gathered here to share in the supper which your only Son left to his Church to reveal his love. He gave it to us when he was about to die and commanded us to celebrate it as the new and eternal sacrifice. We pray that in this eucharist we may find the fullness of love and life.
> (*The Roman Missal*, Collins, London, 1974)
>
> Sacratissimam, Deus, frequentantibus Cenam, in qua Unigenitus tuus, morti se traditurus, novum in saecula sacrificium dilectionisque suae convivium Ecclesiae commendavit, da nobis, quaesumus, ut ex tanto mysterio plenitudinem caritatis hauriamus et vitae.
> (*Missale Romanum*, Città del Vaticano, 2002)

to the Lord's supper, "to ones gathering in great numbers", referring to the assembly, or "to ones celebrating", referring to the supper.

Paul refers to "the Lord's supper" (*dominicam cenam*; 1 Corinthians 11:20; NRS, Vulgate throughout). The invitation to Communion evokes Revelation 19:9: "Blessed are those who are invited to the marriage supper [*cenam nuptiarum*] of the Lamb."

Amplification: Normally amplifying the invocation, here the relative clause amplifies the word "Supper" (*Cenam*): *in qua Unigenitus tuus, morti se traditurus, novum in saecula sacrificium dilectionisque suae convivium Ecclesiae commendavit*, "at which your Only-begotten, about to hand himself over to death, entrusted to the Church the new everlasting sacrifice and the banquet of his love", which is rendered as, "which your only Son left to his Church to reveal his love. He gave it to us when he was about to die and commanded us to celebrate it as the new and eternal sacrifice".

Convivium, "banquet", alludes to Jesus' banqueting with the tax collectors (Luke 5:29), to the feeding of the 5,000 who sat down in groups (*convivia*) of about 50 each (Luke 9:14) and to Jesus' teaching to "invite the poor, the crippled, the lame, and the blind" to our banquet (Luke 14:13). The *Magnificat* antiphon for the feast of the body and blood of Christ says: "O holy banquet [*convivium*], in which Christ is received: the memory of his Passion is recalled, the mind is filled with grace and the pledge of future glory is given to us". Finally, there is a beautiful chiasm in the English translation, lacking to the Latin, of the second eucharistic prayer for Masses of reconciliation: "You have gathered us here around the table of your Son, in fellowship with the Virgin Mary, Mother of God, and all the saints. In that new world where the fullness of your peace will be revealed, gather people of every race, language, and way of life to share in the one eternal banquet [*convivium*]".

Second petition: The parenthetical *quaesumus* is translated literally as "We pray".

Purpose: Our intended purpose for praying, *ut … plenitudinem caritatis hauriamus et vitae*, "that we may draw the fullness of love and life", is rendered as, "that in this Eucharist we may find the fullness of love and life". There is a parallel

between the fullness of love (*caritatis*) and the banquet of his love (*dilectionis*), and a contrast between the fullness of life (*vitae*) and the new sacrifice (*sacrificium*) suggesting a life-giving sacrifice.

Isaiah says: "With joy you will draw [*haurietis*] water from the wells of salvation" (12:3). At the wedding feast of Cana, Jesus told the stewards to draw some of the water out (*haurite*; John 2:8-9). In the story of the woman at the well, there is a play on drawing water from the well and the water of eternal life that Jesus gives (John 4:7-15).

Drawing from the fullness of love alludes to this liturgy's gospel of the washing of the feet and Jesus' instruction: "I give you a new commandment, that you love one another. Just as I have loved you, you also should love one another" (John 13:34), which we sing while washing the feet of one another at this Mass. The last antiphon for the washing of the feet is: "… the greatest of these is love [*caritatis*]".

Motive: God's motive for granting "that we may draw" is the prepositional phrase *ex tanto mysterio* – "from so great a mystery" – translated as "in this Eucharist". The mystery is the supper we celebrate as the new sacrifice and banquet of his love, by which celebration we cooperate with the divine gift that we may come to greater participation in divine life by drawing deeply from its fullness of love and life.

Summary. This prayer does not use the direct language, found in other prayers, that the Church offers Christ's sacrifice, but the more nuanced language that the Church celebrates the Supper, entrusted to her as both sacrifice and banquet. The eschatological imagery of the Eucharist in this prayer is based upon our celebrating a supper, and because a supper, a nuptial banquet of the union between God and humanity. ∎

In newness of life

We consider that of the liturgy of the Triduum through which we might rise to self-transcending love of God and neighbour

In Christ crucified our humanity came to share in the divine life by sharing in this self-emptying love of God (Philippians 2:5-11). This divine-human exchange characterises the Christian life, for "we have been buried with him by baptism into death, so that, just as Christ was raised from the dead by the glory of the Father, so we too might walk in newness of life" (Romans 6:4; NRSV, Vulgate throughout).

History. By the end of the first century the rudiments of an annual one-day celebration of the Lord's passing from death to life had developed. Today that feast is celebrated as a single liturgy over three days: Friday (beginning Thursday evening), Saturday and Sunday. The myrrh-bearing women came to the tomb early in the morning on the third day, Sunday. The day after Christ's Sabbath rest in the tomb, Sunday, is both the first day of Creation and the first day of our recreation in Christ unto everlasting life, but, because there are only seven weekdays, the day of the Resurrection is also the "eighth day", which never ends. This is why baptisteries combine hexagons with octagons, for we are baptised into Christ's death (on the sixth day) and Resurrection (eighth day).

Our Holy Week liturgies are heavily influenced by those celebrated in Jerusalem, as recorded in the diary of a Spanish pilgrim, Egeria, c. 385. As the Jerusalem community celebrated the liturgy in the places where the mysteries happened, so the Church of Rome mapped out over its urban landscape various places where specific mysteries are commemorated. The tomb is the baptistery of St John; the

---

the opening prayer
Good Friday

Lord, by the suffering of Christ your Son you have saved us all from the death we inherited from sinful Adam. By the law of nature we have borne the likeness of his manhood. May the sanctifying power of grace help us to put on the likeness of our Lord in heaven.
(*The Roman Missal*,
Collins, London, 1974)

Deus, qui peccati veteris hereditariam mortem, in qua posteritatis genus omne successerat, Christi Filii tui, Domini nostri, passione solvisti, da, ut conformes eidem facti, sicut imaginem terreni hominis naturae necessitate portavimus, ita imaginem caelestis gratiae sanctificatione portemus.
(*Missale Romanum*,
Città del Vaticano, 2002)

Lateran basilica, the upper room; the basilica of the Holy Cross in Jerusalem, Calvary, where a relic of the true Cross brought from Jerusalem by Helena, the mother of the emperor Constantine, is housed. When I served as parish priest of three parishes in rural Kansas, one church served as the annual station for the Mass of the Lord's Supper, another housed the relic for Good Friday, and the third had an immersion font for the Easter Vigil.

The Good Friday liturgy begins as the ministers prostrate in silence, then, standing, the opening prayer is offered without the invitation "let us pray", as the Church continues its vigilant prayer throughout the one three-day feast (*Triduum*).

Source. Two opening prayer options are given, both originally found in the *Gelasianum*, composed between 628-715 for presbyteral use in the titular churches of Rome, where the first was assigned to Monday of Holy Week and the second, presented here, to Good Friday, when it was offered after the first reading and psalm response.

Analysis of the literary form

Invocation: The simple invocation *Deus*, "God", is rendered "Lord".

Amplification: The relative phrase, *qui peccati veteris hereditariam mortem, in qua posteritatis genus omne successerat, Christi Filii tui, Domini nostri, passione solvisti*, "you who by the Passion of Christ your Son, our Lord, destroyed the hereditary death of the ancient sin, in which the whole race of posterity had followed", which is rendered as, "by the suffering of Christ your son you have saved us all from the death we inherited from sinful Adam". The titles of Christ evoke the confession of the soldier looking upon the deceased Jesus: "Truly this man was God's Son" (Mark 15:39). In Judges 10:6 *peccati veteris* refers to idolatry.

The amplification alludes to God's "passing over the transgression [*peccatum*] of the remnant of your possession [*hereditatis*]" (Micah 7:18), and to Psalm 146:7, "the Lord sets the prisoners free [*solvit conpeditos*]". In Luke 13:15 Jesus asks who would not untie (*solvit*) the ox or donkey from its manger to give it water on the Sabbath; yet Jesus breaks (*solvit*) the doors of death during his Sabbath rest and brings us unto the waters of baptism, who profess faith in Jesus incarnate of Mary, as even "the ox knows its owner, and the donkey its master's crib" (Isaiah 1:3), thus their inclusion with believers in the crèche.

Petition: The imperative petition *da*, "grant", is not translated.

Premise: The purpose clause has two correlative phrases established by *sicut ... ita*, "just as ... so". The first correlative gives the premise: *sicut imaginem terreni hominis naturae necessitate portavimus*, "just as by the necessity of nature we have borne the image of the earthly human person", which is rendered as, "By the law of nature we have borne the likeness".

Purpose: The second half of the correlative expresses the purpose: *ut ... ita imaginem caelestis gratiae sanctificatione portemus*, "so may we carry the image of the heavenly one by the sanctification of grace", which is refashioned as an exhortative petition, "May the sanctifying power of grace help us to put on the likeness of our Lord in heaven". The purpose and premise come from 1 Corinthians 15:49: *sicut portavimus imaginem terreni portemus et imaginem caelestis*, "Just as we have borne the image of the man of dust, we will also bear the image of the man of heaven."

Motive: Expressing God's motive for granting that we may carry the image of the heavenly one is the participial phrase, *conformes eidem facti*: "[we] having been made similar to the same one", which is not translated. The allusion is to Romans 8:29: "For those whom he foreknew he also predestined to be conformed to the image of his Son [*conformes fieri imaginis Filii eius*]." (See 1 Corinthians 15:22).

Summary. We are made similar to Christ when we love as Christ has loved us (John 13:34). He emptied himself suffering death upon a Cross, that, as our humanity is brought to its fullness, we might rise to self-transcending love of God and neighbour. ∎

Eternity unsealed

The collect for Easter Sunday celebrates the Resurrection as part of our present and our future

Source. The *Missale Romanum* of 1570 provides an entirely different opening prayer for Easter Sunday with the option of substituting a prayer against those who persecute the Church or one for the Pope. These prayers were replaced by the 1962 *Missale Romanum* with a variant of the current prayer, which variant dates from the Hadrianum, a sacramentary given by Pope Hadrian I to Charlemagne in 785-786, where it is the only opening prayer given for Easter Sunday. After the Second Vatican Council the current version of the opening prayer was drawn from the Gelasian Sacramentary composed between 628 and 715, where it is given for Easter Sunday, but in other sacramentaries has been appointed to the Easter Vigil Mass.

Analysis of the literary form

Invocation: *Deus*, while simply meaning "God", has been translated as "God our Father".

Amplification: Expressed as the relative clause *qui hodierna die, per Unigenitum tuum, aeternitatis nobis aditum ... reserasti*: literally, "you who on this present day have unsealed the entrance of eternity on our behalf through your Only-begotten". The amplification has been rendered by an independent sentence in English: "By raising Christ your Son you conquered the power of death and opened for us the way to eternal life."

The phrase "On this present day", *hodierna die*, sets the prayer in the present time. The controlling verb, *reserasti*, is the contracted form of *reseravisti* meaning literally "you have unlocked" and thus "you

> *the opening prayer*
> **Easter Sunday:**
> **Mass During the Day**
>
> God our Father, by raising Christ your Son you conquered the power of death and opened for us the way to eternal life. Let our celebration today raise us up and renew our lives by the Spirit that is within us.
> (*The Roman Missal*, Collins, London, 1974)
>
> Deus, qui hodierna die, per Unigenitum tuum, aeternitatis nobis aditum, devicta morte, reserasti, da nobis quaesumus, ut, qui resurrectionis dominicae sollemnia colimus, per innovationem tui Spiritus in lumine vitae resurgamus.
> (*Missale Romanum*, Città del Vaticano, 2002)

have disclosed, revealed something unknown". God unseals the *aditum*, whose basic meaning is "approach, access", then the "possibility or right of approaching", then concretely "the entrance" itself. The entrance is "of eternity": *aeternitatis*. In this God acts "on our behalf" – *nobis*.

The entrance of eternity is disclosed "by means of", *per*, God's "Only-begotten", *Unigenitum tuum*; because the masculine is used, "son" is expressed, but not stated by a separate word in the Latin. The words of Gregory the Great (Pope from 590 to 604) are heard in this amplification clause, who said in his commentary on the first book of Kings: "rising on our behalf, he unsealed the entrance of eternity" (I, 1).

Premise: Inserted into the amplification is the premise for the prayer, *devicta morte*. By itself, *devicta* means "having been conquered completely, overcome, subdued". The two-word ablative absolute then comes to mean "death having been conquered". It coordinates with *hodierna die*: "on this present day, as death has been overcome".

Petition: *Da nobis quaesumus*: "give to us we ask". The imperative *da* – "give!" – is softened by the addition of *quaesumus*: "we ask". The English text rephrases the prayer by adding a full stop after the amplification and rendering the petition in the doxology as, "we ask this".

Purpose: *Ut ... per innovationem tui Spiritus in lumine vitae resurgamus*: "that we may rise again in the light of life through the renewal of your spirit". The English reworks the purpose and motive clauses into an independent sentence in the form of an exhortative petition: "Let our celebration today raise us up and renew our lives by the Spirit that is within us".

In ecclesiastical Latin *resurgamus* has the meaning "may we rise again, rise from the grave". The purpose clause is ambiguous, because Latin has only four subjunctives. *Ut resurgamus* may indicate that our rising is contemporary with our worship, as in rising from the waters of baptism; incomplete, as a pledge of future glory; continual, as an ongoing transformation; perpetual, as heavenly glory is inchoate; and future, as on the last day.

We rise in the "light of life", *in lumine vitae*, which is a rephrasing of Psalm 35/36:10: "because in you is the source of life, in your light we shall see light". Our prayer conflates the verse by combining "of life" from the first part and "in light" from the second. The phrase "in the light of life" appears to be a recent addition to the prayer, for it replaces the phrase "from

the death of the soul", which is in other appearances of this prayer. The substitution seems to have been made to accord with the liturgical renewal of Vatican II.

We pray that we may rise "by means of", *per*, the renewal of God's Spirit. *Innovationem* means "a renewing, alteration, innovation". The reference to the Spirit here complements the reference to the Only-begotten in the amplification.

Motive: Inserted into the purpose clause is the motive: *qui resurrectionis dominicae sollemnia colimus*: "we who celebrate the solemnities of the Lord's Resurrection". In the English prayer this phrase is integrated into the second sentence, but without the force of a motive clause, when it refers to "our celebration today". The controlling verb *colimus* at its root means "we cultivate", as in a garden, then it means "we care for something", then "we regard with care, honour, worship".

Summary. This opening prayer is Trinitarian. It is addressed to God and mentions God's work through the Only-begotten and through the Spirit. The prayer does not simply state that Christ died and rose from the dead, as if to focus on a historical event. Rather it focuses on God's work today on our behalf. The Resurrection is mentioned in reference to our celebration, and our prayer that we may rise through the renewal of the Spirit. God's motive for granting what we ask is our celebration of the Lord's Resurrection, which is not merely an anniversary of a past event. Rather, God is at work in what we are doing.

This prayer tells us what the paschal mystery is: a living reality for us according to which death has been conquered. God has unsealed the entrance of eternity for us, we celebrate the Lord's Resurrection, and we, who have risen with Christ from the waters of baptism, pray to rise from the grave through the renewal of the spirit. ∎

By water, Spirit and blood

The collect for the Second Sunday of Easter marks the first day of the new creation in Christ, that is, the first day of eternity. Here we examine the prayer's significance

Source. This prayer is not found in the ancient Roman books, but comes from the *Missale Gothicum*, a Gallican sacramentary redacted perhaps between 690 and 710 in Burgundy. The inclusion of this prayer of Gallican use in the post-conciliar Roman Missal is an indication of its catholicity or universality in drawing prayers from every era and region of the Latin church. The opening prayer this Sunday replaces one in the *Missale Romanum* of 1962 which dates from the Hadrianum, a sacramentary given by Pope Hadrian I to Charlemagne in 785-786, where it was assigned to the Sunday after Easter. In the current sacramentary that prayer is assigned to Saturday of the seventh week of Easter, the day before Pentecost.

The *Missale Romanum* of 1962 numbers Sundays after Easter, this Sunday being the first, whereas the post-conciliar Roman Missals count the Sundays of Easter, Easter Sunday itself being the first, this the second.

Analysis of the literary form

Invocation: The invocation with a genitive of quality is *Deus misericordiae sempiternae*: "God of everlasting mercy". The adjective, necessary to the Latin construction of a genitive of quality, is dropped in the English translation: "God of mercy". The invocation alludes to Psalm 51/52:10, which says, "I have hoped in the mercy of God for ever and ever".

Amplification: The relative phrase, *qui in ipso paschalis festi recursu fidem sacratae tibi plebis accendis*: means, ""you who enkindle the faith of the people consecrated to you in the very return of the paschal

---

the opening prayer
Second Sunday of Easter

God of mercy, you wash away our sins in water, you give us new birth in the Spirit, and redeem us in the blood of Christ. As we celebrate Christ's resurrection increase our awareness of these blessings, and renew your gift of life within us.
(*The Roman Missal*,
Collins, London, 1974)

Deus misericordiae sempiternae,
qui in ipso paschalis festi recursu
fidem sacratae tibi plebis accendis,
auge gratiam quam dedisti, ut digna
omnes intellegentia comprehendant,
quo lavacro abluti, quo spiritu regenerati,
quo sanguine sunt redempti.
(*Missale Romanum*,
Città del Vaticano, 2002)

---

feast". Part of the amplification is rephrased in the English by a temporal clause: "as we celebrate Christ's resurrection". Here the subject is changed to we, who celebrate the paschal feast, whereas in the Latin this phrase expresses in what condition God rouses the faith of the people: "in the return itself of the paschal feast".

Accendis means "you set on fire" then figuratively "you inflame, incite, rouse up". God rouses up the faith, *fidem*, of the people, *plebis*. The people is *sacratae*, "having been consecrated or devoted to the gods". This people is consecrated to you [God], *tibi*.

Petition: The imperative, *auge gratiam* means, "increase the grace". *Auge* alone means "increase, nourish!" but with the object comes to mean, "furnish abundantly with, heap upon, enrich!". *Gratiam* literally refers to the favour one has in others' eyes, as in "esteem, influence", and the favour one shows to others, as in "kindness, gratitude". This is the root of the word "grace". The prayer is restructured into two sentences in English and the petition is doubled. The first petition is: "increase our awareness of these blessings". Here what is increased is not the favour, but our awareness – perhaps referring to *intellegentia* in the purpose clause. The second is unique to the English: "and renew your gift of life within us".

Motive: The clause describes the favour, *quam dedisti*: "which you have given". God has already given favour, so we ask for its increase. This phrase may be implied in the English when it refers to the "gift of life within us".

Purpose: The classic formula of *ut* followed by the subjunctive. It begins: *ut digna omnes intellegentia comprehendant*: "that all people may comprehend with a worthy understanding". This first part of the purpose is perhaps implied in the choice of the English word "awareness". The controlling verb, *comprehendant*, means at its root: "may they lay hold of something on all sides", then "may they comprehend something intellectually, grasp".

The purpose clause continues with three eloquent relative clauses – "*quo lavacro abluti, quo spiritu regenerati, quo sanguine sunt redempti*" – literally meaning "by which bath [they have been] washed, by which Spirit [they have been] reborn, by which blood they have been redeemed". The phrases are eloquent because the three objects of "may they comprehend" are the washing, the Spirit and the blood. Each of these objects has been tucked into its own relative clause. If we pulled them out of their clauses it would read: "may they comprehend … the bath by which they have been washed, the Spirit by which they

have been reborn, the blood by which they have been redeemed." These three relative clauses are expressed in the English by three independent sentences rephrased into direct address: "you wash away our sins in water, you give us new birth in the Spirit, and redeem us in the blood of Christ". *Abluti … sunt* means, "they have been washed, cleansed" and in ecclesiastical Latin refers to baptism. *Regenerati … sunt* means, "they have been brought forth again", and here refers to being born again by the Spirit (v. 1 Peter 1:3). *Sunt redempti* means, "they have been bought back, ransomed", the root meaning of "to redeem".

The source for these three clauses is 1 John 5:7-8, which says that there are three witnesses to Jesus on earth: the water, the Spirit and the blood. Ambrose of Milan (c. 340-397) cites this passage both in his commentary on Luke and in his treatise On Virgins where he says *aqua ad lavacrum, sanguis ad potum, spiritus ad resurrectionem*: "water for washing, blood for drinking, Spirit for resurrecting".

Summary. Sunday is both the first day of the week, and thus the first day of creation by God, and the eighth day of the week, and thus the first day outside the week, outside time and history, the first day of eternity, the day of the resurrection and the new creation in Christ. This is the basis for celebrating Easter for eight days including this Sunday, the Octave of Easter. The purpose clause refers to those who were baptised in water, anointed in the Spirit and communed in the body and blood of Christ at the Easter Vigil, who traditionally wore a white garment until this Sunday, which was called *Dominica in albis*, "Sunday in whites" in the 1962 Roman Missal. The preaching during this period is called mystagogy, which seeks to guide us back to the places of the mysteries and to comprehend by an ever more worthy understanding the mystery of ourselves in Christ. (Definitions from *A Latin Dictionary* by Lewis & Short.) ∎

With joy and expectation

The collect for the Third Sunday of Easter welcomes the renewal of spirit and looks forward to our resurrection

Source. The opening prayer this Sunday is a combination and revision of two ancient prayers. Most of the text is a revision of a prayer said over the people as part of the final blessing at the end of Mass, and is first found among the prayers for parish use in the Gelasian Sacramentary, of Roman origin and composed between 628 and 715. The purpose clause, however, is an exact citation from a prayer for the dead found only in the so-called Sacramentary of Verona, a collection of booklets each containing the prayers for a specific Mass. These booklets were developed from the papal liturgy between 400 and 560 and compiled between 561 and 574.

Because these Sundays are numbered differently in the two missals, the current prayer for the third Sunday of Easter replaces one for the second Sunday after Easter in the 1962 Roman Missal.

Analysis of the literary form

Petition: The prayer begins with the petition in the exhortative subjunctive: *semper exsultet populus tuus*: "may your people always rejoice". The English omits this phrase.

The first word of the Easter Proclamation during the Easter Vigil, *exsultet*, "may it rejoice", finds its echo in the first two words of our prayer three weeks later, *semper exsultet*, "may it ever rejoice"; there the angelic multitude exults, here God's people rejoice. Moving these words to the beginning emphasises their resonance with the Easter Proclamation.

Invocation: The simple form *Deus*, "God", is translated as "God our Father".

> *the opening prayer*
> ### Third Sunday of Easter
>
> God our Father, may we look forward with hope to our resurrection, for you have made us your sons and daughters, and restored the joy of our youth.
> (*The Roman Missal*, Collins, London, 1974)
>
> Semper exsultet populus tuus, Deus, renovata animae iuventute, ut, qui nunc laetatur in adoptionis se gloriam restitutum, resurrectionis diem spe certae gratulationis exspectet.
> (*Missale Romanum*, Città del Vaticano, 2002)

Premise: A type of premise is expressed by the ablative absolute: *renovata animae iuventute*, "as the youth of spirit [of your people] has been renewed". This is rendered active in English by a causal clause, which is addressed directly to God "for you have ... restored the joy of our youth". It is the basis for our petitioning God in prayer, a basis in what God has already done within us by renewing the vigour of our spirit.

Iuventute, "the age of youth", referred, in the classic world, to those between 20 and 40 years old. *Renovata* means "having been renewed, restored"; it is a "divine passive" because God is the unnamed agent who renews the youth. The difficulty of translating the feminine *animae* and its masculine counterpart, *animi*, is compounded over the centuries. For Cicero (106-43 BC) the feminine *animae* referred to the principle of life, which plants and animals have, whereas the masculine *animi* referred to the immortal soul. By the time of Thomas Aquinas (1225-74) the meanings had reversed.

Purpose: *Ut... resurrectionis diem spe certae gratulationis exspectet* can be translated as "that your people may long for the day of the resurrection in the hope of certain thanksgiving". The English translation restructures the prayer by rephrasing the purpose clause as a petition: "may we look forward with hope to our resurrection".

This is cited directly from the prayer for the dead. *Exspectet* followed by the accusative *diem* "day" means, " to look for with hope, fear, desire, expectation". *Diem* also means "appointed time" and can even refer to the activity done in a day, which is specified here by *resurrectionis*, "of the resurrection". Our longing for the day is characterised by *spe* – "in the hope". *Gratulationis* means, "of a manifestation of joy" and has the specific connotation, "of a religious festival of joy and thanksgiving". What is certain here is not the hope we have today, but the rejoicing and thanksgiving we hope to have on the day of the resurrection.

Motive: The relative clause, *qui nunc laetatur in adoptionis se gloriam restitutum*, means, your people "who now rejoice that it has been raised up unto the glory of adoption". The clause was originally used during the final blessing at Mass. The verb *laetatur* ("it rejoices, is joyful") has, as its complement the object sentence composed of the accusative subject *se* and the infinitive *restitutum esse*; the *esse* has been dropped, as it is understood. *Se* refers to *populus tuus*, "your people". While *restitutum esse* means "to have been restored, revived" and can even mean "to have been raised from the dead" – an allusion to baptism. Baptism, indeed, restores us to a former glory, which is

expressed in the earliest variant of this prayer, *in pristinam gloriam*, "unto the original glory". However, baptism restores us in the new way "of adoption" – *adoptionis*. Thus I have translated *restitutum* as "raised up" rather than as "restored".

Summary. Here the subject is *populus tuus* – "your people", the words that began the ancient prayer over the people. This subject is maintained throughout the prayer. The people's youth of spirit has been renewed by God; in the purpose clause the people await the day of resurrection; God's people rejoices in the motive clause. This emphasis on "your people" belies the origin of the prayer as a blessing over the people.

This prayer confesses what God has done, is doing and will do on our behalf. What God has done is expressed in both past participles, which are divine passives implying God's work: *renovata*, "having been renewed" and *restitutum*, "having been raised up", which is an image of rising from the waters of baptism into eternal life. Our response is to rejoice, *laetatur*, in the now, *nunc*.

We petition to ever rejoice as the angels, on that night of the Resurrection, at the Easter Vigil when the elect are baptised, confirmed and communed, and when Christians renew their baptismal vows. Christian life is lived in this paradox between who we have become in Christ and who we are yet to become fully, between the already and the not yet, rejoicing and expectation. With hope and awe we long for that day of the final resurrection. What, we pray, God will do on our behalf turns the paradox of our lives on its head, for in the midst of today's hope, *spe*, we proclaim a tomorrow of certain rejoicing, *certae gratulationis*. We pray that on the last day of the Resurrection we may have rejoicing and thanksgiving because we will have been raised up definitively. ■

Way of the shepherd

The collect for the Fourth Sunday of Easter proclaims the paschal mystery not merely through its words but also through its structure

---

the opening prayer
Fourth Sunday of Easter

Almighty and ever-living God,
give us new strength from the courage
of Christ our shepherd,
and lead us to join the saints in heaven.
(*The Roman Missal*,
Collins, London, 1974)

Omnipotens sempiterne Deus,
deduc nos ad societatem caelestium
gaudiorum, ut eo perveniat humilitas
gregis, quo processit fortitudo pastoris.
(*Missale Romanum*,
Città del Vaticano, 2002)

This Sunday we proclaim the good news that Jesus, the good shepherd, has laid down his life for the sheep. This paschal mystery suffuses our every prayer. The opening prayer this Sunday is a dense kernel summarising the paschal mystery not only in its words but also in its literary structure. Attention to this prayer before and during its proclamation will open us to receive the Word proclaimed and living anew among us.

Source. I was once asked by neighbouring evangelical pastors about praying from the heart. I responded that when we Catholics come up with a good prayer, we keep it. This Sunday's prayer dates at least to the mid-seventh century, when it was offered in the titular churches of Rome during presbyteral liturgies, as it is listed among prayers for the evenings of Paschaltide in the Gelasian Sacramentary composed between 628-715. This prayer replaces one in the 1962 *Missale Romanum*, which was first assigned to this Sunday in the Sacramentary of Padua c. 670-680, when it was among those used by presbyters celebrating liturgies with pilgrims at the shrine of St. Peter. That prayer is now assigned to the fifteenth Sunday in Ordinary Time.

Analysis of the literary form

Invocation: This is complex – a noun and two adjectives: *Omnipotens sempiterne Deus*. It is rendered literally in the official translation: "Almighty and ever-living God."

Petition: *deduc nos ad societatem caelestium gaudiorum*: "lead us on to the fellowship of heavenly joys". *Deduc* is an imperative meaning "lead forth, escort". Moreover, the petition follows a classic Latin expression for marriage: *deducere mulierem ad...*, literally "to conduct a bride (from her father's house) to (her husband)". The petition replaces *mulierem* "woman" with *nos* "us" and replaces the image of the husband with *societatem*, which means "fellowship, communion, society". This fellowship is *caelestium gaudiorum* or "of heavenly joys". Thus, the allusion is that we petition God as a husband to conduct us as a bride to the communion of heavenly joys, the wedding feast of the lamb. This is rendered in the English translation as the second of two petitions, "and lead us to join the saints in heaven".

Purpose: This is expressed by the classic formula of *ut* followed by the subjunctive: *ut eo perveniat humilitas gregis, quo* *processit fortitudo pastoris*, meaning, "that the humility of the flock may arrive thither, whither preceded the courage of the shepherd". The Latin structure of this purpose clause shows a tight contrasting parallelism, which turns on two fulcra, *eo... quo*, best expressed by the old "thither... whither"whither"; which is easily rendered, "to where the courage of the shepherd has proceeded, to there the humility of the flock may arrive".

This parallelism was not yet developed in the earliest text of our prayer but was fully formed by c.670-680 when the prayer was offered during eucharistic celebrations with pilgrims at St Peter's. The contrasting parallel continues with two verbs: *perveniat* and *processit*, meaning respectively "may it arrive at" and "he has gone before". The contrasting parallel continues with the subjects of these verbs: *humilitas and fortitudo*, meaning "lowness" and "strength" respectively. "Lowness" here is a positive force in opposition to pride, and "fortitude" shows its strength in undertaking hardship. Finally, like the snap of a whip, the force of each contrast is revealed in the last two words: *gregis* and *pastoris*, meaning "of the flock" and "of the shepherd". The purpose clause is translated into English by the first of two imperative petitions, "give us new strength from the courage of Christ our shepherd".

Motive: The motive clause was treated above together with the purpose clause, as what better motive could there be for God to grant that the lowness of the flock may arrive to the communion of celestial joys, than that the fortitude of the pastor has already gone ahead.

Summary. Even though the scripture readings for each Sunday are assigned according to a three-year cycle, the opening prayer is the same each year. In all three years, however, this is Good Shepherd Sunday, as is reflected in different scriptures each year. This prayer, then, corresponds to all three gospels, but in different ways.

In year A (2008) the Gospel was John 10:1-10: "I am the sheepgate." According to John, the shepherd enters the sheepfold by the gate, calls his own by name and leads them out, going ahead of them. Likewise, we petition God to lead us out, *deduc nos*. The tight contrasting parallelism of the purpose clause expresses the intimate relationship between the shepherd who leads and the flock that follows. The evangelist also calls Jesus "the sheepgate", and the pen, then, is an image of the communion of heavenly joys, granted the image in the prayer goes well beyond the joys of a sheep pen.

In year B (2009) the Gospel is John 10:11-18: "The good shepherd lays down his life for the sheep." The choice of *fortitudo* is an allusion to this gospel passage, because it is known in undertaking hardship. Jesus also says that he has other sheep that he will bring into the one fold, that there will be one flock and one shepherd. This is expressed in the prayer by the communion of heavenly joys, and by the insistence on the collective nouns in the prayer: *nos* "we", *societatem* "communion" and *gregis* "of the flock". The prayer does not concern itself with individual sheep as does the Gospel in year A. Rather it expresses the unity of the one flock.

In year C (2010) the Gospel is John 10:27-30: "I give my sheep eternal life." We pray that God may lead us to that society of heavenly joys. While the opening prayers do not always correspond to the Gospel of the day, this one works well all three years and thus prepares the assembly to hear the word of God proclaimed, meditate upon it and offer the word back to God in prayer. ■

Towards eternal joy

The collect for the Fifth Sunday of Easter brings together the new creation of Christ's rising from the grave with the new life that springs from our baptism

Source. The opening prayer this Sunday is an example of the ongoing liturgical renewal. The prayer usually offered in English this Sunday is the translation of a Latin prayer assigned to this Sunday in the *Missale Romanum* of both 1970 and 1975. The same opening prayer was repeated on the twenty-third Sunday in Ordinary Time. After more than 30 years of praying from those missals, the third edition of the *Missale Romanum*, 2002, was revised and augmented. The prayer from Saturday of the fourth week of Easter was transferred to this Sunday. This substitution, however, has not yet been made in the English translation, which is based on the 1970 Roman Missal. Thus, today I offer a commentary on the newly assigned prayer for this Sunday, then on the twenty-third Sunday in Ordinary Time I shall comment on the prayer that still appears in the English translation on this Sunday. Finally, the prayer for this Sunday in the 1962 Missal is now assigned to the twenty-first Sunday in Ordinary Time.

This prayer is indeed new in that it was composed at the time of the Second Vatican Council from parts of two prayers appearing on Tuesday of Holy Week in the ancient Sacramentary of Bergamo, an Ambrosian sacramentary with Carolingian redaction. Neither of these prayers corresponds to any ancient Roman sacramentary, offering yet another example of how the Roman rite appropriates in ways ever new the best of other Latin rites.

Analysis of the literary form

Invocation: The same complex invocation, *omnipotens sempiterne Deus*, translated literally last week as "Almighty and ever-living God", this week is rendered as "Father".

> *the opening prayer*
> **Fifth Sunday of Easter**
> Father, May we whom you renew in baptism bear witness to our faith by the way we live. By the suffering, death, and resurrection of your Son may we come to eternal joy.
> (*The Roman Missal*, Collins, London, 1974)
>
> Omnipotens sempiterne Deus, semper in nobis paschale perfice sacramentum, ut, quos sacro baptismate dignatus es renovare, sub tuae protectionis auxilio multos fructus afferant, et ad aeternae vitae gaudia pervenire concedas.
> (*Missale Romanum*, Città del Vaticano, 2002)

Petition: Given in the imperative, the petition is the phrase *semper in nobis paschale perfice sacramentum*: "ever bring the paschal mystery to completion within us". This phrase is adapted from the preface of the Eucharistic prayer in the Bergamo Sacramentary. The structure of the English prayer has been reworked, as the imperative petition has been omitted, and the paschal mystery has been specified by the phrase "by the suffering, death, and resurrection of your Son".

In classic Latin *sacramentum* is a military oath of allegiance. Tertullian (c. 155-230) used *sacramentum* to translate the Greek *mysterion* referring to hidden things revealed, as in the mystery of faith revealed in Christ. The *paschalis sacramentum* or paschal mystery is the self-emptying of

God and the divinisation of humanity in Christ. This is specified by his death and Resurrection, and is celebrated in the Easter sacraments of baptism, confirmation and Eucharist. Leo the Great combines both the historical and liturgical dimensions when referring to the Easter sacraments as the "paschal feast in which the mystery of human salvation consists" (Epistles, 121, 1, 13).

The rest of the opening prayer is reworked from the prayer over the gifts from the Bergamo Sacramentary.

Motive: Two phrases express the purpose of our praying, and both of them incorporate the word *eos* "they" the antecedent implied in the relative pronoun *quos* – "whom" of the motive, the relative clause *quos sacro baptismate dignatus es renovare*: "whom you have deemed worthy to restore by holy baptism", expressed in the translation as "whom you renew in baptism". *Renovare* is "to renew in strength, recreate"; Christ's rising from the grave is the new creation by which we rising from the waters of baptism are recreated.

The **first purpose** clause is *ut ... sub tuae protectionis auxilio multos fructus afferant*; "that ... they may bear much fruit under the help of your protection". *Afferant* is an example of the very rare classical meaning "may they bring forth as a product, yield, produce". Even though we are the subject of this first purpose clause, we are subordinated to God's action in the dependent motive clause. Thus the purpose for our praying is that God may bring it about that we bear much fruit. Latin uses the same construction, *ut ... afferant*, to express both intention (purpose), expressed in the subjunctive in English as, "that they may bear...", as and result, expressed in the indicative in English as, "that they do bear". I understand this phrase to express intention and the final one to express result. The primary

meaning of *fructus* is "enjoyments", then in a transferred sense "the enjoyment that proceeds from a thing", as in "fruit, results, returns"; while its translation need not be moralised, Scripture often refers to the Christian way of life as a tree or seed bearing good fruit, as in the English rephrasing of the first purpose clause as an exhortative petition: "may we ... bear witness to our faith by the way we live".

Second purpose: A second subjunctive verb establishes another purpose clause, *ut ... et ... concedas* – "and that you may grant" – is not rendered in English. This clause restores God as the subject, in that *concedas* means "may you grant, confirm" or the old "vouchsafe".

Result: What we ask that God grant is expressed by the entire result clause composed of *eos* – "they" – implied in *quos* – "whom" – and the infinitive *pervenire* – "to attain to". Thus, the result of God's granting is [*eos...*] *ad aeternae vitae gaudia pervenire*. While this construction may be expressive of either the intended purpose of God's granting, and thus be expressed in English in the subjunctive, "that they may attain to the joys of eternal life", I take it here to express the result of the entire developmental process of this prayer that results in God's granting "that they attain to the joys of eternal life". The official English renders the clause as an exhortative petition, "may we come to eternal joy".

Summary. All Christian prayer celebrates the paschal mystery ever perfecting the image of Christ's rising from the grave in us who likewise have come up from the waters. The motive for God's granting us to arrive unto the joys of eternal life is God's deeming it worthy to restore us by the sacrament, and our lives in Christ produce fruit only by the help of God's protection, but when we cooperate with divine gift, we bear fruit and enter into eternal joys. ∎

To the rising Lord

We seek God's help at times of sorrow, but we also need him when we rejoice. The collect for the Sixth Sunday of Easter, writes Daniel McCarthy, asks God to enable us to celebrate the Resurrection in such a way that we live what we celebrate

One of my reasons for writing this column is to show how the meaning of an opening prayer comes from the meaning of the words in their grammatical structure or literary form. This is why I detail the correspondence between the grammatical phrases and their literary elements: the invocation, amplification, petition, purpose, motive and premise. My analysis of the prayer conforms to a literary framework expressed in classical grammar, to which even a recent composition such as last Sunday's opening prayer concurs.

Source. The opening prayer this Sunday was composed for the 1970 Roman Missal from fragments of three ancient prayers, as I note below. It replaces a prayer, assigned to this Sunday in the Gelasian Sacramentary, composed between 628 and 715 for use in the titular churches of Rome, but now assigned to the tenth Sunday in ordinary time.

Analysis of the literary form

Petition: The whole prayer springs from the petition *fac*, literally "make", which means variously, "help, enable, bring it about". The verb's object is expressed by the entire phrase *nos ... hos laetitiae dies ... affectu sedulo celebrare*, "that we celebrate with steadfast zeal during these days of great joy", all of which is rendered in the English prayer as "help us to celebrate our joy". The use of *fac* with the accusative (*nos*) and infinitive (*celebrare*) is not classical, but is common in medieval Latin and modern languages such as Italian and English, as above where it is rendered word for word "make us to celebrate". The imperative *fac* typically establishes a result

the opening prayer
Sixth Sunday of Easter

Ever-living God, Help us to celebrate our joy in the resurrection of the Lord and to express in our lives the love we celebrate.
(*The Roman Missal*, Collins, London, 1974)

Fac nos, omnipotens Deus, hos laetitiae dies, quos in honorem Domini resurgentis exsequimur, affectu sedulo celebrare, ut quod recordatione percurrimus semper in opere teneamus.
(*Missale Romanum*, Città del Vaticano, 2002)

clause, wereby we command God to bring about a concrete result. But *fac* may also establish a purpose clause expressive of our cooperating with God's intent: "bring it about that we may celebrate". *Celebrare* here means, "we frequent, go in great numbers to a celebration, celebrate, honour".

The last three words *affectu sedulo celebrare*, here meaning "we celebrate with steadfast zeal", interpreted in the English prayer by the phrase "the love we celebrate", are reworked from the prayer after communion for the feast of St John the Baptist in the so-called Verona Sacramentary, a compilation of individual Mass booklets developed from the papal liturgy between 400 and 560 and compiled together outside Rome between 561 and 574.

Invocation: Tucked inside the object phrase of the petition is the complex invocation consisting of a noun and an adjective, *omnipotens Deus*, "all-powerful God", which is translated as "ever-living God". *Omnipotens* corresponds directly with the petition *fac*, in that, because God is omnipotent, God can surely bring about what we ask.

Premise: Also tucked within the object phrase of the petition is the first of two relative clauses, *quos in honorem Domini resurgentis exsequimur* – "which days we fulfil unto the honour of the rising Lord", represented in the English by the prepositional phrase "in the resurrection of the Lord". Even though its grammar does not conform to the classical model, I have called this a premise clause because our "fulfilling the days" is the context for our asking God to help us to celebrate.

Resurgentis is a present participle meaning "of one rising again, appearing again" and, thus, conveys both that Christ is rising from the dead, implying that he is yet to ascend, and that during these days Christ appears again and again, as recounted in the gospels. This ambivalence was developed by omitting the words *a mortuis*, "from the dead", from the original phrase found in a preface for a fast day following Pentecost, again in the Verona Sacramentary. The original, however, is more fluid: "which days we fulfil unto the honour of the Lord rising from the dead". On Pentecost Sunday perhaps in 441, Leo the Great (Pope from 440 to 461) gives the same text as the Verona Sacramentary in a homily, when he talks about the fast after Pentecost. Both Leo and the prayer continue to mention the Ascension and gift of the Holy Spirit, which have been excised from our pre-Ascension prayer. *Resurgentis* also appears in the Easter sequence *Victimae Paschali*, in which Mary says: "*Gloriam vidi resurgentis*" – "I saw the glory of the one rising".

Purpose: The entire *ut* clause comes from an opening prayer for Easter in the Gelasian Sacramentary. As we fulfil these days unto the honour of the Lord, and God enables to celebrate with steadfast zeal, we celebrate in turn with the intention expressed in the purpose clause, *ut ... semper in opere teneamus*, "that we ever attain in action". The *ut* clause expresses the purpose for which we pray, namely the desired result we wish God to bring about. In this prayer we wish God to enable us to celebrate such that, as a result, we live what we celebrate. The English translation has rephrased the purpose clause as a second infinitive dependent on the petition "help", which gives the prayer the following parallel structure: "help us to celebrate ... and to express in our lives".

Motive: Following the classical structure, God's motive is expressed by a relative clause tucked into the purpose clause, *quod recordatione percurrimus*: "that which we experience by recollection". God's motive for helping us to celebrate in such a way that we live what we celebrate is that we have penetrated it by reflection. *Recordatione*, meaning "by a calling to mind, recollection, remembrance", appears only here in the current Roman Missal, and nowhere in the Vulgate Bible. Its verbal form, however, is frequent, as we often petition God *recordare*, "be mindful of" the Church, for example. In this prayer, we are mindful of the rising Lord by our celebration.

Summary: This prayer differs from others in that we are the subject of all the verbs save *fac*: *exsequimur*, *celebrare*, *percurrimus*, *teneamus*. God's activity (*fac*) enables us to act. The participial describes Christ's rising not as a past event but as contemporaneous reality, which we honour. The prayer shows its force, however, as recollection motivates our lives. There is no separation between liturgy and daily activity. The purpose of our prayer attains to action; may we so celebrate that we live. ∎

Glory and exultation

Some countries have transferred the celebration of the Feast of the Ascension from Thursday to Sunday. or Ascension Day, we ask God to help us rejoice in thankfulness

In many countries, the Feast of the Ascension is celebrated on the Sunday following Ascension Day. Something similar happened with Easter at the turn of the second century, when it was transferred from the Jewish lunar calendar 14 Nissan (regardless of the day of the week) to Sunday. At that time, Easter was a unitary feast, as in John's Gospel where Jesus gives the gift of the Spirit to the disciples on Easter Sunday (20:22). Over time our celebration of Easter was extended to the three days (the *Triduum*) and eventually developed into the Lent and Easter Seasons, as in the Acts of the Apostles, which says that the risen Jesus appeared among the disciples for 40 days before his ascension (1:3), then followed the gift of the Spirit on the fiftieth day, Pentecost.

Source. The 1962 *Missale Romanum* included Mass formularies for both the Vigil of the Ascension (its opening prayer from the seventh-century Gelasian is now used on the tenth Sunday in ordinary time) and for Mass on Ascension Thursday (its opening prayer from the Hadrianum of 785-786 is given today as an option). After the Second Vatican Council the Vigil Mass was dropped until the 2002 *Missale*, when a new Vigil formulary was inserted. This formulary is not included in the English Sacramentary, which ever remains the first translation of the 1970 *Missale*. Here I examine the newly composed opening prayer introduced in the 1970 *Missale*, which only slightly reworks a phrase from a homily given by Leo the Great on this feast in the year 444 (*Tractatus* 73, 3). Leo's preaching still inspires the Church in the composition of new prayers.

the opening prayer
The Ascension of the Lord

God our Father, make us joyful in the ascension of your Son Jesus Christ. May we follow him into the new creation, for his ascension is our glory and our hope.
(*The Roman Missal*, Collins, London, 1974)

Fac nos, omnipotens Deus, sanctis exsultare gaudiis, et pia gratiarum actione laetari, quia Christi Filii tui ascensio est nostra provectio, et quo processit gloria capitis, eo spes vocatur et corporis.
(*Missale Romanum*, Città del Vaticano, 2002)

Analysis of the literary form
Petition: The prayer begins with the imperative petition *fac*: "bring about that", translated literally as "make".

First result: God enables us to act in two ways expressed in two object sentences, composed of two infinitives sharing the same accusative subject *nos*, "us". The first is: *nos … sanctis exsultare gaudiis*, "[make] us to exult with holy joys". The English translation combines both purpose clauses and the first motive clause into one phrase: "make us joyful in the ascension of your Son Jesus Christ".

The construction *fac* followed by the accusative and infinitive is common to late Latin, and in this case modern Latin to express the concrete result of an action, and is expressed in English in the indicative: "Make us to rejoice". It could have been expressed classically by the result clause: *ut exsultemus* …, which, although in the subjunctive in Latin and identical to a purpose clause, as an expression of result is rendered in English in the indicative "[bring it about] that we exult…". Leo exhorted the assembly *exsultemus*, "let us exult", and we pray that God bring it about that we in fact do exult (*fac nos exsultare*).

Invocation: Nestled within the first result clause is the complex invocation added to Leo's text: *omnipotens Deus*, "all-powerful God", rendered as "God our Father".

Second result: The second object sentence, *et pia gratiarum actione laetari*, "and to be happy with devout thanksgiving", likewise could have been expressed classically as the result clause, *ut … laetemur*, "[bring it about] that we rejoice". Leo exhorted the the assembly *laetemur*, "let us rejoice"; we petition and we pray that God bring it about that we in fact do rejoice (*fac nos laetari*). While grammatically these two result clauses are parallel, joined by a simple *et*, "and", their ideas are accumulative in that at first we exult with holy rejoicings, then we rejoice with a dutiful action of thanks: our rejoicing is ordered to our giving thanks to God.

First motive: To refer to the above as result clauses is not to imply that our rejoicing is coerced or in any way not freely given, because the way in which God brings it about that we exult and rejoice, however, is part of the gift in that God elicits joy from us on account of the two motive clauses for which we give thanks. Both are expressed classically as causal clauses with *quia*, "because". The first is: *quia Christi Filii tui ascensio est nostra provectio*, "because the ascension of Christ your Son is our advancement". The Latin root of *provectio* is the verb *veho*, which is related to the English word "wagon". The ascension is, then, a sort of wagon that bears us before (*pro*) or forward. The ascension of Christ is not considered according to its quality as a past historical

deed, but as our reality, our advancement, both in the sense that in Christ our humanity advances to the right hand of God Almighty, and because we advance as we participate in Christ's mystery.

Second motive: The second motive clause composed of the correlatives *quo … eo*, "whither … thither; to where … to there", is a direct quote from Leo: *quia … et quo processit gloria capitis, eo spes vocatur et corporis*: and "because to where the glory of the head preceeded, to there the hope of the body is called". It is translated by the independent sentence, "May we follow him into the new creation, for his ascension is our glory and our hope."

The first motive is expanded in the correlative clauses of the second. Christ is further understood as head (*capitis*) and body (*corporis*), yet Christ the head assumed our humanity and we, Christ's body, share his divinity, for there is but one Christ, fully human and fully divine. The ascension (*ascensio*) expanded temporally is both Christ's having gone ahead (*processit*) and our being called (*vocatur*). *Vocatur* is a divine passive verb for God calls the hope of the body. Moreover, the ascension is understood as both glory (*gloria*) and hope (*spes*), because in hope we already share in Christ's glory. The hope of our future (*spes*) is presently called (*vocatur*) to where he already preceeded (*processit*).

Summary. In the mystery of the Ascension, God assumes our humanity, transformed by Christ's Resurrection, into the triune life of mutual self-gift. In Christ, we the body of Christ already share the glory to which our hope is called. Because of God's saving deeds already brought about in Christ whereby Christ's ascension is our advancement, and where the glory of the head preceded the hope of the body is called, we have good reason to petition that God elicit this concrete result in us: both to exult and to rejoice with thanksgivings. ∎

Till the end of time

The collect for the Seventh Sunday of Easter, three days after Ascension Day, combines an awareness of the fact that Christ is now with the Father, with a trust in his promise to remain with us always

In many regions the Ascension has been transferred to this Sunday. In England, however, it remains on Thursday according to the chronology of Acts 1:3, "[Jesus] appearing to them for 40 days". Thus, I comment here on the prayer for the Seventh Sunday of Easter.

Every act of Christian prayer celebrates the entire mystery of God's self-emptying love for us in Christ and our becoming one with God in Christ through the power of the Holy Spirit. Specific mysteries are remembered during the liturgical year, that we might better reflect upon each, but always in light of the whole. In every collect, then, we recall the entire paschal mystery, even as we are mindful this Sunday of the few days between the Ascension of Jesus and the descent of the Spirit. While rooted in the life of the historical Jesus, according to the differing accounts given in the Scriptures, Christian prayer is centred in the present act of worship with an eye to its consummation at the hand of God.

Source. The opening prayer this Sunday has been redacted from a prayer first appearing in the Gelasian Sacramentary, composed between 628 and 715, originally compiled for use during the presbyteral liturgy in the titular churches of Rome. This prayer is included in an alternative Mass for the Ascension; it does not come, as one might expect, from the Mass given for the Sunday after the Ascension. It replaces the prayer in the 1962 Roman Missal, which first appears in the Gelasian for the sixth Sunday of Easter. That prayer no longer appears in the Roman Missal.

---

the opening prayer
Seventh Sunday of Easter

Father, help us keep in mind that Christ our Saviour lives with you in glory and promised to remain with us until the end of time.
(*The Roman Missal*,
Collins, London, 1974)

Supplicationibus nostris, Domine, adesto propitius, ut, sicut humani generis Salvatorem tecum in tua credimus maiestate, ita eum usque ad consummationem saeculi manere nobiscum, sicut ipse promisit, sentiamus.
(*Missale Romanum*,
Città del Vaticano, 2002)

The scriptural context for this prayer is the last line of the Gospel of Matthew: *Et ecce ego vobiscum sum omnibus diebus usque ad consummationem saeculi*: "and behold, I am with you all days until the consummation of time" (28:20). Matthew's Gospel does not recount the Ascension. Rather, Jesus gives the great commission from a hill in Galilee.

Analysis of the literary form
Petition: The prayer begins with the petition *supplicationibus nostris ... adesto propitius*: "graciously attend ... to our prayers". The entire phrase is omitted in the English. *Adesto* is a "future" imperative, which form we commonly know from the Ten Commandments: "thou shalt". It means, "do be near, attend to, be present with one's aid or support, come".

Invocation: The simple invocation *Domine*, "Lord", is translated, "Father".

First motive: Used as an adverb to mean "graciously", *propitius* is properly an adjective meaning "gracious". God's motive for attending to our prayer is that God is gracious. *Propitius* comes from the adverb *prope*, which means "near", thus reinforcing the imperative "be present".

Second motive: The purpose and motive clauses are comparative phrases that hinge on two adverbs: *sicut ... ita*, "just as ... so". The first, the dependent phrase, gives another motive, *sicut humani generis Salvatorem tecum in tua credimus maiestate*, "just as we believe that the Saviour of the human race is with you in your majesty". This is expressed in the English prayer as a petition in the imperative, "help us keep in mind that Christ our Saviour lives with you in glory". *Credimus* was originally a business term meaning, "we give as a loan", then came to mean "we trust or confide in a person or thing". What we believe is expressed by the accusative with an implied infinitive, *Salvatorem [esse]*, "that the Saviour is".

Purpose: The main phrase of the comparative gives the purpose for our prayer, expressed by a purpose clause according to the classical formula *ut* followed by the subjunctive *sentiamus*: *ut ... ita eum usque ad consummationem saeculi manere nobiscum ... sentiamus* – "so may we perceive him to remain with us until the consummation of the age". This clause is expressed in English by a second phrase dependent on the imperative petition "and promised to remain with us until the end of time". *Sentiamus* means "may we discern by the senses, perceive". What we perceive is expressed by the accusative *eum* followed by the infinitive *manere*, here meaning "that he ... abides, remains".

Third motive: We remind the Lord of the promise of Christ, *sicut ipse promisit*, "just as he promised", which is not rendered in the English translation.

Summary. A contrasting parallelism drives the purpose clause and its motive between what we believe, *credimus*, and what we want to perceive, *sentiamus*. We believe that the Saviour is with the Lord, *tecum*; we want to perceive him remaining with us, *manere nobiscum*. We believe that the Saviour is in the Lord's majesty, *in tua maiestate*, and thus outside of time; we want to perceive him with us until the end of time, *usque ad consummationem saeculi*. The contrasting parallelism continues between the Saviour of the human race, and we who believe and want to perceive. *In tua maiestate*, "in your majesty", alludes to Mark 16:19: "Jesus was taken up into heaven and sits at the right of God", and Romans 8:34, which adds that Jesus intercedes on our behalf. Thus, we ask the Lord to draw near to our prayers, *Supplicationibus nostris adesto*.

Three motives are expressed in this prayer: 1) because the Lord is merciful we pray that God will be near; 2) because we believe that the Saviour is with the Lord; and 3) because the Saviour promised to remain with us, we pray to perceive the Saviour, who has ascended, yet remains with us until the end of time.

While the liturgical year is rooted in the past, our prayer is a present exchange with an eye to the future. In this prayer, the only phrase that looks to the past, to the promise of the Saviour to remain with us always, also looks to the end of time. Otherwise, the prayer engages us in the divine human exchange at the heart of all Christian prayer, here specified as God's presence to our prayers, and our response by believing and praying that God grant us to perceive the Redeemer, already in majesty, yet remaining also with us until the consummation of time.. ∎

Gifts rain down from heaver

*The collect for Pentecost exhorts the Spirit to
continue to work in the world and petitions
God for an outpouring of the Holy Spirit*

Source. By comparing the earliest
recorded source of the opening prayer
for any given Sunday in the *Missale
Romanum* of 1962 – the last before the
Council – with that of 1970, the first fruits
of Vatican II, we may understand in part
the mind of the author of the new Missal.
As we have seen numerous times, so again
the opening prayer of Pentecost in the
1962 *Missale Romanum* first appears
assigned to Pentecost in the Hadrianum, a
sacramentary given by Pope Hadrian I to
Charlemagne in 785-86. The Hadrianum
was a papal sacramentary, with only the
rites proper to the celebration of the liturgy by the Pope. As such, it lacked many of
the elements needed for ordinary celebrations. During the reign of Louis the Pious,
a supplement was added by Benedict of
Aniane with almost 800 prayers for parish
use working to supply the missing parts, all
of which affected the development of the
liturgy in the Middle Ages. Many of the
prayers in the *Missale Romanum* of 1962
that originally came from the Hadrianum
have been replaced by prayers first found
in the Gelasian Sacramentary, of between
628 and 715, originally for use in presbyteral liturgy celebrated in the titular
churches of Rome. The opening prayer for
this Sunday, which was assigned to this
same feast, was among those prayers
replaced. That prayer is no longer included in the *Missale Romanum*. The shift
from the Hadrianum to the Gelasianum
represents a shift from papal liturgy to
parish liturgy, and to an earlier textual
source.

Analysis of the literary form
Invocation: The simple invocation *Deus*,
"God", is translated as "God our Father".

---

the opening prayer
Pentecost: Mass during the Day

God our Father, let the Spirit you sent
on your Church to begin the teaching
of the Gospel continue to work in the
world through the hearts of all who
believe.
(*The Roman Missal*,
Collins, London, 1974)

Deus, qui sacramento festivitatis
hodiernae universam Ecclesiam tuam
in omni gente et natione sanctificas,
in totam mundi latitudinem Spiritus
Sancti dona defunde, et, quod inter
ipsa evangelicae praedicationis exordia
operata est divina dignatio, nunc
quoque per credentium corda
perfunde.
(*Missale Romanum*,
Città del Vaticano, 2002)

Amplification: An extensive amplification is given by the relative clause, *qui
sacramento festivitatis hodiernae universam Ecclesiam tuam in omni gente et
natione sanctificas*: "you who make your
whole Church in every people and nation
holy by the mystery of today's feast", is not
expressed in the English translation.
Sanctificas means "you make holy, conse-
crate, dedicate". *Sacramento* in juridical
language refers to money held in bond; in
military language, the soldier's oath of allegiance to the emperor; in religious language, a mystery revealed; in Christian
language, a sacrament, but more broadly
understood than the seven. The Holy
Spirit is, as it were, God's bond for what is
to come – a security, God's pledge.

First petition: Like many English translations of the opening prayers, this one has two petitions, both in the imperative. The first, *in totam mundi latitudinem Spiritus Sancti dona defunde*, means "pour down into the entire breadth of the world the gifts of the Holy Spirit". Both petitions are reworked in the English into one exhortative subjunctive: "let the Spirit ... continue to work in the world". *Defunde* means "to pour down"; used as as a religious term it means "to pour out", as in a libation to the gods. In this prayer, God pours *in totam mundi latitudinem* – the entire breadth of the world.

Second petition: I find the second petition playful, but it must be considered in unison with the motive clause. First the petition, *et ... nunc quoque per credentium corda perfunde*: "and even now pour out ... over the hearts of the ones believing". This is rendered in the English by "through the hearts of all who believe". The early texts of this prayer used the petition *defunde* twice. Our current version achieves better style by using different verbs. Only the prefix has been changed, however, to *per*, rendering *perfunde*, which both can be accompanied in the same sentence by the preposition *per*, as here, *per corda*, and can be followed by a double accusative as here: *corda* and *quod*. *Perfunde*, however, introduces a new meaning, "pour over, bedew", then it can mean "pour into" and "cause to flow out", as I have rendered it above. *Per corda* here means, "throughout, all over the hearts".

Motive: What we ask God to pour out is given in the motive, a relative clause beginning with the accusative, *quod*, dependant on *perfunde*: *quod inter ipsa evangelicae praedicationis exordia operata est divina dignatio*, which means "that which divine condescension accomplished about during the very beginnings of Gospel preaching". The motive is expressed in English by the relative clause: "[Let the

Spirit] you sent on your Church to begin the teaching of the Gospel". God's motive for filling the hearts of believers today is what God already brought about at the beginning. *Operata est* is a form of the verb *operor*, meaning, "to serve the gods, perform sacred rites" and in church Latin, "to work, operate, have effect". Here it is God's work, not ours. *Dignatio* means, "by a deeming worthy, regard". *Inter ... exordia* here means "during, in the course of ... the origins".

Purpose: There is no purpose clause. The early texts have the word *ut* in place of *et* thus making the second imperative a purpose clause, but the verb remained in the imperative. This has been corrected in the current prayer.

Summary. This prayer is Trinitarian in that it is addressed to God, *Deus*; it recalls the preaching of the good news of Jesus, *evangelicae praedicationis*; and it petitions for the outpouring of the Holy Spirit, *Spiritus Sancti dona defunde*. Our current celebration, *festivitatis hodiernae*, recalls the beginnings, *exordia*, but in the context of petitioning that God act again even now, *nunc quoque ... perfunde*. The mystery, *sacramento*, of this feast is not only what the divine regard brought about, *operata est divina dignatio*, but our petitioning to share in the same Spirit today, *perfunde*. The prayer is broad in its application to God's entire Church, *universam Ecclesiam tuam*, in every people and nation, *in omni gente et natione*. One petition is equally extensive, asking God to rain down the gifts of the Spirit on the world, *in totam mundi latitudinem*, whereas the second petition is intimate, asking that God cause to overflow the hearts of believers: *per credentium corda perfunde*. ■

On earth and in heaven

In our flesh we bear the image of Adam but we also bear the image of Christ. This Sunday's opening prayer, acknowledging God as ruler of heavenly and earthly realities, bears witness to our divine creation and also to our divine recreation

The supplications (*supplicationes*) we ask God to hear are not only the two petitions of this opening prayer, but also the personal prayers made by the faithful during the preceding silence. In this way, the opening prayer is truly a *collecta*, as its Latin title means "things having been gathered up". Thus, after the presider invites the assembly to pray, all pause for silent prayer. When asked how long the silence ought to last, I respond long enough to allow the members of the assembly to formulate their own personal prayers. Furthermore, the silence ought to be so dependable that the people come to trust that the presider, acknowledging their need to formulate their own personal prayer, will provide the silence necessary. These personal prayers, then, are "gathered together", as it were, as the presider offers the opening prayer, which by its very nature is universal so as to give voice to the many private prayers of the assembly. The assembly, then, ratifies the prayer of the presider with its "Amen".

Source. This Sunday's opening prayer is found in both the ancient presbyteral and papal traditions. Its earliest witness is in the Hadrianum, the papal sacramentary given by Pope Hadrian I to Charlemagne in 785-786. In the 1962 *Missale Romanum* it was assigned to the second Sunday after Epiphany. Due to the liturgical reform mandated by the Second Vatican Council, the Advent-Christmas cycle now ends with the feast of the Baptism of the Lord, whereupon the Sundays of ordinary time are numbered until Lent, resuming after the Lent-Easter cycle. The term "ordinary time" comes from the Latin *ordinalis* denoting an order of succession as in

> *the opening prayer*
> ## Second Sunday in Ordinary Time
> Father of heaven and earth, hear our prayers, and show us the way to peace in the world.
> (*The Roman Missal*,
> Collins, London, 1974)
>
> Omnipotens sempiterne Deus,
> qui caelestia simul et terrena
> moderaris, supplicationes populi tui
> clementer exaudi, et pacem tuam
> nostris concede temporibus.
> (*Missale Romanum*,
> Città del Vaticano, 2002)

"ordinal numbers". In Latin, this Sunday is called *dominica II* "*per annum*", "second Sunday 'in the course of the year'".

Analysis of the literary form
Invocation: The complex invocation *Omnipotens sempiterne Deus* means literally "all-powerful ever-living God", which is rendered in English as "Father".

Amplification: The invocation is amplified by the relative clause *qui caelestia simul et terrena moderaris*, "you who regulate heavenly bodies and also earthly realities", which is translated as "of heaven and earth". The deponent form *moderaris* means "you set a measure, bounds", then, "you rule, guide, govern".

The pairing of heavenly bodies with earthly realities does not refer merely to cosmology. Rather, it is an allusion to Paul's distinction between Adam and Christ in 1 Corinthians 15:47-49. First Paul contrasts Adam with

Christ, for Adam, *primus homo de terra, terrenus*, "the first human person, being from the earth, was earthly", whereas Christ, *secundus homo de caelo, caelestis*, "the second human person, from heaven, is heavenly" (Vulgate throughout, translation by author).

Paul then uses this distinction to contrast all people, for *qualis terrenus, tales et terreni*, "as was the earthly person, so are earthly people", *et qualis caelestis, tales et caelestes*, "and as was the heavenly person, so are heavenly people". He then unifies both images in the believer, for *igitur, sicut portavimus imaginem terreni, portemus et imaginem caelestis*, "therefore, just as we have borne the image of the earthly person, may we bear also the image of the heavenly person".

By this simple pairing the prayer first contrasts the creation of Adam with the recreation in Christ, then those who, like Adam, are bound up in this earth, with those enjoying heavenly realities in Christ; then the apostle expresses the desire that we, who share in Adam's image, may share also the image of Christ.

A second allusion gives the Church's response to the question of Christ: "If I have told you about earthly things [*terrena*] and you do not believe, how can you believe if I tell you about heavenly things [*caelestia*]?" (NRSV, John 3:12). Through the process of *lectio divina*, or reflective reading, the Church over the centuries has reflected on Christ's question, and then, drawing upon the very words of Christ, gives her response in prayer by affirming God as ruler of heavenly and earthly realities, creation and recreation, carnal and spiritual, and our conversion unto the image of Christ.

Petition: The first of two imperative petitions, *supplicationes populi tui clementer exaudi*, means "mercifully hear the prayers of your people", and is rendered as "hear our prayers". The root meaning of *exaudi* is "perceive clearly", then variously, "harken to, grant, give heed to, obey, understand". Here, the Church takes the role of Jesus, who "in the days of his flesh, … offered up prayers and supplications [*supplicationesque*], with loud cries and tears, to the one who was able to save him from death, and he was heard [*exauditus*] because of his reverent submission" (Hebrews 5:7). Again according to the process of *lectio divina*, the Church, meditating on the relationship of Jesus to his Father, so assumes the very words of Jesus in our prayer to God, that just as Jesus was heard, so too we, who have been reborn in Christ, trust God to hear our liturgical prayer.

God, already acknowledged as almighty and eternal, is petitioned to act mercifully, for God's omnipotence is exercised in mercy (see the collect for the twenty-sixth Sunday in Ordinary Time).

Second petition: The second imperative petition is *et pacem tuam nostris concede temporibus*, "and grant your peace in our times", which is rendered as "and show us the way to peace in the world". *Nostris temporibus* is the ablative of time when meaning, "in our times" but can also mean, as in English, "in our circumstances". The petition alludes to the embolism following the Lord's Prayer, *da propitius pacem in diebus nostris*, "Grant us peace in our day" (*Missale Romanum* 2002; Roman Missal, Collins 1974).

Summary. God directs our creation and recreation in Christ to bring us from earthly to heavenly realities by that admirable exchange, whereby we come to share in divine life through Christ who humbled himself to share in our humanity. ∎

Human impulse, divinely ordere

It is through cooperating with God's directing of our actions that we, having been saved by grace, come to merit the lavish and abundant gifts that he bestows on us – gifts that allow us to further the cause of peace and unity on earth

We pray to be transformed according to the divine plan in Christ, that we may be worthy of abounding in good works in Christ.

Source. The prayer first appears in the Hadrianum, a papal sacramentary given by Pope Hadrian I to Charlemagne in 785-786, as a prayer for "another Sunday" in January.

Analysis of the literary form

Invocation: The complex invocation *Omnipotens sempiterne Deus* is translated literally as "All-powerful and ever-living God".

Petition: The imperative petition *dirige actus nostros in beneplacito tuo*, "guide our actions in your good will", is rendered as "direct your love that is within us". *Dirige* has two basic meanings: "arrange in distinct lines; give a particular direction to". However, because *actus* refers properly to the impetus to act, we petition God to order and guide the internal impulse driving our actions in relation to God's gracious purpose, which was revealed in Christ, for God "has made known to us the mystery of his will, according to the good pleasure [*bonum placitum*] that he set forth in Christ" (NRSV, Vulgate throughout; Ephesians 1:9).

Purpose: Expressed classically, the purpose clause *ut in nomine dilecti Filii tui mereamur bonis operibus abundare*, "that in the name of your beloved Son we may be worthy of abounding in good works", is translated as a purpose clause: "that our efforts in the name of your Son may bring mankind to unity and peace". *Mereamur* means "may we deserve, merit, be worthy

> *the opening prayer*
> **Third Sunday in Ordinary Time**
> All-powerful and ever-living God, direct your love that is within us, that our efforts in the name of your Son may bring mankind to unity and peace.
> (*The Roman Missal*,
> Collins, London, 1974)
>
> Omnipotens sempiterne Deus,
> dirige actus nostros in beneplacito tuo,
> sut in nomine dilecti Filii tui mereamur bonis operibus abundare
> (*Missale Romanum*,
> Città del Vaticano, 2002)

of". *Abundare* literally refers to a wave overflowing.

While God has placed Jesus "above every name that is named [*nomen quod nominatur*]" (Ephesians 1:21), yet Jesus promised that "where two or three are gathered in my name [*in nomine meo*], I am there among them" (Matthew 18:20). Accordingly, we who gather in the name of Jesus petition God to order our inner impulses to well-pleasing purposes.

During the baptism of Jesus "a voice from heaven said, 'This is my Son [*Filius meus dilectus*], the Beloved, with whom I am well pleased'" (Matthew 3:17. Cf. Luke 3:22). In the Transfiguration of Jesus, not only did the voice from the cloud say, "This is my Son, the Beloved [*Filius meus dilectus*]; with him I am well pleased" but it also gave the command, "Listen to him!" (Matthew 17:5; cf. Mark 9:7), perhaps the first good work.

Furthermore, we, on whom Christ has lavished (*superabundavit*) the richness of his grace (Ephesians 1:8), wish to be worthy of abounding (*abundare*) in good works. We have already been saved by grace, raised up and seated with Christ in the heavenly places that God "might show the immeasurable [*abundantes*] riches of his grace in kindness toward us in Christ Jesus" (Ephesians 2:6-7). "For we are … created in Christ Jesus for good works (*bonis operibus*), which God prepared beforehand to be our way of life" (Ephesians 2:10). For example, when Peter and John went to the temple, they said to the blind man lying at the gate: "What I have I give you; in the name of Jesus Christ [*in nomine Iesu Christi*] of Nazareth, stand up and walk" (Acts 3:6).

Summary. In what sense can it be said that we merit anything from God? After the Reformation polemic, recent ecumenical agreements have nuanced our understanding. Modern analysis of the literary structure of such ancient opening prayers as this Sunday's also offers its contribution. First, only God is omnipotent and ever-living. Second, before any mention of meriting, we first ask God to direct our actions, which implies our cooperation.

Third, the purpose clause expresses our hope to be worthy (*mereamur*) of something. As a first (present) subjunctive, however, our meriting is incomplete, unfinished, ongoing, eternal, future, contemporaneous with regard to God's directing our actions. Only as we cooperate with God's directing our actions do we and will we come to merit. Furthermore, although in early and late Latin *mereamur* may be taken as the passive of an active verb meaning "may we be made worthy", in classical Latin it is a deponent verb, which is passive in form but active in meaning. Nor is *mereamur* a transitive or reflexive verb as if it referred to something we did to something else or even to our-

selves. As it is related to the Greek word, which means "to receive one's share", our meriting involves receiving what is due. My sense is that *mereamur* is what we become only by our cooperating with the gift of God, which involves stages of our transformation into Christ. Thus, all is gift, yet we hope to receive what is due to those who cooperate with divine gifts.

Fourth, our meriting is not for ourselves. To the contrary it is for service, as we hope to become worthy of abounding in good works, for we are worthy of good works to the degree that we comply with God's ordering and directing our impulses leading to action. Fifth, our meriting is in no way extraneous from the good work of God in Jesus Christ, in whose name and according to whose good pleasure we may become worthy.

With so many limitations, one might ask: why even bother to speak of merit? Yet the ancient prayers express our hope of meriting. When considered from the perspective of the divine-human exchange, while our human nature is given by God, through Mary we gave our human nature to Christ its creator, who, by emptying himself to take on our human form, became its redeemer.

While all is gift from God, may all be gift to God, who so assumed our human nature in Christ that we are made worthy of sharing in divine life. ∎

Two commands, one love

Christ told us what we need to do, but we cannot do it – love God with all our heart, mind and soul and our neighbour as ourselves – without God's help. Here we petition God for that help, reminding us of the true measure of the love that is required of us, which is the love of God for us in Christ

Loving God with our whole being and our neighbour as ourselves is realised by our cooperation with divine grace. In asking God for the gift of loving as God has loved us in Jesus Christ, we signal our desire and intention to cooperate with the gift of divine love, and thus with our own transformation ever more into who we are by baptism.

Source. The opening prayer this Sunday is found among the most ancient of all liturgical manuscripts, the Verona compilation of Mass booklets, compiled between 561 and 574 as a collection of Mass booklets, where the prayer is ascribed among the daily prayers for the month of June.

Analysis of the literary form

Petition: The prayer begins with the imperative petition *Concede nobis*, "grant to us", which is translated as "help us". The command form is direct and without qualification that would soften or render honorific our petition of God.

Invocation: The complex invocation *Domine Deus noster* is translated literally as "Lord our God". The invocation begins an extended allusion to the greatest commandment to "love the Lord your God [*Dominum Deum tuum*]" (NRSV, Vulgate throughout; Matthew 22:37; Mark 12:29; Luke 10:27).

First purpose: Expressed classically by *ut*, "that", followed by the subjunctive *veneremur*, "we may worship", the first purpose clause *ut te tota mente veneremur*, "that we may adore you with the whole heart", is translated by the infinitive clause, "to love you with all our hearts". This is a common construction to express

> ### *the opening prayer*
> ### **Fourth Sunday in Ordinary Time**
>
> Lord our God, help us to love you with all our hearts and to love all men as you love them.
> (*The Roman Missal*,
> Collins, London, 1974)
>
> Concede nobis, Domine Deus noster, ut te tota mente veneremur, et omnes homines rationabili diligamus affectu.
> (*Missale Romanum*,
> Città del Vaticano, 2002)

purpose in modern languages. *Mente* means "with the mind, heart, soul, conscience, intention", and thus refers to the whole interior life of a person. *Veneremur* means "we may venerate, worship, adore", but, as this is the only instance in the current *Missale Romanum* where God is the object of the verb *veneror*, this is one case in which English assonance with the Latin *veneremur*, "may we venerate", would confuse, for we venerate the saints and icons, but we worship and adore God alone. The use of *tota mente*, "with the whole mind", continues the allusion to the greatest commandment: "love the Lord your God with all your heart, and with all your soul, and with all your mind [*in tota mente*]" (Matthew 22:37 and parallels).

Second purpose: A second subjunctive verb, *diligamus*, "may we love", establishes another purpose clause: *ut ... et omnes homines rationabili diligamus affectu*, "and that we may love all people with a reasonable affection", which is translate by a second infinitive clause expressing purpose, "and to love all men as you love them". The second purpose clause completes the scriptural allusion as *diligamus* corresponds with both the greatest and the second commandment, "You shall love [*diliges*] the Lord your God ... You shall love [*diliges*] your neighbour as yourself" (Matthew 22:37 and parallels). Thus, our response to Jesus' command is to petition God to grant that we may love him fully and our neighbour as ourselves.

We are to love all human beings with an *affectu*, which refers to a disposition of mind or affection, whether good or bad, but means especially "by love, good will, compassion". This internal affection is characterised as *rationabili*. In their respective studies on the vocabulary of the ancient prayers both Mary Pierre Ellebracht and Christine Mohrmann explain that in ancient Christian prayers the word *rationabilis* means "spiritual". Later on, when its more assonant meaning, "rational", came to predominate, the prayers then use the word *spiritalis*, to maintain the meaning, "spiritual". This ancient use is confirmed in the Roman Canon (Eucharistic Prayer I) where *oblationem ... rationabilem acceptabilemque* is translated as, "an offering in spirit and in truth". Furthermore, *rationabili* is associated with what is pleasing to God, as when Paul urges the Church of Rome: "present your bodies as a living sacrifice, holy and acceptable to God, which is your spiritual worship [*rationabile obsequium*]" (Romans 12:1). Finally, our "genuine mutual love [*in fraternitatis amore simplici*]" is the "pure spiritual milk [*rationale sine dolo lac*]", which makes us grow unto salvation, when we "love one another deeply from the heart [*ex corde invicem diligite attentius*]" (1 Peter 1:22; 2:2).

Loving our neighbour with a compassion pleasing to God is to love another not only as ourselves but as Christ loved us, who said: "I give you a new commandment, that you love [*diligatis*] one another. Just as I have loved you, you also should love [*diligatis*] one another" (John 13:34). This last allusion is rendered more fully in the prayer's translation: "to love all men as you love them", for the measure of our love is God's love for us. As Christ shed his blood for all, so this prayer calls us to universal love of all people (*omnes homines*). Jesus gave the greatest commandment, according to Luke, in response to a lawyer who stood up to test him. In turn the lawyer wished to justify himself and asked, "who is my neighbour?" (10:29). In the parable of the good Samaritan, Jesus turned the lawyer's question around by saying that we are neighbour in our compassion to others in their need (Luke 10:30-37), and thus to all people.

Summary. The four steps of *lectio divina* are to read and meditate on the Scriptures, and then to offer the reflected Word back to God in prayer leading to an ever-deeper appreciation. This opening prayer shows how the Church's *lectio* is not a parroting back of God's Word, but is the result of millennia of meditation on the Word and on the Church's lived experience of the paschal mystery, that by our cooperating with the self-emptying love of God in Christ, we come to participate in the divine life itself. ∎

Just for today

Our desire for God's definitive and ultimate favour is not directed simply towards the future; the longing we experience today, our living faith, allows the divine to exist in the present moment. Our hope can become its own fulfilment

Catalysis is a chemical reaction whereby one agent without change to itself effects a change in another. God's protection is the catalyst freeing our trust, which in turn realises God's steadfast strength.

Source. The prayer is found in the Gregorian (papal) tradition both in the Hadrianum, the papal sacramentary given by Pope Hadrian I to Charlemagne in 785-786, where, in a slightly altered form, it is given as a prayer over the people at the end of Mass on Saturday of the second week of Lent, and likewise in the Sacramentary of Padua, a later redaction of an earlier papal sacramentary adapted around 670-680 for presbyteral ministry to pilgrims to St Peter's basilica. It is also found in the Gelasian (presbyteral) sacramentaries of the eighth century, where it is assigned to the fifth Sunday after Epiphany, whence it was likewise included in the supplement to the Hadrianum compiled by Benedict of Aniane between 810 and 815. Both variants were preserved in the *Missale Romanum* of 1962 respectively on the fifth Sunday after Epiphany and Saturday of the second week of Lent.

Analysis of the literary form

First petition: The prayer begins with the imperative petition *Familiam tuam ... continua pietate custodi*: "preserve your family with ongoing compassion", which is translated by the first of two imperative petitions, "watch over your family". While *pietate* usually refers to "dutiful conduct towards the gods, parents, relatives, benefactors, country, etc", here, to the contrary, it refers to God's sense of duty towards us, which is expressed in tenderness and compassion.

---

the opening prayer
Fifth Sunday in Ordinary Time

Father, watch over your family
and keep us in your care
for all our hope is in you.
(*The Roman Missal*,
Collins, London, 1974)

Familiam tuam, quaesumus, Domine,
continua pietate custodi, ut, quae in
sola spe gratiae caelestis innititur,
tua semper protectione muniatur.
(*Missale Romanum*,
Città del Vaticano, 2002)

Second petition: The parenthetical petition *quaesumus*, "we ask", is translated in the concluding doxology as "we ask this". This simple parenthetical begins a dialectic whereby we ask God to preserve us in divine compassion.

Invocation: Nestled within the petition is the invocation, *Domine*, "Lord", which is translated as "Father".

Purpose: Expressed classically, the purpose of the prayer is *ut ... tua semper protectione muniatur*, "that [your] family ever may be defended by your protection", which is rendered as a second imperative petition: "and keep us in your care". *Muniatur* is a divine passive literally meaning that God builds a defensive wall around the family.

The petition and purpose clauses are closely parallel as *custodi* (preserve) corresponds to *muniatur* (may it be defended), *pietate* (with compassion) to *tua protectione* (by protection) and *continua* (ongoing) to *semper* (forever).

God's word is efficacious accomplishing its desired result (Isaiah 55:11). This could suggest that *ut muniatur* is a result clause stating the concrete result we wish God to bring about; accordingly, the prayer would be translated as "guard your family with the result that it is fortified". Granted that the difference between a result and a purpose clause may be merely one of perspective, I have translated *ut muniatur* as a purpose clause to emphasise not the result of God's action but God's intent in acting. Such a translation also highlights human cooperation with divine intention.

Motive: God's motive, who already preserves the family, for defending the family is expressed by a relative clause inserted at the beginning of the purpose clause: *quae in sola spe gratiae caelestis innititur*, "which family relies upon the sole hope of heavenly favour", which is rendered by an explanatory clause as, "for all our hope is in you". *Innititur* means, "it leans or rests upon", or even "it trusts", as in the passage, "Who among you fears the Lord and obeys the voice of his servant, who walks in darkness and has no light, yet trusts [*innitatur*] in the name of the Lord ...?" (NRSV, Vulgate, Isaiah 50:10).

The dialectic established in the petition clause, where we ask (*quaesumus*) God to preserve (*custodi*) God's family, is developed in the motive clause by adding our cooperation with divine gift by our trusting and relying upon (*innititur*) the hope of heavenly favour. This in turn becomes God's motive for strengthening (*muniatur*) God's family. Thus, interpreting *ut muniatur* as a purpose and not as a result clause respects the reality of human cooperation with divine gift, which in turn leads to greater gifts inviting greater participation, thus rendering our maturation in the faith a dialogical process.

Furthermore, because relative to the imperative verb, *custodi*, the first subjunctive *muniatur* is incomplete, unfinished, ongoing, eternal, future, contemporaneous, this dialectic happens all at once as God's entire self is the gift; it happens over time as our response develops by stages of maturation; and it happens definitively at the end of time. Throughout the process of our transformation, nevertheless, God's steadfastness towards us is emphasised by the use of both *continua*, "ongoing", and *semper*, "always".

Summary. While the modern desire to reclaim the eschatological dimension of the liturgy often focuses on a future vision then understood to be inchoately present, in this prayer, typical of opening prayers, because of the polyvalence of the first subjunctive *muniatur* in regard to the verb on which it depends, *custodi*, we petition God from our present and ongoing reality, which is ever qualified by the hope of heavenly favour. There is no dichotomy, then, between the inchoate – the rudimentary – and its fullness. The interchange between the hope of heavenly favour and our daily reliance upon and trust in God is even more evident in the version of the prayer assigned to Saturday of the Second of Lent prior to 1970, where the purpose line reads, *ut ... caelesti etiam protectione muniatur*, according to which we pray that the one, who relies upon the sole hope of heavenly favour, "even now may be defended by heavenly protection": our heavenly hope is our present surety.

The family of God finds its linchpin in Jesus Christ, Son of God and Son of Mary. In Christ does our petition of God find its satisfaction in God's compassionate protection; in Christ does our trusting reliance upon God become a fortress and we the city of God. ∎

Self-transcending gift

*The mutual exchange between God and man
is implicit on our asking for God's gift of
grace, and offering our cooperation by
conducting upright and sincere lives*

God dwells in us that we may dwell in God, that by this mutual self-gift God's self-emptying love may bring us to self-transcending love.

Source. The prayer first appears in the Gelasian Sacramentary, composed between 628-715, where it is ascribed to the prayers for the Sunday after the Ascension – thus the emphasis on God's abiding presence. The prayer was eventually dropped from use until it was assigned to this Sunday in the *Missale Romanum* of 1970.

Analysis of the literary form
Invocation: The simple invocation *Deus*, "God", is translated as, "God our Father".

Amplification: Amplifying the invocation, the relative clause *qui ... asseris*, "you who declare", is translated in the past tense as "you have promised". The present tense expresses the immediacy of the human heart asking for the gift of God's indwelling. Although the root meaning of *asseris* is "you join [some person or thing] to yourself", here God comes to remain within us.

Premise: What God declares, the complement of *asseris*, is expressed in the object sentence *te in rectis et sinceris manere pectoribus*, "that you remain in upright and genuine hearts", rendered as, "to just and right". In this case, the object sentence is not expressive of purpose or result. It indicates, rather, what God declares, and so is the context or premise for our prayer.

Not appearing in Scripture, this phrase is already the fruit of meditating on the word

> *the opening prayer*
> ### Sixth Sunday in Ordinary Time
> God our Father, you have promised
> to remain for ever with those
> who do what is just and right.
> Help us to live in your presence.
> (*The Roman Missal*,
> Collins, London, 1974)
>
> Deus, qui te in rectis
> et sinceris manere pectoribus asseris,
> da nobis tua gratia tales exsistere,
> in quibus habitare digneris.
> (*Missale Romanum*,
> Città del Vaticano, 2002)

of God and Christian life, now offered back to God in prayer: the Church's *lectio divina*.

The first Letter of John tell us that "God abides [*manet*] in those who confess that Jesus is the Son of God, and they abide in God" (NRSV, Vulgate throughout, 4:15), and that "God is love, and those who abide [*manet*] in love abide in God, and God abides [*manet*] in them" (4:16), and furthermore, that "if we love one another, God lives [*manet*] in us, and his love is perfected in us" (4:12). The indwelling Spirit is the guarantor of the mutual indwelling of God and humanity: "By this we know that we abide [*manemus*] in him and he in us, because he has given us of his Spirit" (4:13).

Petition: The imperative petition *da nobis tua gratia tales exsistere*, "grant us by your grace to be such people", is rendered as, "Help us to live".

Purpose: The relative clause expressing purpose, composed of *in quibus*, "in whom", followed by the first subjunctive *digneris*, "you may deign", *in quibus habitare digneris*, "among whom you may deem it worthy to live", is a substitution for the purpose clause *ut in eis habitare digneris*, "that in them you may deign to dwell", but is translated as "in your presence". What is implied, however, between the imperative *da*, "grant", and *digneris*, "you may deign", is our cooperation with God's grace (*tua gratia*) by living as such people (*tales*) that God, who remains in the upright and sincere hearts (*in rectis et sinceris pectoribus*), may consider it worthy of God's self (*digneris*) to dwell (*habitare*) in us. The verb *digneris* is expressive of the divine-human exchange in that it refers both to God's condescending or self-emptying to dwell among us and to our being enabled by God deeming it worthy of God's self to dwell among us.

Summary. The divine-human exchange is the mutual self-gift in love between God and humanity. I say mutual because, although God's essence is wholly other than our humanity, God's love for us is self-emptying that we may experience in our hearts and according to our capacity the divine love revealed in the incarnation, life and death of Jesus, whereas our love for God is self-transcending as we are ennobled by grace to participate in mutual self-gift and so in the nuptial union between God and humanity.

While God's self-gift is full and immediate, even if adapted to our capacity to host the divine indwelling, our response of self-gift to God, however, happens by stages of maturation. First we ask for God's gift of favour (*gratia*), without which we could not of our own offer ourselves in a way patient of God's indwelling. Because God's favour respects our free will, it then elicits our response, our cooperating by conduct-ing upright and sincere lives, which in turn leads to the gift of God's indwelling.

This contrast between God's complete self-gift and our developmental response along one's own path toward self-transcending love reminds me of the banquet scene in the film Babette's Feast, when the military commander, who had left love behind to pursue his career, in a moment of self-transcendence, gives the toast: "Man, in his weakness and short-sightedness, believes he must make choices in this life. He trembles at the risks he must take … There comes a time when our eyes are opened. And we come to realise at last that mercy is infinite … Mercy imposes no conditions. And see! Everything we have chosen has been granted to us. And everything we renounced has also been granted. Yes, we even get back what we threw away. For mercy and truth are met together. And righteousness and peace have kissed each other."

In the self-transcending gift of ourselves to God, we realise that nothing of good has been lost by the necessity of a particular path as we were yielding by stages to God's self-gift. St Ephrem of Nisibis in Mesopotamia, (d. 373) reminds us of this: "Be thankful then for what you have received, and do not be saddened at all that such an abundance still remains.

"What you have received and attained is your present share, while what is left will be your heritage. For what you could not take at one time because of your weakness, you will be able to grasp at another if you only persevere. So do not foolishly try to drain in one draught what cannot be consumed all at once, and do not cease out of faintheartedness from what you will be able to absorb as time goes on" (*Commentary on the Diatessaron* 1.19, in *The Liturgy of the Hours*, Catholic Book Publishing Company, New York 1975, 3, 200). ■

Giving as one and many

Here we explore the many ways in which the gift of self is at the core of our individual and corporate relationship with God

O nly the gift of "full conscious, and active participation" in liturgy and life expresses and constitutes the self-gift of the Church to her self-giving God (*Sacrosanctum Concilium*, 14).

Source. This prayer has four historical uses. Firstly, it was a daily prayer in the Hadrianum, the Papal Sacramentary given by Pope Hadrian I to Charlemagne in 785-786. Secondly, it was used in time of strife in the Gelasian Sacramentary, composed between 628 and 715 for presbyteral use in the titular churches of Rome, whence it passed into eighth-century variants and the supplement to the Hadrianum. Thirdly, it was used on either the fifth or sixth Sunday after Epiphany from the eighth century until 1962. It was used after Epiphany and in time of strife in the *Paduensis*, a ninth-century redaction of a Sacramentary composed around 670-680 for presbyteral use at St Peter's. Finally, an adaptation praying for the King and Queen was the prayer's only appearance in the missals used at St Augustine's Abbey, Canterbury and Westminster Abbey; in the missal given by Robert, Bishop of London (1044), to his former abbey at Jumiège; and in those missals of Salisbury and Hereford cathedrals, Lesnes Abbey, Rochester diocese, and the church at Arbuthnott, Scotland. Throughout its varied history the prayer has been used as an opening prayer, prayer after Communion and prayer over the people.

Analysis of the Literary Form
Petition: The prayer begins with the imperative petition *Praesta*, "Grant", which is not translated. Granting is God's only direct action in the Latin text, whereas the

---

the opening prayer
Seventh Sunday in Ordinary Time
Father, keep before us the wisdom and love you have revealed in your Son.
Help us to be like him
in word and deed
(*The Roman Missal*,
Collins, London, 1974)

Praesta, quaesumus, omnipotens Deus, ut, semper rationabilia meditantes, quae tibi sunt placita, et dictis exsequamur et factis
(*Missale Romanum*,
Città del Vaticano, 2002)

English text has made God active throughout as the subject of the verbal forms: "keep", "you have revealed", "help".

Petition: The parenthetical *quaesumus*, "we ask", is expressed in the doxology as "we ask this". Even God's granting is requested by us.

Invocation: Sandwiched between the petition and its object is the complex invocation *omnipotens Deus*, "all-powerful God", rendered as "Father". God's omnipotence is exercised by making us capable of both contemplating spiritual realities which are pleasing to God, and then of following them through in our word and deeds.

Purpose: Expressed classically, the purpose clause *ut ... et dictis exsequamur et factis*, ""that we may accomplish things... with words said and with deeds done", inspires the imperative petition, "Help us to be like him in word and deed".

Exsequamur also means "may we pursue, accomplish, fulfil". *Dictis* and *factis* may be either nouns meaning "in words and deeds", or anterior participles emphasising accomplished actions, "in words having been said and deeds having been done".

Latin grammar is limited in that the construction *ut* followed by the subjunctive *exsequamur* can express either a result clause or a purpose clause, and the difference between the two may be merely one of perspective, for what I purpose may seem an unintended result to someone else, and I may be blamed for intending a result I did not wish.

Motive: What we pursue is also our motive for pursuing: *quae tibi sunt placita*, "things which are pleasing to you". The translation parallels our words with Christ's wisdom and our deeds with Christ's love: "the wisdom and love you have revealed in your Son". The object of *exsequamur* is *ea*, "things", implied in the relative *quae*, "which things".

Premise: When this prayer was offered after Communion the participial phrase *semper rationabilia meditantes*, "[we] ever meditating on spiritual realities", inspiring the translation "keep before us", referred back to the sacraments just celebrated as the prayer's premise. The nuance present in the Latin is that we meditate on the spiritual realities (*rationabilia*), which also are the things we pursue (*exsequamur ea*), and the things pleasing to God (*tibi sunt placita*).

In commenting on the phrase "Hallowed be thy name", in his treatise On the Lord's Prayer (c. 251), Cyprian of Carthage says: "And may our impulse not be unworthy of the Spirit, that we, who have begun to be heavenly and spiritual beings [*caelestes et spiritales*], may reflect upon and bring to action [*cogitemus et agamus*] nothing but spiritual and heavenly things [*spiritalia et caelestia*]" (11).

Ancient prayers used *rationabilia* to mean "spiritual realities" until the idea of "rational things" came to predominate the word's meaning; later orations used *spiritalia*, as does Cyprian.

Summary. A result clause states the concrete consequence of an action while leaving the guiding intention in suspense. A purpose clause states the intention while leaving the result in suspension. *Praesta* may introduce either. I understand *ut exsequamur* to express intention, leaving its realisation in suspense, and thus translate it in the subjunctive. Were it an expression of result, referring to the concrete consequence of God's action, it would be expressed in the indicative in English; such concrete, factual language is at variance with prayer. In either case, because the prayer involves human co-operation with divine gift, the faithful are called to active participation in the liturgy. The verb *exsequamur*, "may we fulfil", suggests full participation; the participles *meditantes*, "we meditating", and *dictis*, "by words said", suggest conscious participation; and *factis*, "by deeds done", suggests active participation. Indeed, in this prayer, God, having granted (*praesta*), takes a passive role as we both contemplate and accomplish things pleasing to God.

We participate in liturgy as in life by responding to God's self-gift to us by giving ourselves to God-made-present both in liturgical celebrations and in our neighbour, which suggests the criterion for good liturgy is that it foster through rites and prayers this mutual self-gift, the nuptial union of God and humanity. Furthermore, we give ourselves to God not only personally, but, overcoming individualism, we as a corporate body, this assembly, the Church, gives itself to Christ in the liturgical encounter, even as Christ is present in the assembly. ∎

Without him we falter

Our mortal weakness finds completion in God's strength, as the opening prayer for this Sunday emphasises. Here is revealed the subtlety in the Latin and its translation

In England the feast of the Body and Blood of Christ is celebrated on the preceding Thursday; in some countries the feast is this Sunday. This prayer for the eleventh Sunday in Ordinary time shows how the Christian assembly acknowledges its dependence on God for every good deed.

Source. The opening prayer this Sunday comes from the Gelasian Sacramentary, composed between 628 and 715 for use during presbyteral liturgies in the titular churches of Rome, where it is given for the seventh Sunday of Easter. Because the numbered Sundays of Ordinary time in the post-Vatican II *Missale Romanum* do not correspond directly with the Sundays after Pentecost in the pre-conciliar Missale, I can no longer say that the opening prayer for this Sunday replaces a specific opening prayer in the 1962 *Missale*. Such a comparison between opening prayers is possible only during the seasons before and after Christmas and Easter and in the cycle of feasts, when there is a direct correspondence between the Sundays or feasts both before and after the Second Vatican Council.

Analysis of the literary form
Invocation: The simple invocation *Deus*, literally "God", is translated here as "Almighty God".

Amplification: The invocation of God is amplified by a phrase in apposition, *in te sperantium fortitudo*, meaning "strength of ones hoping in you", and translated as, "our hope and our strength". Strength is a common attribute of God in the scriptures as in *diligam te, Domine, fortitudo mea* (Psalm 17/18:2), often translated in the present tense, "I love you, Lord, my strength".

---

the opening prayer
11th Sunday in Ordinary Time
Almighty God, our hope and our strength, without you we falter.
Help us to follow Christ
and to live according to your will.
(*The Roman Missal*,
Collins, London, 1974)

Deus, in te sperantium fortitudo,
invocationibus nostris adesto propitius,
et, quia sine te nihil potest mortalis
infirmitas, gratiae tuae praesta semper
auxilium, ut, in exsequendis mandatis
tuis, et voluntate tibi et actione
placeamus.
(*Missale Romanum*,
Città del Vaticano, 2002)

First petition: Two petitions are given, each with a motive. First we petition God *invocationibus nostris adesto propitius*: "graciously attend to our prayers", which is not rendered in the English.

First motive: While *propitius* is used as an adverb meaning "favourably, graciously", it also works as an adjective in apposition describing God as "favourable, gracious": God's first motive for attending to our prayers is God's graciousness.

The **second petition** is *et … gratiae tuae praesta semper auxilium*, meaning, "ever grant the help of your favour". The English text rephrases the ideas expressed in the second petition, the purpose clause and final motive, rendering an independent sentence with an imperative petition in two parts: "Help us to follow Christ and to live according to your will".

Second motive: The second petition includes a second motive, expressed by the relative phrase *quia sine te nihil potest mortalis infirmitas*, meaning "because without you mortal weakness can do nothing", which is translated as, "without you we falter". *Infirmitas* means, "want of strength", and finds its completion in God's *fortitudo*, "strength", whereas *mortalis*, "mortal" contrasts with *semper*, "always". Human life comes from God, even if mortal weakness is limited and in need of God's fullness. The prayer applies to God that which Jesus said of himself, the true vine: *sine me nihil potestis facere*, "without me you can do nothing" (John 15:5).

Purpose: We pray to God *ut … et voluntate tibi et actione placeamus*: "that we may be pleasing to you in intention and action". *Voluntate*, meaning, "in free will, desire", coordinates with *actione*, "in action, deed", to indicate that our action is freely desired and that what we desire we put into action. The purpose clause contrasts with the second motive clause, because mortal weakness can do nothing without God, whereas with the help of God's favour we may be pleasing to God in both desire and deed. I have translated this as a purpose clause, "we may be pleasing", to highlight freedom in choosing to do God's will.

A **third motive** is expressed by the *gerundive in exsequendis mandatis tuis*: "in carrying out your commands". The infinitive *exsequi* means, "to engage busily, carry into effect". The motive for God's deeming us pleasing is our carrying out his commands. Jesus says that the greatest commandment is to love God with our whole heart, soul and mind (Matthew 22:38), thus, in the words of the prayer, we are pleasing to God by fulfilling the commandment to love God in both desire and deed. Jesus also gives a new commandment to love others as he has loved us (John 15:12); thus, in the words of the prayer, we are pleasing to God when we freely show to others the love God has shown us in Christ. Only by God's help, however, are we capable of freely living by God's commandments.

Summary. The prayer refers to us, the praying assembly, in various ways. One of two direct references is in the first petition, which explicitly asks God to be present (*invocationibus nostris*) "to our prayers". The second direct reference is found in the purpose clause *ut … placeamus*, "that … we may be pleasing".

The second petition does not specifically mention to whom we ask God to grant help. However, *nobis*, "to us", is implied in the petition and then expressed in the purpose clause, which asks "that … we may be pleasing". The implied *nobis* has been made explicit in the English translation: "help us".

Another reference to the praying assembly is indirect. The motive clause refers to all humanity when it says *mortalis infirmitas*, "mortal weakness". Thus, the prayer states the human condition without directly attributing weakness to the assembly. Nor is *mortalis*, "mortal", directly attributed to the assembly. This phrase has been made personal in the translation, "we falter".

Finally, the praying assembly is also mindful *sperantium*, "of one's hoping". The assembly is neither strictly identified with those hoping, nor is it an attribute of the human condition. Rather, the indefinite use here renders the phrase an admonition to hope in God, even as it affirms God as strength for those who in fact do hope in God. This phrase has been made personal in the English translation: "our hope", "our strength".

Where the English translation maintains the reference to the praying assembly, it expresses it personally, whereas the Latin employs the indefinite with subtle finesse. ∎

Love and awe

It was so revered in the Jewish tradition that it was uttered only once a year when the high priest entered the Holy of Holies. Here is explained how the opening prayer for this Sunday helps us to respond today to the divine name

The revelation of the divine name to the Jewish people is a sign of the Lord's closeness and yet wholly otherness. To call upon the name of the Lord evokes the intimate relationship of the covenant formula: you will be my people and I shall be your God. Yet so revered is the divine name, so freely other, that it used to be pronounced but once annually when the high priest entered the Holy of Holies. Otherwise pious Jews and Christians to this day substitute for the divine name the title "Lord", or in Latin, *Domine*. The opening prayer this Sunday asks that we may have awe and love for the divine name, as the Lord has received us in divine love.

Source. This prayer is first assigned to the Sunday after the Ascension in the Gelasian Sacramentary originally composed between 628-715 of earlier elements for use in the presbyteral liturgies celebrated in the titular churches of Rome. In most other sacramentaries, however, it is assigned to the second Sunday after Pentecost where it is found in the 1962 *Missale*.

Analysis of the literary form

Petition: This opening prayer has a nestling construction. We begin in the second line with the Petition, the imperative *fac*, which means "make, bring it about", and is translated as "grant".

The petition is nestled within its own object constructed as a sentence in the accusative *nos* with the infinitive *habere* that expresses either God's intention (purpose) in acting or the result of our cooperation with God's action: *sancti nominis tui … timorem pariter et amorem … nos habere*

> *the opening prayer*
> ## 12th Sunday in Ordinary Time
> Father, guide and protector of your people, grant us an unfailing respect for your name, and keep us always in your love.
> (*The Roman Missal*, Collins, London, 1974)
>
> Sancti nominis tui, Domine, timorem pariter et amorem fac nos habere perpetuum, quia numquam tua gubernatione destituis, quos in soliditate tuae dilectionis instituis.
> (*Missale Romanum*, Città del Vaticano, 2002)

perpetuum. Since God respects human freedom, I have translated it as a purpose clause with the subjunctive "may": "[make] us have perpetual awe and likewise love of your holy name", which is translated in the official English text as "[grant] us an unfailing respect for your name".

Invocation: Nestled within the object sentence is the invocation *Domine* meaning "Lord" and translated as "Father". The beauty of Latin is that it can vary the word order in ways that English cannot. Thus, the beginning of the Latin text follows this word order: "of holy name your, O Lord, awe equally and love …" While nonsensical in English, the Latin begins by invoking the holy name of the Lord, and immediately adds awe balanced with love.

Fear and love can be exclusive as *perfecta caritas foras mittit timorem*, "perfect love casts out fear" (NV, New Revised Standard Version 1 John 4:18), or as in the Resurrection story when the guards shook with fear but the angel told the women *nolite timere vos*, "do not fear" (NV, Matthew 28:4-5). Whereas here *timorem* means "awe", as in "the fear of the Lord is the beginning of wisdom" (NV, NRSV Psalm 110/111:10). *Amorem* recalls Jesus' asking Peter twice *diligis me*, "Do you love me?", and a third time *amas me*, "Do you love me?". Peter's response each time was *amo te*, "I love you" (NV, John 21:15-19).

In his homily on this prayer, Baldwin of Ford (Archbishop of Canterbury, died 1190) said that this fear gathers what is scattered, unites what is dispersed, casts out and excludes what is evil; nurtures good things, and guards what is nurtured. In his Sunday sermon on this prayer, Godefrid of Admont (c. 1100-1165) said that awe is not sufficiently perfect unless love is present, nor love, unless awe is included.

The love, then, and the awe we have for God's name are part of the gift that God enables.

Motive: The object sentence ends with *perpetuum*, "uninterrupted", which is immediately contrasted in the Motive clause by *numquam*, "never": *quia numquam tua gubernatione destituis, quos in soliditate tuae dilectionis instituis*, which means, "because you never forsake in your guidance whom you establish in the steadfastness of your love". The motive is rephrased in the English translation as an amplification of "Father": "guide and protector of your people".

The motive clause turns on two verbs with the same root *statuis*, meaning "you cause to stand"; *destituis*, "you set down, forsake", and *instituis*, "you set up, take upon yourself, educate". *Gubernatione* refers to steering a ship, and evokes the image of one on the poop deck laying the hand to the tiller; clearly an allusion to God's guiding the Church. *Soliditate*, meaning "steadfastness", echoes both *perpetuum*, "constant", and, expressed negatively, *numquam … destituis*, "you never forsake".

Summary. Whose is the sacred name? In the Hebrew Scriptures, the sacred name refers to God. This passed into Christianity as a reference to the triune God, as in Jesus' Great Commission to baptise *in nomine Patris et Filii et Spiritus Sancti*, "in the name of the Father and of the Son and of the Holy Spirit", which we also repeat in the Sign of the Cross. Several ancient eucharistic prayers interpret the holy name in terms of the Trinity, such as the oldest extant eucharistic prayer, that of Addai and Mari, ever in constant use in Iraq and then in south-west India.

Only in the fourteenth century did the veneration of the holy name of Jesus enter into the Latin liturgical calendar on 2 January. Perhaps because of its recent origin, this feast was omitted in the calendar reform of Vatican II, but was reinstated on 3 January in the 2002 edition of the *Missale Romanum*, which is not yet promulgated in English. The opening prayer this Sunday predates the veneration of the holy name of Jesus by at least 800 years, and thus refers to the Lord, as it says *Domine*.

Given the prayer's original context on the Sunday after the Ascension, it affirms that God does not forsake believers whom God has received and formed, nor the Church, which God continues to guide even after the ascension of Jesus. The prayer uses balance to express the wonderful exchange in a fundamentally unequal divine-human relationship. We pray that God, who has formed us in the steadfastness of divine love, will help us to respond with love and awe for the divine name. ■

Liberating light

The opening prayer for this Sunday expresses simply, directly and powerfully that the way out of darkness is through the truth and radiant splendour of God, who is the guardian of our souls and, in loving us, makes us children of light

The liturgy is the result of centuries of that Benedictine form of prayer *lectio divina*, and we who celebrate are beckoned to share in its transformative power. The four stages of *lectio divina* are paralleled in the various parts of the liturgy. First, the word of God is proclaimed. Second, we meditate on the word as an assembly during the silence after each proclamation, during the homily, and in our daily lives. Third, we offer the digested scriptures back to God in prayer. The prayer is the outpouring of the heart thoroughly formed by the scriptures to God in prayer. The opening prayer this Sunday is a wonderful example of such prayer meant to lead the assembly to the fourth stage: the contemplation of God.

> *the opening prayer*
> ## 13th Sunday in Ordinary Time
> Father, you call your children
> to walk in the light of Christ.
> Free us from darkness and keep us in
> the radiance of your truth.
> (*The Roman Missal*,
> Collins, London, 1974)
>
> Deus, qui, per adoptionem gratiae,
> lucis nos esse filios voluisti,
> praesta, quaesumus, ut errorum non
> involvamur tenebris, sed in splendore
> veritatis semper maneamus conspicui.
> (*Missale Romanum*,
> Città del Vaticano, 2002)

Source. The prayer does not appear in any of the ancient Roman sacramentaries. Rather, it comes from the Ambrosian Sacramentary of Bergamo, dating from the tenth to the eleventh century, where it is the first of many prayers of a litany assigned to the week before Pentecost. The inclusion of prayers from the Bergamo Sacramentary is a sign of how the liturgical reform of the Second Vatican Council was truly universal in scope.

Analysis of the literary form
Invocation: The simple invocation *Deus*, meaning literally "God", is translated as "Father".

Amplification: A relative phrase amplifies the simple invocation: *qui... voluisti*, "you have desired ...".

First purpose: What God desired is presented by the entire phrase with a subject in the accusative *nos*, "us, we", and the verb in the infinitive *esse*, "to be", expressive of God's intention or purpose: *per adoptionem gratiae, lucis nos esse filios*, "[you have desired] us to be daughters and sons of light through the adoption of grace". Taken together, the amplification and first purpose clause are rephrased in the English: "you call your children to walk in the light of Christ". The first purpose pairs *filios*, "children", with *adoptionem*, "adoption", and evokes the scriptural image of *lucis filios*, "children of light". The root meaning of *gratiae* is "of favour, love, beauty" and thus, "of grace".

Two petitions: The imperative petition *praesta*, "grant", is followed by the parenthetic *quaesumus*, literally, "we ask", which simply means, "please". The petition *praesta* is omitted in translation, but *quaesumus* is rendered as, "we ask this" in the doxology.

Second purpose: The purpose clause is constructed classically with *ut* followed by, in this case, two subjunctives, *involvamur* and *maneamus*, producing two purposes. The first is *ut errorum non involvamur tenebris*: "that we may not be enveloped by the darkness of errors". Both purpose clauses have been rephrased in the English as imperative petitions in an independent sentence. The first, "free us from darkness", uses the active voice indicating that the praying assembly is in darkness, whereas the Latin uses the passive voice in the subjunctive "we may not be enveloped", which maintains the possibility that we are not in darkness and wish to avoid it. *Non involvamur* can also mean "may we not be entangled" or, "may we not devote ourselves to". *Errorum* literally means "of goings astray, departings from the truth, errors", as in: "you were going astray [*errantes*] like sheep, but now you have returned to the shepherd and guardian of your souls" (All quotes are from the NRSV and the New Vulgate, 1 Peter 2:25).

Third purpose: In contrast to that purpose clause, this one is positive: *ut ... sed in splendore veritatis semper maneamus conspicui*: "but that we always remain conspicuous in the splendour of truth". The English renders the purpose clause expressed in the subjunctive, "may we remain", as an imperative: "and keep us in the radiance of your truth". The first and third purpose clauses form a literary "sandwich" or inclusion of the second purpose clause. On the one hand, the phrase *lucis filios*, "children of light", from the first purpose clause, interprets the phrase *splendore veritatis*, "the splendour of truth", in the third purpose clause not only because light and splendour reinterpret one another, but also because we are adopted children in the Only-begotten who, as the Word of God, is truth. On the other hand, as a literary inclusion the first and third purpose clauses enclose and

constrast with the second purpose clause, because light and splendour contrast with *tenebris*, "in the darkness", and *errorum*, "of straying ways", contrasts with *veritatis*, "of truth". Our being enveloped in darkness (*involvamur tenebris*) contrasts with our prayer that we may remain conspicuous (*maneamus conspicui*).

Summary. The nexus of scriptural passages behind this prayer explores the image of the light and splendour of truth shining in the darkness as seen in creation and our recreation in Christ. As when "darkness covered the face of the deep" and God said "Let there be light'; and there was light, so "God is light" in whom "there is no darkness at all" (Genesis 1:2-3; 1 John 1:5). "The God who said 'Let light shine out of darkness'... has shone in our hearts" (2 Corinthians 4:6). We "live as children of light – for the fruit of the light is found in all that is good and right and true" (Ephesians 5:8-9). As children of light we are sisters and brothers, for "if we walk in the light ... we have fellowship with one another", but "whoever says, 'I am in the light', while hating a brother or sister, is still in the darkness. Whoever loves a brother or sister lives in the light" (1 John 1:7; 2:9-10).

The prayer also synthesises the scriptural images of the children of light by the adoption of grace, for we "have beheld his glory, the glory as of a father's only son, full of grace and truth ... From his fullness we have all received, grace upon grace" (John 1:14, 16). Furthermore, Paul writes that God sent the Son that we might receive adoption as children [*adoptionem filiorum*] through Jesus Christ (Romans 8:15, Galatians 4:5, Ephesians 1:5). We become *lucis filios*, "children of light" when we believe in Jesus, the light that shines in the darkness (John 12:36; 1:5), and "the way, and the truth, and the life" (John 14:6). ∎

By humility to eternity

Just as Christ gave us life by humbling himself,
so we must be prepared to stoop low if we are to
be raised up to everlasting joy

---

the opening prayer
14th Sunday in Ordinary Time

Father, through the obedience of Jesus, your servant and your Son, you raised a fallen world. Free us from sin and bring us the joy that lasts for ever. (*The Roman Missal*, Collins, London, 1974)	Deus, qui in Filii tui humilitate iacentem mundum erexisti, fidelibus tuis sanctam concede laetitiam, ut, quos eripuisti a servitute peccati, gaudiis facias perfrui sempiternis. (*Missale Romanum*, Città del Vaticano, 2002)

The opening prayer this Sunday emphasises the humility of Christ and the exaltation of humanity in Christ. This text is a recapitulation in prayer of the canticle from Philippians 2.5-11.

Source. The prayer first appears in the Gelasian Sacramentary, compiled between 628 and 715 for presbyteral use in the titular churches of Rome, where it was offered on the Sunday after the octave of Easter. It was reassigned in the 1970 *Missale Romanum* to both Monday of the fourth week of Easter and this Sunday. With the slight revisions in the *Missale* of 2002, the duplication was eliminated, and it is assigned to this Sunday only.

Analysis of the literary form
Invocation: The simple invocation is *Deus*, literally "God", which is translated "Father".

Amplification: A relative clause amplifies the invocation: *qui in Filii tui humilitate iacentem mundum erexisti*, which means "you who in the humility of your Son have raised up the ailing world". This is translated as "through the obedience of Jesus, your servant and your Son, you raised a

fallen world". *Erexisti* means "you have raised up, constructed, encouraged". *Iacentem* means "one lying" and even "one lying ill, dead, in ruins". In ecclesial Latin *humilitate* is opposed to pride, and has the positive meaning of "lowness, humility".

Petition: Given as an imperative, the petition is: *fidelibus tuis sanctam concede laetitiam*, which means "grant holy joy to your faithful". The petition is not expressed in the English. Here *concede* means "grant" or "vouchsafe". The adjective *fidelibus* used as a substantive means "to trustworthy people, to the faithful", its noun, *fides*, refers to those who place their trust in someone, thus characterising the trust the faithful place in God. *Laetitiam* refers to unrestrained joyfulness.

Purpose: Expressed classically by *ut* followed by the subjunctive, *facias*, the purpose for our praying is *ut ... gaudiis facias perfrui sempiternis*, literally meaning "that you may make ... to thoroughly enjoy eternal joys". The purpose clause is translated in the official English text as an imperative petition: "and bring us the joy that lasts for ever". The object of *facias*, "may you bring it about", is the entire object sentence, whose accusative subject is not explicit, but is perhaps the *fideles*, "faithful", implied in the relative *quos* "whom". The implied subject is followed by the verb in the infinitive, *perfrui*, here meaning, "they enjoy fully, thoroughly". Tucking the implied subject into the relative clause can be done in English as well: "may you make, whom you saved, to enjoy eternal life". *Gaudiis* is a synonym of *laetitiam* in the petition.

Motive: God's motive for bringing us to eternal joys is that we are those *quos eripuisti a servitute peccati*: "whom you snatched from the slavery of sin". In the English translation, this is an imperative petition, "free us from sin". *Eripuisti* means "you have snatched away, delivered, set free". *A servitute* means "from slavery, servitude, dominion".

Summary. To bring back to life the son of the woman of Shunem, Elisha had to humble himself (2 Kings 4:8 ff). Basil of Caesarea (469/ 470-542) saw in this a parallel with Christ who humbled himself to restore us to life, as Basil says in the words of this prayer: "Elisha stooped low that he might raise the boy to life; Christ humbled himself that he might raise up the world lying in sins" (*humiliavit se Christus, ut mundum in peccatis iacentem erigeret*, Sermon 128.8). Basil says that what Elisha prefigured in the boy's regard, Christ fulfilled on behalf of the entire human race. Basil then interprets the canticle that Christ Jesus "humbled [*humiliavit*] himself and became obedient to the point of death" (NRSV Philippians 2:5-11), to mean that because we were small, so Christ made himself small, to us lying in death – no one can raise the fallen who does not wish to bend down.

This prayer is based on several contrasts and comparisons. God has raised up the ailing world (*iacentem mundum*). This is then said of the faithful whom God has

snatched (*eripuisti*) from servitude to sin (*a servitute peccati*). This is done in the humility of God's Son (*in filii tui humilitate*). The canticle from Philippians 2, however, continues to say that because Christ humbled himself, God has exalted him above all creation. We likewise are raised up, but in two stages. We pray that God grant holy joy in this life, that those who trust in God (fideles) may enjoy eternal joys (*gaudiis perfrui sempiternis*) in the next.

Two modifications appear in the post-Second Vatican Council text of this prayer. First, the motive clause, formerly *quos perpetuae mortis eripuisti casibus*, "whom you have snatched from the calamities of eternal death", now reads *quos eripuisti a servitute peccati*, "whom you have snatched from the slavery of sin", thus shifting the emphasis from salvation from eternal death in the afterlife to salvation in the struggle with sin in the present life. Second, in the 1962 *Missale Romanum* the petition includes the phrase *perpetuam laetitiam*, "perpetual joy", which is contrasted with *perpetuae mortis*, "of eternal death", and paralleled with *gaudiis sempiternis*, "eternal joys". The current missal replaces *perpetuam* with *sanctam laetitiam*, "holy joy", which contrasts with *a servitute peccati*, "from the slavery of sin" and is developed by *gaudiis sempiternis*, "eternal joys". Thus, the current text highlights three distinct times: the past, because God has already snatched us from the slavery of sin; the present, as we ask for holy joy in this life; and the future, for we hope to attain eternal joys. While these three times were present in the pre-Vatican II version, the actions of each were considered in the light of their consequences in the after-life: eternal death or life. ■

Guided by the light of truth

The Church's reflection on the experience of praying can lead to the development of the liturgical texts themselves, as they have done through the centuries and have continued to do since the Second Vatican Council

Today, discussion of the translation of liturgical texts is best situated in the context of the history of developing the Latin texts upon which all translations are based. The gradual evolution of the opening prayer this Sunday teaches us of the ecclesial task of developing these texts by the Church's reflection on the experience of praying them.

Source. The oldest form of this prayer is found in the so-called Verona Sacramentary, a collection of booklets developed for individual Masses compiled between 561 and 574. The prayer was included among other Masses for the month of April. We can trace the development of the prayer through the changes to the original phrase: *errantes in via posse redire*, ""the ones erring that they would be able to return in the way". The prayer was then included in the Gelasian Sacramentary, composed between 628 and 715, for presbyteral use in the titular churches of Rome, where it was assigned to the second Sunday after the Easter Octave, where it remained in almost all liturgical books until the reform of Vatican II. There the same phrase reads: *errantes ut in via possent redire* – "that erring ones would be able to return on the way". Here we see the addition of *ut* followed by the subjunctive, which is incorrectly given as *possent*; it should read *possint*.

This seventh-century Gelasian was carried into Gaul and was mixed with other Gallican rites, then further developed there during the eighth century. For example, the Gelasian Sacramentary of Gellone reads: *errantes ut in viam possent redire iustitie*, "that erring ones would be able to return unto the way of justice". Here, *in*

---

the opening prayer
16th Sunday in Ordinary Time

God our Father, your light of truth
guides us to the way of Christ.
May all who follow him reject
what is contrary to the gospel.
(*The Roman Missal*,
Collins, London, 1974)

Deus, qui errantibus, ut in viam possint
redire, veritatis tuae lumen ostendis, da
cunctis qui christiana professione
censentur, et illa respuere, quae huic
inimica sunt nomini, et ea quae sunt
apta sectari.
(*Missale Romanum*,
Città del Vaticano, 2002)

---

via, "on the way", yields to the preferable *in viam*, "unto the way". The way is specified by *iustitie*, "of justice", spelled phonetically, but classically spelled *iustitiae*.

When Charlemagne (742-814) wished to unify his empire he asked Hadrian I (pope from 772 to 795) for a sacramentary and in 786 received a papal sacramentary, the Hadrianum. Because this book included only the prayers used by the Bishop of Rome, it was ill-suited for parish use in Gaul; his successor, Louis the Pius, charged Benedict of Aniane (d. 821) to supplement the book. Benedict included this Sunday's prayer from the Gelasian Sacramentary tradition of the eighth century then circulating in Gaul and changed the phrase to read *errantibus, ut in viam possint redire iustitiae*, correcting *possent* and *iustitie* and making *errantibus* the indirect object of *ostendis*: "you reveal … to ones erring that they would be able to return unto the way of justice".

During the liturgical reform of Vatican II Benedict's version of the prayer was maintained, but the word *iustitiae*, "of justice", was dropped. In the 1975 *Missale Romanum* the prayer was assigned both to this Sunday and to Monday of the third week of Easter. After the slight revision of the *Missale Romanum* 2002, the prayer remains assigned to this Sunday alone. The historical development of this prayer continues today as the whole Sacramentary is undergoing its first major revision since the *Missale Romanum* was first translated into English and many other vernacular languages after the Council.

Analysis of the literary form

Invocation: Expressed simply, the prayer addresses *Deus*, literally "God", which is translated as "God our Father".

Amplification: The invocation is amplified by the relative clause, *qui errantibus ... veritatis tuae lumen ostendis*, which means "you who extend the light of your truth to ones wondering from the truth", rephrased in the English as "your light of truth guides us". *Errantibus* by itself means "to ones wandering from the truth" and thus relates to *veritatis tuae* – "of your truth"; it also means "to ones going astray", thus relating to *in viam redire* "to return unto the way" in the next phrase.

First purpose: The amplification includes its own purpose clause expressed classically by *ut* followed by the subjunctive *possint*: *ut in viam possint redire*; literally, "that they be able to return to the way", rephrased as "guides us to the way of Christ". The subject of *possint*, "they may be able", is the word *errantes*, "erring ones", implied in *errantibus*.

Petition: The imperative petition *da cunctis*, meaning "grant to all", is rendered

as an exhortative subjunctive of a second English sentence: "May all". *Cunctis*, here, refers to all Christians as we shall see in the motive clause.

Second purpose: The petition is followed by two infinitives expressive of purpose. The first is: *et illa respuere, quae huic inimica sunt nomini*, which means "both to reject those things, which are hostile to the name", which is rephrased in English by the exhortative subjunctive "May all ... reject what is contrary to the gospel". *Respuere* means "to spit out", hence "to reject".

Third purpose: The second infinitive phrase, not expressed in the English, is: *et ea quae sunt apta sectari (huic nomini)*, meaning "and to pursue ones which are fitting".

Motive: The motive for God's granting that all Christians reject and pursue ... is expressed by a relative clause amplifying *cunctis*: *qui christiana professione censentur*, meaning "to all who are known by Christian profession", and is rephrased in English as "who follow him". In the post-Vatican II *Missale Romanum*, the term "Christian" can refer to all the baptised as is evident in the post-Communion prayer of the Mass for Christian Unity, which prays for "all who find their glory in the name Christian", *omnes qui christiana gloriantur nomine*. This prayer, indeed, resonates with the baptismal imagery of first rejecting what is hostile to, and then professing the Christian faith that the judge may not spit us out as lukewarm water (Revelation 3:16).

Summary. The Church lives by her prayer, and this prayer develops by her reflection on the act of praying itself. I hope that these weekly commentaries help the Church to pray fully conscious, and then to deepen her reflection on the experience of praying. ∎

Gifts of the Lord's favour

In the collect for the sixteenth Sunday in ordinary time we ask that we, fervent in faith, hope and love, may persevere in obeying God's commands. We examine the nuances of the original Latin and how it is rendered in translation

The opening prayer this Sunday quickly draws the assembly into the mystery of the love of God, who increases our faith, hope and love.

Source. Of the three opening prayers included in the post-Vatican II *Missale Romanum* from the ancient Bergamo Sacramentary of the Ambrosian rite, the opening prayer this Sunday is one of two originally from the litanies for the three rogation days of prayer and fasting in preparation for the feast of Pentecost. I wonder if these three prayers were included in homage to the Good Pope John XXIII, who attended seminary in Bergamo, where the Ambrosian rite is still celebrated.

Analysis of the literary form

First petition: The prayer begins with two imperative petitions, the first in the passive voice. *Propitiare … famulis tuis* means "be favourable to your servants", and is translated as "be merciful to your people". *Propitiare* as an active verb means "to render favourable, appease" as in "to appease the gods". Here, on the contrary, we invoke the Lord to be favourable. Nowhere does the Latin text of this prayer refer to "us" or "we", rather it uses the third person *famulis tuis*, "to your servants".

Invocation: Tucked into the first petition is the simple invocation *Domine*, translated literally as "Lord". The invocation is not amplified.

Second petition: An active imperative, the second petition, *et clementer gratiae tuae super eos dona multiplica*, means "and mercifully increase the gifts of your

> *the opening prayer*
> **16th Sunday in Ordinary Time**
> Lord, be merciful to your people.
> Fill us with your gifts and make us
> always eager to serve you in faith,
> hope and love.
> (*The Roman Missal*,
> Collins, London, 1974)
>
> Propitiare, Domine, famulis tuis,
> et clementer gratiae tuae super eos
> dona multiplica, ut, spe, fide et caritate
> ferventes, semper in mandatis tuis vigili
> custodia perseverent.
> (*Missale Romanum*,
> Città del Vaticano, 2002)

grace upon them". "Them" refers to "your servants", which is made personal in the English translation: "fill us with your gifts". *Clementer* is an adverb meaning "with forbearance, indulgence", which the OED defines as abstaining "from enforcing what is due", especially "the payment of a debt". *Dona*, in general, means "gifts, presents" and in particular "presents brought to a deity" as in the gifts of bread and wine we offer in the Eucharist. Here, however, the gifts are given by the Lord, and it anticipates the gift of the Spirit celebrated at Pentecost.

Purpose: Our purpose for asking the Lord to be favourable and to increase the gifts of the Lord's grace is expressed classically by *ut* followed by the subjunctive *perseverent: ut … semper in mandatis tuis vigili custodia perseverent*, meaning "that they may always persevere with vigilant observance in your commands".

The purpose is rendered in English by a third imperative, "and make us always eager to serve you".

Perseverent followed by *in* and the ablative *mandatis* means "to abide by, adhere strictly to, continue steadfastly, persist, persevere". The word is reminiscent of the crowd that remained (*perseverant*) with Jesus for three days to hear his teaching and then was abundantly fed on seven loaves and a few small fish (Matthew 15:32), or of the one who endures (*perseveraverit*) to the end that will be saved (Matthew 10:22. Biblical citations from NRSV, Vulgate). More specific to the original context of this prayer between the Ascension and Pentecost are the stories of the disciples returning to Jerusalem after the Ascension. They persevered in prayer (*erant perseverantes … in oratione*, Acts 1:14), and after the descent of the Spirit, persevered in the apostles' teaching (*erant … perseverantes in doctrina apostolorum*, Acts 2:42).

The combination *vigili custodia* evokes the image of the shepherds keeping watch by night (*vigilantes et custodientes vigilias noctis*), when the Angel of the Lord announced the birth of the Saviour (Luke 2:8), or of those who stay awake and clothed (*beatus qui vigilat et custodit vestimenta sua*) for the Lord will come as a thief in the night (Revelation 16:15).

Moreover, some form of the words *custodia* and *mandatum* occurs often in the Bible, calling us to obey the Lord's commands. The one, for example, who professes Jesus, but does not obey his commands (*mandata eius non custodit*) is a liar (1 John 1:24). Also, we receive what we ask for because we obey God's commands (*quoniam mandata eius custodimus*, 1 John 3:22). Perhaps the strongest affirmation is: "the love of God is this, that we obey his commandments" (*haec est enim caritas Dei ut mandata eius custodiamus*, 1 John 5:3).

Motive: The manner in which the Lord's servants persevere in the Lord's commands is given in apposition to the *ii*, "they", implied in *perseverent*, "may they persevere": *spe, fide et caritate ferventes*, meaning "burning with hope, faith and love" and translated simply as, "in faith, hope and love". The reference is to the scriptural text: "and now faith, hope, and love abide, these three; and the greatest of these is love" (*nunc autem manet fides spes caritas tria haec maior autem his est caritas*, 1 Corinthians 13:13. Cf. 1 Thessalonians 1:3, 5:3).

Summary. How do we keep God's commands? The greatest commandment is to "love the Lord your God with all your heart, and with all your soul, and with all your mind", and the second is to "love your neighbour as yourself" (Matthew 22:37, 39). Furthermore, Jesus gave a new commandment: "Just as I have loved you, you also should love one another" (John 13:34). In Christ our humanity is joined to his divinity in the very revelation of the self-emptying love of God for us, and so we learn how to love God, neighbour and self as Christ has loved us. We sing of this new commandment when we wash feet on Holy Thursday, as Jesus at the Last Supper, prefiguring his humble service on the Cross.

In this prayer we ask the Lord to increase the gifts of the Lord's favour, interpreted as faith, hope and love. Moreover, the purpose of our prayer is that we, fervent with faith, hope and love, may persevere in the Lord's commands, to love as the Lord has loved us, for in the end there remain faith, hope and love, and the greatest of these is love. ∎

The Lord is our steersman

The metaphor of God as our guide and rudder in the journey of life appears in the collect for this Sunday's Mass, drawing on imagery used since the early days of the Church. Here we examine its sources and how it exemplifies the tradition of the renewal of prayers

The opening prayer this Sunday shows how the liturgical renewal mandated by Vatican II draws deeply upon the Church's tradition that her prayer ever may be renewed.

Source. This prayer was redacted during the liturgical renewal mandated by the Second Vatican Council from parts of three ancient prayers. Most of the text comes from a prayer assigned to the fourth Sunday after Pentecost in the Sacramentary of Padua, originally composed c. 670-680 to adapt the papal liturgy to presbyteral use for the pilgrims to St Peter's Basilica, Rome. The last two lines come from two other prayers found in the so-called Verona Sacramentary, a collection of Roman Mass booklets compiled between 561 and 574, as noted below.

Analysis of the literary form

First amplification: The prayer begins with an amplification in apposition to the invocation which follows: *Protector in te sperantium* means "protector of ones hoping in you", which is rendered in the English as "and protector". The line comes from Psalm 18:30: "The Lord is a protector of all hoping in the Lord" (*protector est omnium sperantium in eum*), which is frequently translated as "he is a shield for all who take refuge in him" (Vulgate, NRSV throughout).

Invocation: The invocation is simply *Deus*, and rendered in English as "God our Father".

Second amplification: The invocation is amplified by the relative clause *sine quo nihil est validum, nihil sanctum*, which

---

the opening prayer
17th Sunday in Ordinary Time
God our Father and protector, without you nothing is holy, nothing has value. Guide us to everlasting life by helping us to use wisely the blessings you have given to the world.
(*The Roman Missal*, Collins, London, 1974)

Protector in te sperantium Deus, sine quo nihil est validum, nihil sanctum, multiplica super nos misericordiam tuam, ut, te rectore, te duce, sic bonis transeuntibus nunc utamur, ut iam possimus inhaerere mansuris.
(*Missale Romanum*, Città del Vaticano, 2002)

---

means "without whom nothing is strong, nothing holy", as in the English, "without you nothing is holy, nothing has value". *Validum* means "robust, in good health, effective". The phrase evokes the image of the vine and the branches, as Jesus says: "Those who abide in me and I in them bear much fruit, because apart from me you can do nothing", where *sine me nihil*, "without me nothing", parallels *sine quo nihil*, "without whom nothing", in the prayer (John 15:5). In the Hebrew Bible, life is holy, *sanctum*, and that which generates life.

Petition: Given in the imperative, we petition God: *multiplica super nos misericordiam tuam*, which means "increase your mercy upon us". The phrase is not expressed in the English. *Misericordiam* also means "tender-heartedness, pity, compassion". The phrase evokes the Vulgate version of Psalm 35:8: "how you have multiplied your mercy, O God" (*multiplicasti misericordiam tuam Deus* – compare with Psalm 36:7). The rest of the verse echoes the first amplification as it refers to those "who will hope in the shelter of God's wings" (*in tegmine alarum tuarum sperabunt*), again the image of refuge in God.

Result: Drawn mostly from a preface in the Verona Sacramentary, the result clause is expressed classically by *ut* followed by the subjunctive *utamur*: *ut … sic bonis transeuntibus nunc utamur*, meaning, "that we so use passing goods now" and is rephrased in the English as, "by helping us to use wisely the blessings you have given to the world". Gregory the Great (540-604) uses similar words in his reflections on Job, "For if the heart were under discipline, it would seek higher things, it would not long for acquiring passing goods [*bonis transeuntibus*]" (13.33).

Purpose: The result clause leads to a result clause expressed classically by *ut* followed by the subjunctive *possimus*: *ut iam possimus inhaerere [bonis] mansuris*. Although the Latin grammar is the same for a result clause, translated in the indicative, I take it to be a result clause, and, thus, translate it in the subjunctive: "that already we may cling to ones going to remain". *Mansuris* is the one word derived solely from the third ancient prayer also from the Verona Sacramentary; its inclusion gives a stunning force to this prayer when its core meaning as a future participle is maintained, even though it is used as an adjective describing *bonis* and thus parallel to the present participle *transeuntibus*. While parallel, their times contrast, as *bonis transeuntibus*, "passing things", contrasts with *bonis mansuris*, "good things going to remain", which are the

eschata-logical joys of heaven. What is stunning is that through this paralleling contrast the prayer asks that we now use passing goods with the result that we are able to grasp even now eschatological goods going to remain. Furthermore, taking it as a result clause heightens the contrast between the result we wish to attain now, and the "not-yet" of things about to come. The clause is perhaps expressed in the current translation by the phrase: "to everlasting life".

Premise: Included in the purpose clause is the premise on which the prayer is based, expressed by two ablative absolutes *te rectore, te duce*; the verb "being" is typically omitted. Literally, "you the steersman, you the navigator", the English translation alludes to them by the imperative petition "guide us". The *rectore* is similar to the *gubernatore*, who steers the ship with the rudder, whereas the *duce* is the leader out front, in this case navigating the ship. This same image is found in Cyprian's (d. 258) commentary On the Lord's Prayer: "that …we illuminated by the light of grace might continue the journey of life with the Lord, as navigator and steersman [*duce et rectore Domino*]" (1).

Summary. God is our protector and source of strength and life. In God's abundance, we are to use the passing goods of this world in such a way as to already enjoy eternal goods, going to remain. God is both the one who navigates out front and steers in the back of the ark, the Church, wherein we find refuge. Continuing the metaphor of the ship, we pray to use the goods along the journey in such a way as to already enjoy the bounty of the promised land. ∎

To our origin and guide

The opening prayer for the eighteenth Sunday in Ordinary Time, was replaced in 2006's calendar by that of the Feast of the Transfiguration

Reminiscent of Eucharistic Prayer IV: "in the name of every creature under heaven, we too praise your glory as we sing", in the opening prayer this Sunday we pray that God may restore and preserve all things for us who acknowledge God as Creator and director.

Source. Tracing the changes of just one word, among the variants of this prayer, helps to map its historical development. The oldest source of this prayer is the Verona collection of Mass booklets compiled between 561 and 574, where it appears as a prayer over the people for the fast of the seventh month, September (*septem* = seven), according to the old Roman calendar. During the redaction of the Gelasian Sacramentary between 628 and 715 for presbyteral celebration in the titular churches of Rome, the prayer was transferred to Wednesday of the second week of Lent and the word *creata* was changed to *grata*, thereby breaking the original parallelism, which was restored only in 2002. Sometime shortly before the pontificate of Pope Gregory II (715-731), prayers were composed for the Thursdays of Lent. Accordingly, this prayer was transferred to Thursday of the second week of Lent, and *grata* was changed to *congregata*. This use spans from the Hadrianum, the papal Sacramentary given by Pope Hadrian I to Charlemagne in 785-786, until 1970. In 1970 this prayer over the people offered at the end of Mass became an opening prayer and was transferred to this Sunday, which falls at the beginning of August (the Roman sixth month, *sextilus*, was renamed after Emperor Augustus in 8 BC). In 1970 *congregata* was restored to *grata* of the

---

the opening prayer
18th Sunday in Ordinary Time

Father of everlasting goodness, our origin and guide, be close to us and hear the prayers of all who praise you. Forgive our sins and restore us to life. Keep us safe in your love
(*The Roman Missal*, Collins, London, 1974)

Adesto, Domine, famulis tuis, et perpetuam benignitatem largire poscentibus, ut his, qui te auctorem et gubernatorem gloriantur habere, et creata restaures, et restaurata conserves.
(*Missale Romanum*, Città del Vaticano, 2002)

Gelasian, and in 2002 to *creata* of the Verona. As the prayer continued to evolve, this one word made a full sweep.

Analysis of the literary form

First petition: The prayer begins with the second (future) imperative *Adesto … famulis tuis*, "be present to your servants", which is personalised as "be close to us". The divine-human exchange is God's presence for us, and our response of self-gift as God's servants.

Invocation: Inserted into the first petition is the simple invocation *Domine*, literally, "Lord", which is elaborated as "Father of everlasting goodness".

Second petition: The imperative, *et perpetuam benignitatem largire poscentibus*: ""and lavish perpetual goodness on the ones desiring", is translated as "and hear the prayers of all who praise you". Again, according to the exchange, God gives bountifully, whereas we offer our need petitioning that God's continuous favour be lavished upon us.

The deponent imperative *largire*, "give bountifully, lavish", and the contemporaneous participle *poscentibus*, "to ones asking for urgently, desiring", can each have as its object the entire *ut* clause, but because *largire* already has a direct and indirect object (*benignitatem... poscentibus*), I have translated the *ut* clause as depending on *poscentibus*. This is important in that were the *ut* clause dependent on *largire*, it would express God's intention in lavishing, but depending on *poscentibus* it expresses the desire of ones urgently asking.

Double purpose: Our desired purpose is expressed in the entire phrase *ut his ... et creata restaures, et restaurata conserves*, "so that for these ... created things you may restore and ones restored you may preserve", which perhaps suggests the three imperatives, "Forgive our sins and restore us to life. Keep us safe in your love." The pronoun *his* is a dative of interest for we ask that God restore creation in the interest of the ones desiring (*poscentibus*) and boasting (*gloriantur*). The first purpose clause yields to the second in that "things having been made" becomes "things having been restored", and God's restoring leads to maintaining. The phrase is a chiasm centring on restoration (*restaures, restaurata*), which is sandwiched by *creata*, things made by God, and by God's maintaining, (*conserves*). The one purpose building on the other evokes God's lavishing (*largire*) time and again, or continually (*perpetuam*), in both creation and redemption.

Motive: Nestled within the purpose clause is the relative clause supplying God's motive for restoring and maintaining

according to our desire: *qui te auctorem et gubernatorem gloriantur habere*, "they who boast to have you as origin and guide", which is rendered as "our origin and guide". In a ship the *gubernator*, putting hand to the rudder, is the "steersman". God's servants (*famulis*) are the ones who acknowledge God as Creator (*auctorem*) and governor (*gubernatorem*), whereas as petitioners (*poscentibus*) they acknowledge that the Creator restores (*restaures*) and maintains (*conserves*). Restoring the text to read *creata* instead of *grata* restores the parallelism between the motive and purpose clauses, for as the Creator (*auctorem*) restores things having been made (*creata*), so the moderator (*gubernatorem*) preserves things having been restored (*restaurata*).

The phrase alludes to the *Hexameron* of Ambrose, "Let us follow, therefore, the one who knows both the author (*auctorem*) and the director (*gubernatorem*)" (2.7), and to Augustine, "the Lord Jesus Christ, director, author [*gubernator auctor*]" (Sermon 293D). John Cassian echoes the creed saying: "believe, that Jesus Christ is Lord [*dominum*] of all things ... the Creator [*creatorem*] of things, who is the maintainer [*conservatorem*] of human people ... formerly the Creator of the entire world, who thereafter is the redeemer of the human race" (*De incarnatione*, 6.19).

Summary. The exchange between God's presence to us, and our response as servants, God's lavishing and our need, continues in the interplay between the purpose and motive clauses, for God who created all things, first restores them in Christ and then preserves them for our benefit, because we who have been lavished with God's continuous favour find our boast in having God as both Creator and director, a parallelism regained after 14 centuries. ■

Intimate with a majestic God

In this analysis of the collect for this Sunday is described how in the prayer we call on God in intimate terms as our father. In the role of children we ask him to perfect us in the spirit of adoption and to make us worthy of entering into the promised inheritance

Confidently we invoke God in the most intimate of terms. The opening prayer this Sunday shows the genius of the Roman rite, its noble simplicity, and its integration of majesty and intimacy, as seen in the majestic invocation, and its intimate amplification and in the petition.

Source. The oldest version of this prayer is found in the Sacramentary of Padua, an adaptation of the papal sacramentary for presbyteral use at St Peter's Basilica between 670-680. Our version is closest to that in the Sacramentary of Bergamo, a pre-Carolingian, Ambrosian sacramentary. The petition clause was reworked after Vatican II, and this prayer is one of the few whose text was altered in the 2002 *Missale* now being translated into English.

Analysis of the literary form

Invocation: The complex invocation *Omnipotens sempiterne Deus* is directly translated as "Almighty and ever-living God".

Scriptural background: The primary scriptural allusion is from Paul's Letter to the Romans: "For all who are led by the spirit of God are children of God. For you did not receive a spirit of slavery to fall back into fear, but you have received a spirit of adoption [*spiritum adoptionis filiorum*], when we cry, "Abba! Father!" it is that very Spirit bearing witness with our spirit that we are children of God, and if children, then heirs [*heredes*], heirs of God and joint heirs with Christ – if, in fact, we suffer with him so that we may also be glorified with him" (NRSV, Vulgate unless noted; 8:14-17). The Hebrew word "abba" is what children call their father, rather like "daddy"; majesty and intimacy are

---

the opening prayer
19th Sunday in Ordinary Time

Almighty and ever-living God,
your Spirit made us your children,
confident to call you Father.
Increase your Spirit within us and bring
us to our promised inheritance.
(*The Roman Missal*,
Collins, London, 1974)

Omnipotens sempiterne Deus,
quem, docente Spiritu Sancto,
paterno nomine invocare praesumimus,
perfice in cordibus nostris spiritum
adoptionis filiorum,
ut promissam hereditatem ingredi
mereamur.
(*Missale Romanum*,
Città del Vaticano, 2002)

---

united when we call the eternal God "Daddy".

Amplification: Given as a relative clause, the amplification, *quem ... paterno nomine invocare praesumimus*, means "whom we are confident to call by a paternal name", and is translated as, "confident to call you Father". *Praesumimus* is related to the English "we presume", but can also mean "we dare, trust, are confident", as in the Vulgate of Judith 6:15: *quia non derelinquis praesumentes de te et praesumentes de se ... humilias* [literally: "because you do not neglect ones trusting you, but you humble ones trusting themselves"] (cf. 6:19). While *invocare* can mean "to call upon, invoke", its transferred meaning is "to call by name" or "to name". I suggest that in the degree to which we are daughters and sons of God, our calling God by an intimate name shows confidence rather than presumption.

The prayer alludes to the request: "Lord, teach [*doce*] us to pray… He said to them, 'When you pray, say: Father [*Pater*], hallowed be your name'" (Luke 11:1). Even this opening prayer, however based on the Scriptures, telling us to call God "Abba" and "Pater", does not so directly address God.

Motive: The ablative absolute, *docente Spiritu Sancto*, gives our motive for calling upon God on intimate terms: "as the Holy Spirit teaches". This clause is found in the ancient texts of this prayer, but was excised for the 1970 *Missale*, of which the current English version is a translation. By this omission the prayer concurs more closely with Romans 8:14-17; its omission, however, removed a rare reference to the teaching role of the Holy Spirit in the Roman liturgy. The *Missale* of 2002 has reinserted this phrase, which should debut in the next English translation. The allusion is to John 14:26: "but the Advocate, the Holy Spirit [*Spiritus Sanctus*], whom the Father will send in my name, will teach [*docebit*] you everything, and remind you of all that I have said to you". The Spirit teaches us to pray, by urging us to pray as Jesus taught.

Petition: *perfice in cordibus nostris spiritum adoptionis filiorum* means "bring to perfection in our hearts the spirit of adoption as daughters and sons", which is the basis of two phrases in the English: "your Spirit made us your children" and "increase your Spirit within us". *In cordibus nostris* is an allusion to *in corda nostra* in the Letter to the Galatians: "… so that we might receive adoption as children [*adoptionem filiorum*]. And because you are children, God has sent the Spirit of his Son into our hearts [*misit Deus Spiritum Filii sui in corda nostra*],

crying, 'Abba! Father! [*Pater*]'. So you are no longer a slave but a child, and if a child then also an heir [*heres*], through God" (4:5-7).

Filiorum can refer to sons alone or to a mixed group of daughters and sons, as my translation makes explicit. The scriptural passages cited in this article translate all forms of *filii* by corresponding forms of "children". The unfortunate aspect of such a translation is expressed in the axiom: "once a child always a child", whereas daughters and sons of God may mature to become adult Christians.

Purpose: We petition that God make perfect in us the Spirit of adoption, *ut promissam hereditatem ingredi mereamur* – "that we may be worthy to enter into the promised inheritance". The purpose is expressed classically by *ut* followed by the subjunctive *mereamur*, and is translated by another imperative petition: "and bring us to our promised inheritance".

Summary. At the heart of the paschal mystery is God's self-emptying in Jesus Christ and our becoming one with God in Jesus (Philippians 2:6-11). This prayer characterises our intimacy with the majestic God.

The state of the pilgrim church is that we pray to become more fully who we already are, that we may enter fully into the inheritance we already enjoy; or, we, who in our baptism have become adopted daughters and sons of God and are taught by the Holy Spirit to trust and confide in the name of God, call upon God to bring to perfection within us that spirit of adoption that we, who already enjoy the promised inheritance, may come to share its fullness. ■

From him all good things come

The opening prayer for the twentieth Sunday in ordinary time expresses our desire to love God above all things and to be transformed by him, but acknowledges that our desire is exceeded by his abundance

---

the opening prayer
20th Sunday in Ordinary Time

God our Father,
may we love you in all things
and above all things
and reach the joy you have prepared for us beyond all our imagining.
(*The Roman Missal*,
Collins, London, 1974)

Deus, qui diligentibus te bona invisibilia praeparasti, infunde cordibus nostris tui amoris affectum, ut, te in omnibus et super omnia diligentes, promissiones tuas, quae omne desiderium superant, consequamur.
(*Missale Romanum*,
Città del Vaticano, 2002)

Through words we come to the ineffable, through the visible to the invisible, through desire to the satisfaction of desires not yet known, through love to fulfilment of the promises of God.

Source. The prayer first appears in the Gelasian Sacramentary, an adaptation of the papal liturgy compiled between 628-715 for presbyteral celebration in the titular churches of Rome. During the eighth century, as the Gelasian was carried north and adapted, the prayer was widely diffused. When Charlemagne sought to unify his kingdom by a common liturgical practice, in 757/758 Pope Hadrian sent to him a papal sacramentary, the Hadrianum; the book was problematic as its Latin was poor and it contained only those elements needed by the bishop. The opening prayer this Sunday received its definitive corrections and was inserted into the supplement compiled by Benedict of Aniane under the reign of Louis the Pious between 810-815. The Hadrianum, with its supplement, became the basis for the future *Missale Romanum*, which was by then a Romano-Gallo-Germanic Missal.

Analysis of the literary form

Invocation: The simple invocation, *Deus*, "God" is translated as "God our Father".

Amplification: The relative clause *qui diligentibus te bona invisibilia praeparasti*, literally "you who have prepared unseen good things for the ones loving you", amplifies the invocation, but is not expressed in the translation. *Praeparasti* is the syncopated form of *praeparavisti*, meaning "you have made ready beforehand, prepared, equipped". The reference is to 1 Corinthians 2:9: "but, as it is written, 'What no eye has seen [*non vidit*], nor ear heard, nor the human heart conceived, what God has prepared for those who love him [*quae praeparavit Deus his, qui diligunt illum*]'" (RSV, New Vulgate, unless noted). Yet God is the unseen good above all goods, "whom, although you have not seen, you love [*quem cum non videritis diligitis*]" (1 Peter 1:8, my translation).

Petition: The imperative petition *infunde cordibus nostris tui amoris affectum* means literally, "pour into our hearts the disposition of love of you", which also is lacking in the English. *Tui amoris* may be translated as "of your love", as in God's love for us, or "of love of you", as in our love for God. *Infunde* means "to pour in, upon or into; to impart". *Affectum* refers to "a state or disposition of mind" and especially, "love, desire, compassion".

Purpose: Expressed classically by *ut* followed by the subjunctive *consequamur*, the purpose clause is *ut … promissiones tuas … consequamur*. It means, "that we may obtain your promises" and is translated as "and reach the joy you have prepared for us". In classical Latin *promissiones* refers to the act of promising, and thus keeps to the divine-human exchange as a present act; God's promises are ever true, whereas, had the prayer used *promissa*, "things having been promised", it would have referred to the promises as a past event. In later Latin *promissiones* comes to mean simply "promises".

God's motive: Included within the purpose clause are two motive clauses, one giving God's motive, the other ours. God's motive for granting what we ask is given as a participial phrase: *te in omnibus et super omnia diligentes*, meaning "[we] loving you in all things and above all things", and translated as a subjunctive petition "may we love you in all things and above all things". The phrase alludes to the Apostle, who says that there is "one God and Father of all, who is above all and through all and in all [*qui super omnes et per omnia et in omnibus*]" (Ephesians 4:6).

Our motive for asking is given in the relative clause: *quae omne desiderium superant*: [promises] "which exceed all desire", and is translated, "beyond all our imagining". *Desiderium* means variously, "an ardent desire, request, pleasure".

Summary. The prayer tells the same story from the perspective of two motives, ours and God's. We petition, but even our desire is excelled by God's abundance. We petition to be transformed by his love, that our rightly ordered loving might be his motive for granting even more. We pray that once our love is transformed we might attain to God's promises, the good things prepared for those loving him. We pray for the good things he promises, knowing they are beyond what we can see, and even excel our desire, because above all we desire God.

God's motive for granting that we attain to his promises is that we are the ones loving him in all things and above all things, which is already the gift of God for which we pray in the petition. Thus we pray that he instil the character of divine love deeply within, that we might become lovers of God in and above all things, which in turn becomes the reason for his granting that we attain to his promises.

"The Word became flesh", moreover, "and dwelt among us, and we have beheld his glory [*vidimus gloriam eius*]" (my translation; John 1:14), and "whoever has seen me has seen the Father" [*qui vidit me vidit et Patrem*] (John 14:9), for Christ Jesus "is the image of the invisible God [*est imago Dei invisibilis*]" (Colossians 1:15).

The genius of our sacramental liturgy is that it moves *per visibilia ad invisibilia*, "through visible things to invisible realities". The Vatican II Constitution on the Liturgy says: "finally, visible signs, which the sacred Liturgy uses to signify invisible divine realities … (*Signa tandem visibilia, quibus utitur sacra Liturgia ad res divinas invisibiles significandas …* ; *Sacrosanctum Concilium* 33), thus the Eucharist is *futurae gloriae pignus*, "a pledge of future glory" (from the antiphon for the feast of the Body and Blood of Christ). ∎

Hearts and minds freely won

The joys and sorrows of our changing world are contrasted with the one true joy available to us when we learn to desire what God has already promised

---

the opening prayer
21st Sunday in Ordinary Time

Father, help us to seek the values
that will bring us lasting joy
in this changing world.
In our desire for what you promise
make us one in mind and heart.
(*The Roman Missal*,
Collins, London, 1974)

Deus, qui fidelium mentes unius efficis
voluntatis, da populis tuis id amare
quod praecipis, id desiderare quod
promittis, ut, inter mundanas varietates,
ibi nostra fixa sint corda,
ubi vera sunt gaudia.
(*Missale Romanum*,
Città del Vaticano, 2002)

Latin poetry at its best, the opening prayer this Sunday is richly interconnected and grounded in the Scriptures, urging us to "love the Lord your God with all your heart [*corde*], and with all your soul, and with all your mind [*mente*], and with all your strength" and "your neighbour as yourself" (Mark 12:30-31).

Source. The prayer is first documented in the Gelasian Sacramentary, an adaptation of the papal sacramentary compiled between 628 and 715 for the presbyteral liturgy in the titular churches of Rome. In the 1975 Missale this prayer was prescribed both for this Sunday and for Monday of the fifth week of Lent. With the revision of the *Missale* of 2002 another prayer has been supplied for that Monday.

Analysis of the literary form

Invocation: The simple invocation *Deus*, meaning "God", is translated as "Father".

Amplification: The invocation is amplified by the relative clause *qui fidelium mentes unius efficis voluntatis*, which means "you who make the minds of the faithful [to be] of one will", and is translated by the imperative petition, "make us one in mind and heart". *Mentes* means variously "minds, hearts, souls", and corresponds to *voluntatis* meaning, "of free will, desire, inclination". *Efficis* followed by the accusative *mentes* (hearts) and the implied infinitive *esse* (to be) means "you form, bring it about that …", and expresses God's purpose for acting: that the hearts of the faithful may be of one desire.

Petition: The imperative petition *da populis tuis*, "grant to your people", is followed by two infinitive clauses. The first, *id amare quod praecipis*, means "to love that which you command", and somewhat corresponds to the English, "help us to seek the values". The second is *id desiderare quod promittis*, meaning "to desire that which you promise", which is expressed as a prepositional phrase in English, "in our desire for what you promise".

The root meaning of *praecipis* is "you take beforehand", then "you give precepts to; admonish, teach, enjoin", and *promittis* means "you say beforehand, hold out"; both actions are in the present and express an anticipation; God is instructing us in how to love him and our neighbour now, while God's promises of future joys inspire steadfastness in our hearts now. *Praecipis* (you instruct) corresponds to *mentes* (minds), whereas *desiderare* (to desire) corresponds to *voluntatis* (of free will), as God's gift respects our free will in teaching and promising, loving and desiring.

Purpose: Expressed classically by *ut* followed by the subjunctive *sint*, the purpose clause, *ut ... ibi nostra fixa sint corda*, means "so that our hearts may there be fixed" and is not expressed in the English. *Fixa* means "fixed, immovable" and characterises our hearts and our desiring and loving in the petition clause, and corresponds to the unity of our desire in the amplification. *Corda* and *mentes* can each refer to the whole person or to the emotions or intellect separately. *In tandem* they express both "minds" and "hearts" and correspond with *voluntatis* (of free will) to describe the whole person in its complexity. *Nostra* corresponds to *populis* in the petition and *fidelium* in the amplification; all three identify us as God's people (*populis tuis*), who trust in God (*fidelium*).

Premise: The premise of the prayer is *inter mundanas varietates*, meaning "among wordly changes", and is rendered in English by, "in this changing world". *Varietates* refers to "fickleness, vicissitudes" and contrasts with *fixa* (immovable) in the purpose, *unius* (of one) in the amplification, and *vera* (true) in the motive clause.

Motive: Our motive for praying is expressed by the correlative, *ubi vera sunt gaudia*, meaning, "where joys are true" and expressed in English by "that will bring us lasting joy". *Vera* means "true, real, genuine". The adverbs *ibi* and *ubi* are correlatives expressing either time, "then ... when", or place, "there ... where". They express the time when desired promises are fulfilled, including the present. They

express the place of true joys (*vera gaudia*), namely heaven, in contrast to the fickleness of this world (*mundanas varietates*).

There is a subtle shift from the subjunctive *sint* (may they be) and *sunt* (they are), as the first expresses our purpose, and the second the genuine reality. While the genuine joys are real, realising their promise requires the divine-human exchange whereby we ask God to give us to love and desire. *Gaudia* (delights) are "inner joys", but the word is also used for things that produce joy: "causes, occasions of joy". They are the promised desires of the petition clause and the one desire (*unius voluntatis*) of the amplification. The first and last words of the prayer are united in that *Deus* – God – is the one true joy of the human heart and mind and will.

Summary. God's instruction and the scriptural basis for the prayer is the gospel injunction: "store up for yourselves treasures in heaven (*thesauros in caelo*), where (*ubi*) neither moth nor rust consumes and where thieves do not break in and steal [i.e. *fixa, vera*]. For where your treasure (*thesaurus*) is, there (*ibi*) your heart (*cor*) will be also" (NRSV, New Vulgate, Matthew 6:20-21). The prayer exchanges joys for treasures, and summarises the treasures as genuine and permanent.

While the invocation "O God" may seem stark, it is like a blank canvas on which the rest of the prayer can paint the image of God revealed in the *mirabilia Dei*, "marvellous deeds of God". In the amplification God forms the minds of people trusting in God; in the petition he not only teaches and promises, but gives to his people to love and desire. In the purpose clause God grants our hearts to rest in him. In the ancient basilicas of Rome God is represented only by a hand, for he is known in his works, and by the image of Christ, for whoever has seen him has seen the Father (John 14:9). ■

Nourish good things in us

In this opening prayer we ask God to nurture in us the seed of love of his name, and in doing so increase our reverence for him.

---

the opening prayer
22nd Sunday in Ordinary Time

Almighty God, every good thing comes from you. Fill our hearts with love for you, increase our faith, and by your constant care protect the good you have given us. (*The Roman Missal*, Collins, London, 1974)	Deus virtutum, cuius est totum quod est optimum, insere pectoribus nostris tui nominis amorem, et praesta, ut in nobis, religionis augmento, quae sunt bona nutrias, ac, vigilanti studio, quae sunt nutrita custodias. (*Missale Romanum*, Città del Vaticano, 2002)

Source. The opening prayer this Sunday is first found in the presbyteral liturgy of the titular churches of Rome as represented by the Gelasian Sacramentary, compiled between 628 and 715. Its corrupt Latin was corrected when it was copied for use with the pilgrims to St Peter's as seen in the Sacramentary of Padua (c. 670-680). As the Gelasian Sacramentaries circulated to the north of Rome, the prayer spread and was finally included in the supplement to the Hadrianum (810-815). The prayer was reworked for its inclusion in the *Missale* of Pius V after the Council of Trent, then restored to its ancient form in the *Missale* of Paul VI after Vatican II.

Analysis of the literary form
Invocation: In the Old Testament, the complex invocation *Deus virtutum*, "God of powers", conveys the image of angel hosts ready to do God's command (cf. Psalm 25/24:10). The New Testament develops this idea by emphasising the subjection of powers to God, and especially to Christ, whom God seated "at his right hand in the heavenly places, far above all rule and authority and power [*virtutem*]

and dominion, and above every name [*omne nomen*] that is named" (Ephesians 1:20-21), which inspires the English translation: "Almighty God".

Amplification: Given as a relative clause, the amplification *cuius est totum quod est optimum* means "to whom is all which is most noble" and is translated as "every good thing comes from you". The phrase recalls James 1:17: "Every generous act of giving [*omne datum optimum*], with every perfect gift, is from above." *Est* with the genitive *cuius* is a special construction meaning "it belongs, pertains to".

First petition: Two petitions are given. The first, *insere pectoribus nostris tui nominis amorem*, means, "sow in our hearts the love of your name", which is translated as "fill our hearts with love for you". *Pectoribus* refers to the breast, then the heart, stomach, spirit and mind; in short, one's interior life. So, too, the name of God stands for God's self and self-revelation, for Jesus has made known God's name (*manifestavi nomen tuum*; John 17:6), because Jesus "is the image of the invisible God" (Colossians 1:15).

God's transcendent power and goodness intimately touches the human heart with a transforming love for God, which also finds expression in the love of neighbour as self. We petition almighty God to ingraft or sow seed as a gardener (as the resurrected Christ appeared to Mary; John 20:15), but intimately, within our selves. As this prayer develops, so does the seed germinate and mature by God's vigilant care.

Second petition: Lacking in the English translation, the second petition, *et praesta*, "and grant", or even "and guarantee", which God can do because of God's power and willingly does because of God's goodness.

First result: The twofold result clause is expressed classically by *ut* and the two subjunctives *nutrias* and *custodias*. Each clause contains a motive expressed as a relative clause. The first, *ut in nobis, religionis augmento, quae sunt bona nutrias*, means "[guarantee] that by an increase of reverence you may nourish in/among us things which are good", and is expressed in English by, "increase our faith". The direct object *ea*, "those things", is implied in the relative *quae*, "things which". *In nobis* can mean "in us" or "among us"; the former emphasises the interior transformation, the latter the social. *Religionis* means "of reverence for God, piety, religion" and comes to refer to the celebration of the liturgy as well. Furthermore, "religion [*religio*] that is pure and undefiled before God, the Father, is this: to care for orphans and widows in their distress, and to keep oneself unstained by the world" (James 1:27). Thus, we petition God to nurture the seed of the love of his name, and to do this by increasing our reverence for him, which is expressed in liturgical worship and by the two commandments of Jesus to love God above all things and our neighbour as ourselves (Leviticus 19:18, Matthew 22:39, Mark 12:33, Luke 10:27). God, indeed, nourishes us in the Eucharist through communion with God, neighbour and self in Christ.

First motive: The motive, *quae sunt bona*: "which are good", is not in the English translation. Our motive for petitioning God to sow love in us is that he may then see to it to nourish the good things we desire because of our love of his name. Because God is the greatest good, he desires to nurture good things in us.

Second result: The second result and motive clause is *ut in nobis … ac, vigilanti studio, quae sunt nutrita custodias*, meaning, "and may guard with vigilant attention things which are nourished", and is rendered by the English, "and by your constant care protect the good you have given us". Again, the direct object *ea*, "the things", is implied in the relative *quae*, "things which". Because God has first sown in us the love of God's name, and then has nurtured this love, which is expressed in love of neighbour as self and in worship, we ask God to guard these things vigilantly, even as we keep vigil until the eternal dawn. Indeed, unless the Lord guards [*custodierit*] the city, the guard keeps watch [*vigilavit*] in vain.

Second motive: God's motive for guarding our love of God, neighbour and self is because God, who is all good, has already sown and nourished good things within us.

Summary. The prayer unites the love of God, neighbour, self and the orphan and widow, with liturgical worship, and God's transcendence and intimacy within the human heart, all in an image of sowing, nurturing and guarding, echoing the Apostle: "he who supplies seed to the sower and bread for food will supply [*praestabit*] and multiply your seed for sowing and increase [*augebit*] the harvest of your righteousness" (2 Corinthians 9:10). ∎

Reborn into freedom

The opening prayer for this week reveals a change in the Latin with important theological implications. The original "reborn in Christ" emphasised God's action, whereas the modern "believing in Christ" stresses our own. Either way, it is through our baptism that we are redeemed

Every Sunday celebrates the Resurrection, and thus our baptism, redemption and adoption as God's daughters and sons in Christ. This prayer, originally from the Easter season, highlights the paschal dimension of every Sunday.

Source. Throughout most of its history, this prayer was offered during Easter vespers, as is the case in its earliest witness, the Gelasian Sacramentary (Rome, 628-715). For the *Missale Romanum* of 1970 the prayer was revised and assigned to both the Saturday of the second week of Easter and this Sunday. The duplication was omitted in the *Missale* of 2002.

Analysis of the literary form

Invocation: The simple invocation *Deus*, "God", is translated as "God our Father".

Amplification: Expressed by a relative clause, the amplification *per quem nobis et redemptio venit et praestatur adoptio*, "through whom both redemption comes and adoption is given to us", is translated as, "you redeem us and make us your children in Christ". *Redemptio* refers to "releasing the debtor from the demand, by paying the creditor", and then "a release from sin, a rescuing from death". The phrase is an allusion to Galatians 4:5 – "in order to redeem [*redimeret*] those who were under the law, so that we might receive adoption as children [*adoptionem filiorum*].

Petition: Given in the command form, the petition *filios dilectionis tuae ... intende*, "be attentive to the children of your love", is rendered in English as "Look upon us". *Intende*, at its root, means

---

the opening prayer
23rd Sunday in Ordinary Time

God our Father, you redeem us
and make us your children in Christ.
Look upon us, give us true freedom
and bring us to the inheritance you
promised.
(*The Roman Missal*,
Collins, London, 1974)

Deus, per quem nobis
et redemptio venit et praestatur
adoptio, filios dilectionis tuae benignus
intende, ut in Christo credentibus
et vera tribuatur libertas,
et hereditas aeterna.
(*Missale Romanum*,
Città del Vaticano, 2002)

"stretch forth", and thus, "exert yourself for". *Filios* can refer to sons only or to daughters and sons as here.

The original petition was: *respice in opera misericordiae tuae*, "turn your attention towards the works of your mercy". The *opera misericordiae tuae*, "works of your mercy", are both the works of salvation in Christ, and the people redeemed, whereas the new petition specifies the daughters and sons (*filios*) of God's love. The addition of *filios dilectionis tuae* adds an allusion to the baptism of Christ, when the voice said: "This is my Son, the Beloved [*Filius meus dilectus*]" (NRSV, Vulgate throughout, Matthew 17:5; cf. Mark 9:7; 2 Peter 1:17; Colossians 1:13).

First motive: God's good nature is expressed by the adjective *benignus*, "kind, generous one", used as an adverb to mean "kindly".

Purpose: Expressed classically by *ut* followed by the subjunctive *tribuatur*, the purpose clause *ut in Christo credentibus et vera tribuatur libertas, et hereditas aeterna*, "so that both true freedom and an eternal inheritance be given to ones believing in Christ", is translated by the imperative petition: "give us true freedom and bring us to the inheritance you promised". Reworked for the 1970 *Missale*, the original text was: *et aeterna tribuatur hereditas et vera libertas*. By transposing *hereditas* and *libertas* and their adjectives, the phrase parallels the amplification clause, as redemption (*redemptio*) corresponds to freedom (*libertas*) and adoption (*adoptio*) to inheritance (*hereditas*). This parallel structure simplifies the stylistically more beautiful chiasm present in the original order: redemption, adoption, inheritance, freedom, where the first and last elements correspond and sandwich the other two corresponding elements. The purpose clause is an allusion to Galatians 4:30-5:1 – "the child of the slave will not share the inheritance [*heres*] with the child of the free woman [*filio liberae*] … we are children [*filii*] … of the free woman [*liberae*]. For freedom Christ has set us free [*qua libertate nos Christus liberavit*]".

Second motive: The original phrase *in Christo renatis*, "to people having been reborn in Christ", was changed in the *Missale* of 1970 to *in Christo credentibus*, "to people believing in Christ", creating a grammatical problem because here *credentibus* takes *in* with the accusative (*in Christum*) but not *in* with the ablative (*in Christo*) as in the current prayer. While the new phrase is found in Vulgate of Galatians 2:16 (*in Christo Iesu credidimus*), the Latin has been corrected in the New Vulgate to *in Christum Iesum credidimus*. As often happens in liturgical

development, one part of the liturgy changes, in this case the participle, but not its interconnecting parts, here the dependent phrase *in Christo*, creating a mismatch in Latin and giving rise to the conundrum of whether to translate accurately the awkwardness of the official Latin text. Modern languages such as Italian and English, on the other hand, easily accommodate the change from "reborn in Christ" to "believing in Christ". Perhaps the problematic Latin here reveals the editor's thinking in a modern language. Regardless, the phrase was omitted in the English translation.

Furthermore, the substitution of *credentibus* for *renatis* changes the prayer in several ways. The baptismal association of being "reborn in Christ" is exchanged for a more general "belief in Christ". *Renatis* is the divine passive emphasising God's action, for we are reborn by an act of God, whereas *credentibus* is active, placing greater emphasis on our action, our trusting in Christ. Finally, *renatis* is a past divine passive contrasting with the future divine passive of the purpose clause "may be given", whereas the contrast with the present tense active *credentibus* is not as marked.

Summary. True to its Eastertide origin, the lynchpin of this prayer is baptism by which we are redeemed and adopted as God's daughters and sons. As the prayer has been excised from its original context of paschal vespers, diminishing its outward coherence, so too the changes to the prayer, to the degree to which they largely diminish the baptismal imagery, diminish also its internal coherence. A further purpose is implied in the prayer that gives a greater coherence with our daily lives, as the Apostle admonishes: "For you were called to freedom [*in libertatem*], brothers and sisters; only do not use your freedom as an opportunity for self-indulgence, but through love become slaves to one another" (Galatians 5:13). ∎

The gift of service

Thanks to the sacrifice of Jesus Christ, we can know God's favour, we experience this not only spiritually but with our senses, as we are led into the total love of God and our neighbour

---

the opening prayer
24th Sunday in Ordinary Time

Almighty God, our creator and guide, may we serve you with all our heart and know your forgiveness in our lives. (*The Roman Missal*, Collins, London, 1974)	Respice nos, rerum omnium Deus creator et rector, et, ut tuae propitiationis sentiamus effectum, toto nos tribue tibi corde servire. (*Missale Romanum*, Città del Vaticano, 2002)

Source. Prior to the *Missale* of 1970, this prayer is found in only one source in the history of the Western Church; there it is given as an optional opening prayer in Mass booklet number 15 for the month of September in the Verona compilation of Mass booklets used in the papal liturgy of Rome compiled between 561 and 574.

Analysis of the literary form
First petition: The prayer begins with the imperative petition, *respice nos*: "be mindful of us", which is not rendered in the English. The root meaning of *respice* is "look back, behind", then, "look at with solicitude, be mindful of".

Amplification: As Latin has a more elastic word order than English, the invocation is nestled within the amplification, which is given in apposition: *rerum omnium ... creator et rector*: "creator and guide of all things", which is translated as "our creator and guide". *Rerum* has broad meaning: "of things, beings; events, facts; circumstances, conditions". A *rector* is a "guide, leader, ruler", the helmsman who steers the ship, or, in this case, the guide who directs human history to its fulfilment.

Invocation: The simple invocation *Deus* is translated by the complex invocation: "Almighty God".

Purpose: The purpose clause is placed before the second petition on which it depends. Expressed classically by *ut* followed by the subjunctive *sentiamus*, *ut tuae propitiationis sentiamus effectum*, "that we may experience the effect of your restoring favour", it is translated by a second exhortative subjunctive petition, "and know your forgiveness in our lives" (NRSV, Vulgate throughout; cf. 1 John 2:2). The allusion is to 1 John 4:10: "In this is love, not that we loved God but that he loved us and sent his Son to be the atoning sacrifice [*propitiationem*] for our sins" (cf. 1 John 2:2). *Propitiationis* refers to an act of conciliation or atonement, and is derived from the verb *propitiare*, "to render favourable".

Here, we are not rendered favourable to God, but God is rendered favourable to us by Jesus Christ. *Effectum* refers to "a doing, or the result of an action", even its "operative influence" and thus its power. The effect of God's favour is not limited to the spiritual; rather, we hope to experience it with the senses, as *sentiamus* means, "may we discern by the senses, perceive the effects of anything". The Creator's favour restored by Christ is expressed in regarding us with solicitude and bringing us to experience the power of God's favour.

Second petition: Following the purpose clause, which depends upon it, the second petition given in the imperative: *et … toto nos tribue tibi corde servire*, ""and … grant us to serve you with a whole heart", is translated with an exhortative subjunctive, "may we serve you with all our heart". The allusion is to the two greatest commandments: "You shall love the Lord your God with all your heart [*ex toto corde*], and with all your soul, and with all your mind … You shall love your neighbour as yourself" (Matthew 22:37-39; cf. Luke 10:27), which in turn is an allusion to the commandment of God through Moses: "to serve the Lord your God with all your heart and with all your soul [*servias Domino Deo tuo in toto corde tuo*]" (Deuteronomy 10:12; cf. 11:13).

Serving God, then, is to keep God's commandments, especially by loving God with our whole being, and our neighbour as our self; such love is the gift of God for which we petition, and leads to our experiencing God's favour both in lives of service and in the celebration of the liturgy.

Summary. In the invocation and amplification clauses all of creation goes out (*exitus*) from God the creator (*rerum omnium creator*) and is maintained by God (*rector*). The petitions and purpose clause concern the return of creation to God (*reditus*). After God created all things and humanity fell from grace, Christ restored the favour of God (*tuae propitiationis*). While the redemption won by Christ is the turning point of salvation history, its historical aspect is only implied in the purpose clause. Rather, we ask for the gift of service with the whole heart (*toto tibi corde servire*) in order that we might perceive

with the senses (*sentiamus*) the favour of God accomplished (*effectum*) in Christ. Our incorporation into the economy of salvation is achieved by none other than the gift of service, which is to love God with our whole being, and our neighbour as our self.

There is an interplay between the first petition, where we ask God to look with solicitude upon us, and the purpose clause, where we express our hope to know the power of our being restored to God's favour. By the gift of wholehearted service we hope to pass from our awareness of God's mindfulness of us to directly encountering the power of redemption.

This passage is mediated by our love of God and neighbour as our self, so that such service might lead us to encounter the full power of our redemption intended (*effectum*) by God. Without the purpose clause, our prayer to serve God and to know forgiveness become parallel actions, as in the English translation, and do not build one upon the other. With the purpose clause the gift of service leads to a proper ordering of our love, which prepares us for the gift of the more powerful encounter (*sentiamus effectum*), even as grace leads to grace (John 1:16) and we are transformed time and again on our journey of faith.

God's gift as creator and guide is to all of creation, but to us who believe is given first the gift of God's favourable regard, and then the gift of loving service leads us, in the name of all creation, to the contemplation of the divine favour. ∎

Love of our neighbour

The focus of the collect for this Sunday is on the two great commandments. The theology behind these instructions is built into the grammar – and deliberate ambiguities – of the original Latin. Here we explore a prayer that contains within itself the history of salvation

The opening prayer this Sunday re-orientates our love for God to love for neighbour as a response to the revelation of God's love for us in Christ. For our love for God is not the measure of our lives or liturgical prayer. Rather, God's love for us in Christ is the measure of our love for one another.

Source. The prayer, a new composition in the *Missale Romanum* of 1970, is composed from two ancient prayers. The invocation, amplification and petition are from an optional prayer from Mass booklet 14 for the month of July in the Verona compilation of Mass booklets made between 561 and 625 for the papal liturgy in Rome. The purpose and motive clauses come from the Mozarabic liturgy of the ninth to tenth centuries, where it is given as a prayer for the exchange of peace. These are the only known occurrences of each source prayer.

Analysis of the literary form

Invocation: The simple invocation *Deus*, "God", is rendered "Father".

Amplification: The relative clause *qui sacrae legis omnia constituta in tua et proximi dilectione posuisti*, "you who stated that all things of the holy law had been established in your love and [love] of neighbour", amplifies the invocation and is rendered as an imperative petition, "guide us, as you guide creation according to your law of love". The complement of *posuisti* (you have stated) is the entire phrase of the accusative *omnia*, "all things", with the passive antecedent infinitive *constituta* [*esse*], "to have been established".

There is a subtle play between *tua dilectione*

---

the opening prayer
25th Sunday in Ordinary Time

Father, guide us, as you guide creation
according to your law of love.
May we love one another
and come to perfection
in the eternal life prepared for us.
(*The Roman Missal*,
Collins, London, 1974)

Deus, qui sacrae legis omnia constituta
in tua et proximi dilectione posuisti,
da nobis, ut, tua praecepta servantes,
ad vitam mereamur pervenire
perpetuam.
(*Missale Romanum*,
Città del Vaticano, 2002)

(your love) and *proximi dilectione* (love of neighbour). The couplet *tua dilectione*, with the adjective *tua* (your), refers to God's love for us, whereas our love for God was not expressed as it could have been by the objective genitive *tui* (of you) to parallel *proximi* (of neighbour). The couplet *proximi dilectione*, "in love of neighbour" is bivalent in that *proximi* may be considered an objective genitive, refering to one's love for one's neighbour, or a subjective genitive refering to the love my neighbour has for me, thereby echoing in one word the mutual love of Christ's precept "I give you a new commandment, that you love one another [*ut diligatis invicem*]. Just as I have loved you, you also should love one another" (NRSV, Vulgate throughout; John 13:34). This commandment was given in the Gospel of John at the Last Supper when Christ humbly washed the disciples' feet, thus giving example of mutual love rendered in humble service.

Surprisingly, what is missing in this prayer is a direct reference to our love for God, as commanded through Moses, "you shall love the Lord your God with all your heart, and with all your soul, and with all your might" (Deuteronomy 6:5), which became the basis of Jesus' great commandment, "you shall love the Lord your God with all your heart, and with all your soul, and with all your mind" and his second, "you shall love your neighbour as yourself" (Matthew 22:37-39). Rather, the prayer focuses on the measure of God's love for us in Jesus Christ and on our mutual love. Of course, our love for God is implied in the prayer as our response to God's love for us in Christ, but, for all the emphasis given to our worship of God in the liturgy, a direct reference here to our love for God is all the more strikingly absent.

Petition: The imperative petition *da nobis*, "grant to us", is not expressed in the English.

Purpose: Expressed classically by *ut* followed by the subjunctive *mereamur*, *ut … ad vitam mereamur pervenire perpetuam*, "that we may be worthy to attain eternal life", is translated by the second exhortative subjunctive: "May we … come to perfection in the eternal life prepared for us." In the Latin, the use of the first (present) subjunctive *mereamur* is correlated to the use of *da* (grant) in the petition clause. The use of *mereamur* indicates that the action (our being made worthy) relative to God's granting (*da*) is incomplete, unfinished, ongoing, eternal, future, contemporaneous. Theologically this implies our having being made worthy in Baptism, and affirms that our being worthy is both a process in this life and the desired result in eternal life.

Motive: Tucked within the purpose clause is God's motive for granting us eternal life:

tua praecepta servantes, "people observing your precepts", which is perhaps the basis of the first petition in the exhortative subjunctive, "May we love one another". The allusion is to John 15:10, "If you keep my commandments [*praecepta mea servaveritis*], you will abide in my love, just as I have kept my Father's commandments and abide in his love"; the new commandment, as above, is to love mutually as Christ has loved us. *Servantes* agrees with *mereamur* as we pray that we, observing God's precepts, may be worthy. Both actions, our observing and our being worthy, are contemporaneous, for, as we observe the command to love one another in the measure of God's love for us in Christ, we are ever made worthy. Because the motive clause is tucked into the purpose clause, our observing God's commandments is also a gift for which we pray *da nobis*, "grant to us".

Summary. This prayer depicts the sweep of salvation history. Christ synthesised the law and the prophets in the two great commandments, but the revelation of a new commandment in his teaching and saving passion reorientates the love of God and neighbour-as-self to mutual love according to the measure of God's love for us in Christ. We, who have been made worthy in Baptism, petition God to grant now that we, loving mutually now, may be worthy now, and, ever so loving, may be worthy evermore. Relative to God's granting, as we observe the divine precepts, we merit to arrive unto eternal life, which has already begun for us in baptism. As we mature as Christians, and so as we mature in our ability to observe the devine precepts, so too do we mature in meriting the eternal life we already share. ∎

Running towards God

Divine omnipotence is expressed above all through mercy and compassion, and Christ's compassionate willingness to take up our suffering means that we can participate in his divinity

---

the opening prayer
26th Sunday in Ordinary Time

Father, you show us your almighty power in your mercy and forgiveness Continue to fill us with your gifts of love Help us to hurry towards the eternal life you promise and come to share in the joys of your kingdom. (*The Roman Missal*, Collins, London, 1974)	Deus, qui omnipotentiam tuam parcendo maxime et miserando manifestas, multiplica super nos gratiam tuam, ut, ad tua promissa currentes, caelestium bonorum facias esse consortes. (*Missale Romanum*, Città del Vaticano, 2002)

While the fulcrum of salvation history is the paschal mystery, the death and resurrection of Christ, the divine human exchange is encountered today in this prayer.

Source. The prayer first appears in the Gelasian Sacramentary, compiled between 628 and 715 for presbyteral use in the titular churches of Rome, where it is listed among various opening prayers for Sundays. It was reproduced in various Gelasian sacramentaries of the eighth century used in northern Italy and north of the Alps, whence it was included in the supplement to the Hadrianum, compiled by Benedict of Aniane between 810 and 815, and thence it passed to the *Missale Romanum*. During the liturgical reform of the Second Vatican Council, the petition clause was changed, but was restored to the original Gelasian text in the *Missale Romanum* of 2002.

Analysis of the literary form

Invocation: The simple invocation *Deus*, "God", is translated as "Father".

Amplification: The invocation is ampli-

fied by the relative clause *qui omnipotentiam tuam parcendo maxime et miserando manifestas*, "you who manifest your almighty power most of all by showing mercy and compassion", is translated as, "you show your almighty power in your mercy and forgiveness". *Parcendo* and *miserando* are both gerunds with similar yet contrasting meanings as *parcendo* refers to showing mercy by withholding one's self, "by sparing, forbearing to punish", whereas *miserando* refers to showing mercy in the form of suffering with, "by commiserating".

While in Scripture Christ "is the image of the invisible God" (Colossians 1:15), who "revealed [*manifestavit*] his glory" at the wedding of Cana (John 2:11) and has made God's name known (*manifestavi*; John 17:6), in the prayer, the verb *manifestas*, "you manifest", is in the present and the gerunds "by sparing" (*parcendo*) and "by commiserating" (*miserando*) are contemporaneous, emphasising God's self-manifestation today.

In the prayer God's sparing is not a response to our confession, but is a manifestation of omnipotence, as in the book of

Wisdom: "You spare [*parcis*] all things, for they are yours [*quoniam tua sunt*]" (NRSV, New Vulgate throughout; 11:26). Similarly God's mercy is a manifestation of omnipotence: "But you are merciful [*misereris*] to all, for you can do all things [*omnia potes*]" (Wisdom 11:23). The prayer is the contrary to a series of declamations in the prophet Ezekiel where God swears "my eye will not spare [*non parcet*], and I will have no pity [*non miserebor*]" (Ezekiel 5:11; cf. 7:4, 9, 8:18, 9:10). The reason for this reversal is that God, did not "withhold [*pepercit*] his own son, but gave him up for all of us" (Romans 8:32). From its origin, this prayer has been offered on Sunday; similarly Nehemiah says: "I commanded the Levites … to keep the Sabbath day holy. Remember this also in my favour, O my God, and spare me [*parce mihi*] according to the greatness of your steadfast love [*secundum multitudinem miserationum tuarum*]" (13:22).

Petition: The current text in the third edition of the *Missale Romanum* restores the original imperative petition from the Gelasian Sacramentary, *multiplica super nos gratiam tuam*, "multiply your favour upon us". Our current English sacramentary offers a translation of the petition found in the 1970 *Missale Romanum*, *gratiam tuam super nos indesinenter infunde*, literally, "ceaselessly pour out your favour upon us", translated as, "continue to fill us with your gifts of love". We petition that God's favour, already given by sparing and being compassionate, be multiplied upon us as grace upon grace (John 1:16).

Purpose: Expressed classically by *ut* followed by the subjunctive *facias*, the purpose clause *ut … caelestium bonorum facias esse consortes*, "that you may make to be sharers of the heavenly goods", is rendered in English by the third imperative petition, "and come to share in the joys of your kingdom". *Consortes* refers to

"people sharing property" as in sharing heavenly goods, and to "living in community of goods, having an equal share, colleagues". God who spares and is compassionate, now makes co-heirs. The allusion is to 2 Peter 1:4: "Thus he has given us, through these things, his precious and very great promises [*promissa*], so that … you … may become participants of the divine nature [*efficiamini divinae consortes naturae*]".

Motive: God's motive for making us to share the heavenly goods is expressed by the participial phrase at the beginning of the purpose clause, *ad tua promissa currentes*, "the ones running towards your promises", and is rendered in English by the second imperative petition, "Help us to hurry towards the eternal life you promise".

Our response to God's self-manifestation and multiplying favour upon us is to run towards the promises, which in turn becomes God's motive for granting their fulfilment. Thus, the motive clause finds its resolution in the purpose clause in that "running towards" (*ad … currentes*) finds its fulfilment in being made equal sharers (*consortes*), and "your promises" (*tua promissa*) are fulfilled in the "good things of Heaven" (*caelestium bonorum*).

Summary. The Christian journey in its development by stages is flattened in the English translation to three commands we make of God. The Latin text, however, shows how the wondrous exchange [*admirabile commercium*] between God and humanity develops. First we experience God as sparing and compassionate, especially in Christ who took up our suffering (*miserando*), and we pray for an abundance of such favour, in order that we may run towards the promises offered, and therefore be made participants in the divine life. ∎

Abundant in his compassion

The human divine exchange is the subject of the collect for this week, and in it we see how God's love can cast out our fears and transform us into the image of his divine compassion

---

the opening prayer
27th Sunday in Ordinary Time

Father, your love for us
surpasses all our hopes and desires.
Forgive our failings,
keep us in your peace and lead us
in the way of salvation
(*The Roman Missal*,
Collins, London, 1974)

Omnipotens sempiterne Deus,
qui abundantia pietatis tuae
et merita supplicum excedis et vota,
effunde super nos misericordiam tuam,
ut dimittas quae conscientia metuit,
et adicias quod oratio non praesumit.
(*Missale Romanum*,
Città del Vaticano, 2002)

The *admirabile commercium*, the divine-human exchange, whereby God became human that we might share in divine life, is synthesised in this opening prayer, a *summa brevis*, a brief compendium of salvation history.

Source. This prayer made its debut in the Gelasian Sacramentary, an adaptation of papal liturgy for presbyteral use in the titular churches of Rome, compiled between 628 and 715. Thence it passed into several Gelasian sacramentaries of the eighth century used north of the Alps, whence it was included in the supplement to the Hadrianum compiled by Benedict of Aniane between 810 and 815 as part of the Carolingian synthesis of the Roman rite, which in turn became the basis of the *Missale Romanum*.

Analysis of the literary form

Invocation: The complex invocation, *Omnipotens sempiterne Deus*, "all-powerful ever-living God", is rendered in English as "Father".

Amplification: The invocation is amplified by the relative clause: *qui abundantia*

pietatis tuae et merita supplicum excedis et vota, "you who exceed in the abundance of your compassion the merits and prayers of humble petitioners", is translated as "your love for us surpasses all our hopes and desires". God's qualification for answering our prayer is his tenderness. *Merita* refers to "that which one deserves; that by which one deserves, merit", and refers to the fruit of our cooperation with God's favour.

Pietatis refers to our "love and duty towards God", but here it describes God's love toward humanity, expressed in "kindness, tenderness, compassion" as revealed ultimately in Jesus Christ of whom it is said: "without any doubt, the mystery of our religion [*pietatis mysterium*] is great: He was revealed in flesh ... taken up in glory" (NRSV; New Vulgate throughout; 1 Timothy 3:16). The divine-human exchange flows from God's compassion for us, which so exceeds the fruit of our cooperation with God's grace, our merits and prayers, even as Christ exceeds us by uniting the fullness of our human nature, without sin, to the fullness of divinity that in Christ God is wed to humanity thereby divinised.

Petition: Expressed in the imperative, the petition *effunde super nos misericordiam tuam*, "pour out your mercy upon us", is not expressed in translation. *Misericordiam* also means "pity, compassion, tender-heartedness".

First purpose: Two desired effects of God's mercy are expressed in two purpose clauses corresponding to the merits (*merita*) and prayers (*vota*) that God exceeds (*excedis*) in the amplification. Both are expressed by *ut* followed by the subjunctive. The first, *ut dimittas quae conscientia metuit*, "that you may dismiss things which conscience fears", is translated as an imperative: "Forgive our failings".

The clause may be understood morally, as the conscience fears (*conscientia metuit*) that it merits (*merita*) punishment, but God forgives (*dimittas*) our sin, as in the Lord's Prayer where we say "forgive [*dimitte*] us our debts, as we also have forgiven our debtors" (Matthew 6:12); however, a broader interpretation is also possible, both because *dimittas* means "may you break up, dissolve, dismiss", as tender-heartedness shatters the hard heart, dissolves fears and dismisses obstacles, and because *merita* refers to the just deserts of those who cooperate with the abundant love of God. What we fear is shattered, as we learn divine compassion.

Second purpose: The second, *ut ... et adicias quod oratio non praesumit*, means "and that you may further do that which prayer does not presume". Two allusions suggest two reasons for our not presuming. First, we depend upon the spirit to move us in prayer: "for we do not know how to pray as we ought, but that very spirit intercedes with sighs too deep for words" (Romans 8:26). Second, God is not bound by our limited imagination: "to him who by the power at work within us is able to accomplish abundantly far more [*potens est omnia facere superabundanter*] than all

we can ask or imagine" (Ephesians 3:20).

The second purpose is not translated, but two other imperative petitions are substituted in the English: "keep us in your peace and lead us in the way of salvation". The English text, by omitting the petition with its reference to God's mercy, and by specifying what we fear as our failings, weakens the sense of God's super-abounding self-communication and emphasises our moral failure. Furthermore, the developmental faith journey is flattened as the petition is omitted and the two purpose clauses are rendered as three parallel petitions.

Summary. The divine-human exchange begins with God's self, omnipotence all exceeding (*excedis*). *Pietatis*, then, implies a communication of God's compassion towards us in Jesus Christ, who took upon himself our suffering. God in turn fills us with divine compassion. God then shatters (*dimittas*) our fears and adds even more (*adicias*) beyond our presumption. On the other side of the wondrous exchange, we come to share in the divine life by stages. First, by our cooperation with divine favour we come to merit and to pray humbly before God, then we presume to petition that God's abounding love wash us and thus transform us into the image of divine compassion. By the practice of God's love, we hope both to surrender what we fear to God's purgation and what we dare not petition to be transformed into God's superabundance, implying that we come to share in God's excelling.

God's motive for sharing the divine life is his omnipotence (*omnipotens*) expressed in compassion (*pietatis, misericordiam*), echoing last Sunday's opening prayer: "you who manifest your omnipotence [*omnipotentiam*] most of all by being merciful and compassionate [*miserando*]". ∎

God's love unfolding

The understanding that our good works are performed in response to a divine initiative, and are prompted by the gift of God's favour, is built into the structure of this prayer. The human and the divine do not ultimately run in parallel, but intertwine

The opening prayer of the Mass takes about 10 seconds to offer, if said in a hurry. Thus it is barely noticed in many assemblies. Offering the prayer involves not only understanding the text, but also participating in offering it.

The Latin term for the opening prayer is *collecta*, meaning "things having been gathered up", and refers to the gathering of prayers together into a single prayer at the end of a litany or period of silent prayer. The term also refers to the members of the assembly who have gathered and so are 'collected' into an assembly.

The opening prayer of Mass involves a series of four elements. First, the invitation to pray given by the presider, who says *oremus*, "let us pray". Then the whole assembly observes silence ample enough for personal prayer. Only after an adequate silence does the presider gather the prayers together by offering the collect, thereby giving voice to the prayer of the Church; the collect concludes with a doxological formula. Finally the assembly ratifies the prayer with its "Amen".

Two major difficulties befall the opening prayer. First, insufficient silence is allowed for personal prayer, as if the printed text were the only prayer. Secondly, if the prayer is not gently unfolded by the presider, in its hearing the assembly will not be able to make the prayer its own. Not only is the process dialogical, it involves the participation of the whole assembly; as a human act its effective proclamation requires patience for the human heart to formulate its own personal prayer and to own our common prayer.

the opening prayer
28th Sunday in Ordinary Time

Lord, our help and guide,
make your love the foundation
of our lives. May our love for you
express itself in our eagerness to do
good for others.
(*The Roman Missal*,
Collins, London, 1974)

Tua nos, quaesumus, Domine, gratia
semper et praeveniat et sequatur,
ac bonis operibus iugiter praestet
esse intentos.
(*Missale Romanum*,
Città del Vaticano, 2002)

Because the opening prayer itself draws together our personal prayers, the genre is intentionally universal, as is this Sunday's prayer.

Source. The prayer was included in the Hadrianum, a papal sacramentary (containing only those elements proper to papal liturgy) given by Pope Hadrian I to Charlemagne in 785-86, but the prayer is widely attested not only in later redactions of earlier papal sacramentaries, but in many Gelasian sacramentaries of the eighth century used in northern Italy and north of the Alps, and in sacramentaries of the Ambrosian rite.

Analysis of the literary form
Double exhortative petition: The prayer begins with the double petition of two exhortative subjunctives, *praeveniat* and *sequatur*: *tua nos ... gratia semper et praeveniat et sequatur*, meaning "may

your grace always both precede and follow us". The English translation restructures the prayer by expressing the double petition as an amplification placed in apposition to the invocation "Lord, our help and guide", and by adding the imperative petition "make your love the foundation of our lives", thereby changing the subject from *gratia* (favour) to "the Lord" implied in the imperative "make!"

Invocation: Nestled parenthetically within the double petition is the simple invocation, *Domine*, translated literally as "Lord".

The parenthetical petition: *quaesumus*, "we ask, please" and is rendered in the doxology as, "we ask this".

Third exhortative petition: In addition to God's grace preceding and following, we petition that it *ac ... iugiter praestet*, "and may it likewise guarantee".

Result: What we ask God's grace to ensure is expressed by the entire sentence with an accusative subject *nos* and the infinitive verb *esse*: *nos bonis operibus esse intentos*, "that we are intent upon good works", rendered as, "may our love for you express itself in our eagerness to do good for others". This Latin construction may be used to express either the intent and thus purpose in ensuring or the concrete result of ensuring, as I have interpreted it here. To understand this clause as expressive of result, however, does not negate the freedom of human cooperation with divine gift. It states, rather, the concrete result of a process of gift and cooperative response; the result being that we are intent upon good works. Our doing good works, then, is the result of our cooperating with divine gift.

Summary. The exchange between God and humanity in the official English text occurs between God's love for us, and our parallel love for God expressed by the prayer's two independent petitions; our good works, then, are an expression of our love for God. The Latin text, in contrast, by making *tua gratia* (your favour), the subject of the three final verbs, *praeveniat* (may it anticipate), *sequatur* (may it follow) and *praestet* (may it ensure), focuses on God's favour towards us; our good works, accordingly, express our cooperation with the divine initiative and follow-up. This sandwiching of our good works within the divine milieux is expressed even in the Latin word order of the first line: *tua nos ... gratia*, literally, "your us ... favour", where "us" is interposed within "your favour".

Not only are we surrounded by God's favour, but, even as the three independent verbs establish the dominant idea of the sentence as God's favour towards us, our response is both to petition, as expressed in the parenthetical petition *quaesumus* (we ask), and to do good works, as expressed in the result clause *nos ... bonis operibus ... esse intentos* (that we be attentive to good works), which is fragmented into three parts and dispersed throughout the prayer: *nos* is the second word, the words *bonis operibus* are near the centre of the prayer and *esse intentos* are at the end; only upon reading the last word (*intentos*) can one read backwards through the prayer to find its subject *nos* and predicate *bonis operibus* and thereby discern our response.

Thus although both ideas unfold concurrently our response is subordinated to God's favour, and is even read backwards from the end of the prayer; the divine-human exchange in the Latin text is characterised by the subordination and concurrence of our good acts as a response to their surety in the ever-prevalent favour of God. ∎

Perfect freedom

This week's opening prayer wrestles with the question of compulsion in the divine-human encounter. We are reminded of Christ's teaching and example, that shows us how the road to liberty is through service

---

the opening prayer
29th Sunday in Ordinary Time

Almighty and ever-living God,
our source of power and inspiration,
give us strength and joy
in serving you as followers of Christ.
(*The Roman Missal*,
Collins, London, 1974)

Omnipotens sempiterne Deus,
fac nos tibi semper et devotam gerere
voluntatem, et maiestati tuae sincero
corde servire.
(*Missale Romanum*,
Città del Vaticano, 2002)

Not all ancient prayers are of the same literary quality. Because this Sunday's opening prayer uses a medieval Latin grammatical construction, it forces those responsible for translation to make difficult decisions. However one understands this prayer, our free cooperation with divine gift is fundamental to the understanding of the prayer.

Source. This prayer was included in many ancient manuscripts, and appears three times in its earliest source, the Gelasian Sacramentary, composed between 628 and 715 as an adaptation of the papal liturgy for presbyteral celebration in the titular churches of Rome. As the Gelasian and its descendants circulated to the north of Rome and north of the Alps, many of its prayers were subsequently joined to the papal tradition represented by the Hadrianum, a sacramentary given by Pope Hadrian I to Charlemagne in 785-786, by their inclusion in its supplement compiled by Benedict of Aniane between 810 and 815. The Hadrianum (papal) and its supplement (presbyterial) became the basis for the *Missalia Romana*.

Analysis of the literary form
Invocation: The complex invocation *omnipotens sempiterne Deus* is literally translated as "Almighty and ever-living God".

The English, however, adds the amplification "our source of power and inspiration".

Petition: The prayer uses the medieval Latin construction which begins with the imperative *fac*, "make, ensure, enable, cause", and continues in the two purpose clauses as we shall see.

First purpose: What we request God to ensure is expressed by a compound sentence that has the accusative subject *nos*, "us, we", followed by two infinitives, *gerere*, "to have, exercise, conduct", and *servire* "to serve". This medieval Latin construction substitutes for the more classical construction of the imperative *fac* followed by a purpose clause composed of *ut* and the subjunctive, in this case *geramus* and *serviamus*.

The first part of this compound purpose, then, is [*fac*] *nos tibi semper et devotam gerere voluntatem*, "[make] us always both exercise a free-will devoted to you". Were this clause, moreover, expressed classically, its character as a purpose clause comes to the fore: [*fac*] *ut tibi semper et devotam geramus voluntatem*, "[enable] that we may always both conduct a free-will devoted to you". This is how I understand the phrase, because the purpose of our prayer is to express a wish that we behave in a certain way, which behaviour is possible only by our cooperating with the gift of God.

This same Latin construction, nevertheless, may also be understood to express a concrete result, which would be expressed in English in the indicative as, "[bring it about] that we always both exercise a free-will devoted to you". In this example, moreover, the expression of result is particularly clear. Essential to the idea of 'free-will' is that the will be free and not coerced. The idea that God could coerce us to behave freely is an oxymoron. Thus, even if one were to understand the sentence as an expression of result, *fac nos gerere voluntatem*, literally, "make us to conduct a free-will", far from indicating a divine coersion of human free-will, expresses the desired concrete result of our free cooperation with divine initiative. Thus, whether understood as expressive of purpose or of result, our free cooperation with divine gift is ensured.

Second purpose: The second part of this compound purpose is *[fac] nos … semper … et maiestati tuae sincero corde servire*, "[make] us always… and to serve your majesty with a sincere heart". Again, Were this clause to be expressed classically, its character as a purpose clause comes to the fore: *[fac] ut tibi semper … et maiestati tuae sincero corde servire*, "[enable] that we may always… and serve your majesty with a sincere heart".

Of course, this same Latin construction could equally be understood to express a concrete result, again expressed in the indicative in English as, "[bring it about] that we always… and serve your majesty with a sincere heart". Service is distinguished from slavery once again by our free self-offering. So even the desire to serve God requires a freedom on our part whereby we offer ourselves in our service freely.

The free gift of ourselves to God, whether by serving God or by conducting a free-will devoted to God, is in response to the eternally begotten Word of God, who freely became our servant, accepting even our death. Whereas the Apostle Paul understands the death of Christ to be an act of self-emptying, John presents Christ's being lifted-up on the cross as his exultation, as his glory. We too, then, are coaxed to find our glory in service, our glory in our free-will devoted to God.

Summary. Our service of God is ever in the context of God's service towards us in Christ, who "emptied himself, taking the form of a slave *[formam servi]*, being born in human likeness he humbled himself and became obedient to the point of death – even death on a cross. Therefore God also highly exalted him" (NRSV, New Vulgate; Philippians 2:7-9); the divine-human exchange consists in the revelation of divine love in self-emptying service, for Christ is among us "as one who serves" (Luke 22:27), and in our sharing in divine love by our service in imitation of Christ the humble servant, who, having washed our feet, taught us to wash one another's feet (John 13:14). Furthermore, the Scriptures often translate *maiestas* as "glory", as in "the glory *[maiestas]* of the Lord entered the temple" (Ezekiel 43:4). As Christ is now seated "at the right hand of the Majesty *[Maiestatis]* on high" (Hebrews 1:3), whence "all the tribes of the earth will see 'the Son of Man coming on the clouds of heaven' with power and great glory *[maiestate]*" (Matthew 24:30), so our service is to worship God in glory and prepare for Christ's return, for whatsoever we do to the least of these we do unto Christ (Matthew 26:45).

The divine-human exchange, then, respects human freedom while offering a share in the divine life revealed and lived in self-emptying service. God the all powerful, then, both entices and enables us to co-operate freely and sincerely in the gift of our transformation. ∎

Constant promise

Loving actions make us worthy of what God has undertaken for us. But, as this week's opening prayer reveals, we cannot perform these actions without God. Our future fulfilment breaks into the present, in a single moment and over the course of our lives

The opening prayer this Sunday names the objects of our faith and hope and then shows how our loving God's commands makes us worthy of the fulfilment of our hope.

Source. First recorded in the Gelasian Sacramentary composed between 628 and 715 for presbyteral liturgies in the titular churches of Rome, this prayer passed into many eighth-century Gelasian Sacramentaries and then into the supplement to the Hadrianum, compiled by Benedict of Aniane 810-815.

Analysis of the literary form

Invocation: The complex invocation *Omnipotens sempiterne Deus* is translated literally as "Almighty and ever-living God".

First petition: The imperative petition *da nobis fidei, spei et caritatis augmentum*, "give to us an increase of faith, hope and love", is translated as "strengthen our faith, hope, and love". The allusion is to the first letter of Paul to the Corinthians: "And now faith [*fides*], hope [*spes*], and love [*caritas*] abide, these three; and the greatest of these is love" (NRSV, New Vulgate, 13:13).

Second petition and result: As in last week's prayer, the second petition is a late Latin construction consisting of the imperative *fac* followed by the accusative *nos* and the infinitive *amare*: *et ... fac nos amare quod praecipis*, "and make us love that which you instruct". This construction may express either God's intention or the concrete result of our free cooperation with God's action. If expressive of intention or purpose, it can be translated in the

---

> *the opening prayer*
> ### 30th Sunday in Ordinary Time
> Almighty and ever-living God, strengthen our faith, hope, and love. May we do with loving hearts what you ask of us and come to share the life you promise.
> (*The Roman Missal*, Collins, London, 1974)
>
> Omnipotens sempiterne Deus, da nobis fidei, spei et caritatis augmentum, et, ut mereamur assequi quod promittis, fac nos amare quod praecipis.
> (*Missale Romanum*, Città del Vaticano, 2002)

---

subjunctive, "bring it about that we may love". Such an interpretation leaves the concrete results of our cooperation with divine gift in suspension. Here, however, I take it to refer to the concrete result of our free and thus loving cooperation with divine enabling, which may be translated in the indicative, "bring it about that we do love". It is translated as an exhortative subjunctive in an independent sentence: "May we do with loving hearts what you ask of us". The object of *amare* (to love) is the unexpressed *id* (the thing, reality) implied in the relative pronoun *quod* ([the thing] which). *Praecipis* means variously "you give precepts to, teach, command".

Purpose: The divine-human cooperation that produces the result of our loving that which God commands, is directed towards a further purpose, which is placed first in the sentence. Expressed classically by *ut* followed by the subjunctive *mereamur* the clause *ut mereamur assequi quod promittis*, "that we may be worthy to attain that which you promise", is translated by a second exhortative petition, which is placed last in the prayer, "and [may we] come to share the life you promise". The object of *assequi* (to obtain) is an unexpressed *id* (the thing, reality) implied in the relative pronoun *quod* ([the thing] which).

Summary. The first petition replicates the biblical ordering of faith, hope and love, but the primacy of love is the lynch-pin verb the result clause giving rise to the purpose clause, and the objects of faith and hope are subordinated in two dependent and corresponding relative clauses. First the dependent relative clauses imply that the objects of faith are God's precepts (*quod praecipis*), and the objects of hope are God's promises (*quod promittis*). Then, just as the purpose clause is grammatically dependent on the result clause, so are their verbs, in that our being worthy (*mereamur*) is dependent on our loving (*amemus*, implied in *amare*), which is in turn dependent on God's enabling (*fac*). Thus, our transformation by loving actions is the means by which we become worthy.

Furthermore, the use of the present subjunctive *amemus* and *mereamur* means that the action of each verb in respect to the verb on which each depends is incomplete, unfinished, ongoing, eternal, future or contemporaneous. Thus, our loving (*amemus*) is to God's enabling (*fac*) incomplete, unfinished, ongoing, eternal, future, or contemporaneous, just as our being worthy (*mereamur*) is to our loving (*amemus*). The logical sequence is that first God enables, then we cooperate with divine enabling by loving, which in turn makes us worthy, but, according to the grammar, all of this may happen simultaneously, as well as over the course of our lifetime: we are worthy now in our loving, even as our loving lives bring us to eternal worthiness.

Not only does future fulfilment break into the present in this prayer, but all that has gone before is ever present in our prayer to God, for the text does not say *quod promisisti*, "what you promised", referring to promises made long ago, nor does it say *quod praecepisti*, "what you taught", referring to teachings given long ago. Rather, as the verbs are in the present tense, so God's promising and teaching are ever-present realities. This prayer, then, affirms that as we pray, teachings once given are as ever present as is God's enabling us to love the teachings, and, as we so love, promises once made are as ever present as we become worthy of their fulfilment both in our act of loving and after loving lives. I suggest that this is at the heart of God's real presence in the liturgy, which unites both the past and the future in our cooperating now with divine enabling in every act of love. The divine-human exchange comes about in our sharing in the self-emptying love of God in every loving action, whereby we are transformed by our loving actions to become worthy.

This prayer reveals that *lectio divina* is an inter-generational dialogue of the Church with God in that we meditate on the Scriptures proclaimed and offer back to God in prayer the fruits of that meditation both imbued with the Scriptures yet brought to a new synthesis, as is the inter-relationship between faith, hope and love. This synthesis, then, is tested by the community and if found worthy, informs our further reflection upon the Scriptures, even in subsequent generations, as this prayer has done for over 1,285 years. ∎

The one we serve

God's gift is humble service. We, in turn, serve him, according to the first commandment. We discover the emphasis in the opening prayer for this week is on what God does, and how we participate in his self-revelation

Source. The opening prayer is first found in the Verona Sacramentary, a collection of Mass booklets of Roman origin compiled between 561 and 574.

Analysis of the literary form
Invocation: The complex invocation *omnipotens et misericors Deus*, ""almighty and merciful God", is translated as "God of power and mercy". *Misericors* also means "tender-hearted, merciful". The invocation echoes the amplification of the opening prayer of the 26th Sunday in Ordinary Time: "You who manifest your omnipotence [*omnipotentiam*] most of all by being merciful [*parcendo*] and compassionate [*miserando*]."

Amplification: Expressed by a relative clause, the amplification *de cuius munere venit…*, "from whose gift-service it comes about…", is translated as "only with your help…". *Munere* refers either to a "duty, function, service", for example, the presider's *munus* is to preside in the assembly and to lead the prayer (*General Instruction on the Roman Missal* 310), or to a "present, gift", as in the gifts of bread and wine we offer in the Eucharist (cf. Matthew 5:23-24). God's gift is humble service, for Christ "emptied himself, taking the form of a slave [*servi*]" (NRSV, Vulgate throughout; Philippians 2:7). *Venit* is impersonal and here, as when referring to events, means "it happens": its subject is the entire purpose clause.

First purpose: An unusual element of this prayer is that the subject of the amplification is the entire clause constructed classically by *ut* followed by the subjunctive *serviatur*, which expresses the purpose

> *the opening prayer*
> ## 31st Sunday in Ordinary Time
> God of power and mercy,
> only with your help can we offer you
> fitting service and praise.
> May we live the faith we profess and
> trust your promise of eternal life.
> (*The Roman Missal*,
> Collins, London, 1974)
>
> Omnipotens et misericors Deus,
> de cuius munere venit,
> ut tibi a fidelibus tuis digne et
> laudabiliter serviatur, tribue,
> quaesumus, nobis, ut ad promissiones
> tuas sine offensione curramus.
> (*Missale Romanum*,
> Città del Vaticano, 2002)

of God's service: *ut tibi a fidelibus tuis digne et laudabiliter serviatur*, "that service may be rendered worthily and praise-worthily to you by your trusty people", which is translated as, "can we offer you fitting service and praise?". *Serviatur* is an impersonal passive translated literally by teasing out the idea of service, then making it passive, as in "may service be rendered". We serve God in several ways. The first of the commandments is "to serve [*servias*] the Lord your God with all your heart and with all your soul" (Deuteronomy 10:12; cf. 11:13), which Christ interpreted in terms of love (*diliges*), then added a second: "you shall love your neighbour as yourself" (Matthew 22:37-39, Mark 12:30-31, Luke 10:27). To serve God is also to worship God (*serviunt ei*; Revelation 7:15), and to give thanks to God is to "offer to God an acceptable worship [*serviamus*]" (Hebrews 12:28).

Understanding *munere* in terms of service is strengthened by *serviatur*, because God's serving enables any service worthily rendered to God, a reinterpretation of the divine-human exchange in terms of service. Thus both clauses may be reordered, placing the subject clause first: "that service is rendered worthily and praiseworthily to you by your trusty people, comes about from God's service". God's people are trusting, I suggest, because the way of self-emptying service is so contrary to our natural inclination, especially when it leads to death, that only the compassionate would undertake it and the omnipotent could make it salvific.

Petition: The imperative petition *tribue, quaesumus, nobis,* "grant, we ask, to us", is rendered in the doxology as, "we ask this".

Second purpose: Expressed classically by *ut* followed by the subjunctive *curramus,* the purpose for our prayer is *ut ad promissiones tuas sine offensione curramus,* "that we may run unto your promises without stumbling". It is represented in translation by an independent sentence with two exhortative subjunctives: "May we live the faith we profess and trust your promise of eternal life." *Offensione* refers either to our action, "stumbling, offence" or to an offence received, "misfortune, stumbling-block"; we might say that the Almighty gives the strength to run without stumbling and the merciful removes stumbling-blocks. *Promissiones,* "promises", is derived from the verb *promittere,* "to promise, to send before". Jesus is the one sent before and to run after him is also to follow in his way: "let us run [*curramus*] with perseverance the race that is set before us, looking to Jesus … , who for the sake of the joy that was set before him endured the Cross, disregarding its shame, and has taken his seat at the right hand of the throne of God" (Hebrews, 12:1-2).

The promises are not only glory, but that the way of self-emptying love is ultimately salvific.

Summary. The difficulty in this prayer is the impersonal passive *serviatur,* invariant since the prayer's first appearance. I suggest that the reason for the impersonal passive lies in the prayer's literary form. The first purpose appears in the amplification clause of the prayer as an expansion of the invocation *Deus,* "God". Thus the emphasis is on what God does, not on what we may do, which would have been expressed by the active subjunctive *serviamus,* "we may serve", nor on the more abstract idea of what the faithful may do, similarly expressed by serviant, "they may serve". Rather, according to the literary genre of the opening prayer, the amplification clause is about God's self-expression in humble service in order that worthy service may be rendered to God. What is stated of God's self in the amplification is then applied to us in the petition (*tribue nobis* – "grant to us" – and *quaesumus,* "we ask") and second purpose, which parallels the word-order of the first purpose, this time, however, using the active subjunctive *curramus,* "we may run". Ours is a participation in God's purpose for self-revelation. ∎

Freed from snares

Through God's removal of things that are hostile to what is truly in our interests, we are able to cooperate in our own redemption. In this week's prayer is an understanding of the link between the freeing of the mind and the pursuit of what God wants for us

The opening prayer this Sunday reminds us that God removes the obstacles and frees us that we may accomplish God's work.

Source. Ancient Roman sacramentaries are classed according to two traditions, though each example is typically an admixture of both. The papal tradition was centred on the papal stational liturgy celebrated on certain days according to an established sequence in the various churches (stations) of Rome.

As the pastoral needs of Christians grew in Rome, so the papal tradition was adapted for presbyteral use (when a priest presides) in the titular churches. In ancient times there came to be 25 titular churches, most within the walls, some preserving the earliest house church tradition of apostolic times and bearing the name of the home owner, the titular, inscribed in stone at the door. One can visit the recently excavated house church, among the foundations of the church of John and Paul on the Caelian hill. The oldest sacramentary representing the presbyteral tradition is the Gelasian compiled between 628 and 750, whose sole surviving copy was redacted c. 750 in the nunnery of Chelles, now part of greater Paris.

When Charlemagne sought to unify liturgical practice based on that of Rome, Pope Hadrian sent a papal sacramentary, the Hadrianum. Because it represented the living Latin language, its Latin was twice corrected to a more classical form by Charlemagne's court. One full copy of the first correction remains, that commissioned by Hildoard, Bishop of Cambrai

> *the opening prayer*
> ## 32nd Sunday in Ordinary Time
>
> God of power and mercy,
> protect us from all harm.
> Give us freedom of spirit
> and health in mind and body
> to do your work on earth.
> (*The Roman Missal*,
> Collins, London, 1974)
>
> Omnipotens et misericors Deus,
> universa nobis adversantia propitiatus
> exclude, ut, mente et corpore pariter
> expediti, quae tua sunt liberis mentibus
> exsequamur.
> (*Missale Romanum*,
> Città del Vaticano, 2002)

c. 811-812. It was inadequate for the intended pastoral reform and unification, because it contained only those prayers proper to the papal stational liturgy. A supplement was then compiled by Benedict of Aniane under the reign of Louis the Pious in Septimania in southern France between 810 and 815, lifting texts from the Gelasian, already adapted in Gaul, and its further eighth-century Gallican adaptations. The resulting Hadrianum and Supplement became the basis of the *Missale Romanum*, representing both papal and presbyteral traditions from Rome as adapted for pastoral use in Gaul and the Germanic regions.

The opening prayer this Sunday is first found in the Gelasian Sacramentary, and in many of its eighth-century variants, whence it was included in the Supplement.

Analysis of the literary form

Invocation: The complex invocation *Omnipotens et misericors Deus*, "All-powerful and compassionate God", is translated as "God of power and mercy". *Misericors* also means "tender-hearted, compassionate".

Petition: The imperative petition *universa nobis adversantia … exclude*, "keep away all things opposing us", is rendered as, "protect us from all harm". The imperative *exclude* means, "shut out!, drive out! remove!". While *exclude* takes the ablative *nobis*, "from us", I take *nobis* here to mean "to us", the dative complement of *adversantia*, which, although *adversantia* may refer to a simple turning toward, here it refers to a turning against: "things being in hostile opposition to, unfavourable to".

Motive: The antecedent passive participle *propitiatus* by itself means, "having been rendered favourable, appeased", yet in the passive it becomes like a deponent verb with the active meaning: "having been propitious" or in a transferred sense "having atoned for". Thus *propitiatus* in a word sums up both salvation history (because God's motive in removing obstacles now is his favour already shown, atonement already given) and the divine-human exchange (for in Christ God gives to humanity atonement before God, God brings humanity to favour with God). Because humanity is already swept up in his redeeming act, we petition him to remove all obstacles.

Purpose: Expressed classically by *ut* followed by the subjunctive *exsequamur*, the purpose clause *ut … quae tua sunt liberis mentibus exsequamur*, literally "that … we may carry out with free spirits things which pertain to you", is translated by an independent sentence with an imperative petition, "Give us freedom of spirit … to do your work on earth". The direct object of *exsequamur* is the unexpressed word *ea*, "the things, realities, elements", implied in the relative pronoun *quae*, "which realities". The deponent verb *exsequamur* conveys the active meaning of "may we follow to the end, pursue, accomplish", yet it also conveys the more passive idea of "may we endure" or more positively "undergo". Whether we are transformed as we "undergo God" or cooperate with divine favour by pursuing God's realities, or accomplish God's tasks, as in the official translation, is a matter of perspective and the larger structure of the prayer.

Motive: The motive for God's granting that we accomplish divine things is that we have been further prepared: *mente et corpore pariter expediti* "[we] having been freed equally in mind and in body", which is translated by a second petition, "and [give us …] health in mind and body". The original meaning of the verb *expedire* is "to free the feet" as in "from a snare". Its antecedent passive participle *expediti* means "people having been set free, made ready, set right".

Summary. To do God's will in freedom of heart and mind is the goal of our transformation in Christ possible only by the gift of God who removes all obstacles hostile to us, then prepares us by freeing us from that which binds, that every good and just action of ours arises from our own free will even as God enables us to co-operate in our redemption, who already has set omnipotence to the service of compassion in Christ.

We mature, according to this prayer, first as God removes obstacles, then grants that we be prepared. Only after we are prepared in our whole selves, equally in body and mind, do we arrive at the pursuit of divine things, which we pursue freely. Coming to such freedom requires freedom from what inhibits, then being equipped for the freedom to pursue the good. ■

A talent for joy

In prayer, it is necessary to distinguish between our own devotion towards God, and a different kind of rejoicing, in God's faithfulness towards us. The reading of this week's prayer in Latin helps to discern the difference

By affirming God's faithfulness, the opening prayer this Sunday gives the Church's response to the Gospel of the master who gave the talents to three servants, and upon his return demanded an accounting, casting the fearful servant into outer darkness (Matthew 25:14-30; proclaimed on this Sunday every third year, 2008 inclusive).

Source. The prayer first appears in the Verona Sacramentary, the oldest extant collection of Mass booklets compiled between 561 and 574.

Analysis of the literary form

Two petitions: The prayer begins with the imperative petition, *Da nobis, quaesumus … in tua semper devotione gaudere*, "Give to us ever to rejoice in your faithfulness", translated as, "keep us faithful in serving you". Just as in the Gospel the master gave talents to the servants (*uni dedit …* "to one he gave …" [25:15; New Vulgate; NRSV throughout]), so the prayer applies the narrative to the praying assembly: *Da nobis*, "grant to us". Just as the first two servants returning doubled talents to the master were told, *intra in gaudium domini tui*, "enter into the joy of your master" (25:21, 23), so the prayer asks God to grant that we rejoice (*gaudere*).

The construction composed of the verb *dare* (to give) followed by the dative (here, *nobis*, "to us") and the infinitive (*gaudere*, "to rejoice") is first used poetically, but is common in later Latin. Another common shift in later Latin is the phrase in tua *devotione*, "in your devotion", where the possessive adjective *tua* (your) substitutes for the objective genitive *tui*, "of you",

> ### the opening prayer
> ### 33rd Sunday in Ordinary Time
>
> Father of all that is good, keep us faithful in serving you, for to serve you is our lasting joy.
> (*The Roman Missal*,
> Collins, London, 1974)
>
> Da nobis, quaesumus, Domine Deus noster, in tua semper devotione gaudere, quia perpetua est et plena felicitas, si bonorum omnium iugiter serviamus auctori.
> (*Missale Romanum*,
> Città del Vaticano, 2002)

referring to our devotion towards God. If this is a later Latin construction then the petition means "Give us ever to rejoice in our devotion towards you". Given that *devotione* can refer to "any form of prayer, piety", the petition unfortunately evokes the image of the Pharisee boasting in prayer of his fasting and tithing (Luke 18:10-14).

However, if the phrase *in tua devotione* is classical Latin, it refers to the devotion that God has, literally, "your devotion", or, as its root verb *devoveo* can mean, "your faithfulness", and means "give us ever to rejoice in your faithfulness". Thus, the cause for our rejoicing is not our devotion towards God, but God's faithfulness towards us.

Invocation: The complex invocation *Domine Deus noster*, "Lord, our God", is translated as "Father". The praying assembly assumes the voice of each of the three servants when invoking God as *domine* (25:20, 22, 24). Furthermore, the faithful servants enter into the *gaudium domini tui*, "joy of your master", which is interpreted in the assembly's invocation, *Deus noster*, "our God".

Motive: The motive for our prayer is expressed classically by the causal phrase beginning with *quia*, "because", *quia perpetua est et plena felicitas*, "because happiness is abiding and full", rendered as, "… is our lasting joy". The adjective *plena*, "full", is an allusion to the reward of the faithful stewards: *supra multa te constituam*, "I will put you in charge of many things" (25:21,23), as *perpetua*, "lasting", contrasts with the fearful servant, whose burying the one talent leads to its loss (25:28).

Purpose: The purpose for our praying is expressed by the conditional, *si bonorum omnium iugiter serviamus auctori*, "if we serve directly the author of all good things", translated in part by the causal clause "for to serve you …" and in part by the relative clause amplifying the invocation, "of all that is good". While the Gospel narrative recounts how the master called his servants (*vocavit servos suos*) and gave his goods to them (*et tradidit illis bona sua*; 25:14), the prayer acknowledges God as the author of all good things (*bonorum omnium*); our response is to serve (*serviamus*) the one, who enables us to serve. As it stands, the phrase is an ideal conditional, meaning, "if we should serve you", expressing a more or less fanciful wish. However, it is a later Latin construction whereby the indicative *servimus*, "we serve", has been substituted by the subjunctive *serviamus*, "we should serve", by modal attraction. The phrase must be translated from its classical construction si *servimus*, "if we serve".

Summary. If the phrase *in tua devotione* is understood as a later Latin construction

referring to our faithfulness towards God, its theology is problematic, for its undue self-satisfaction, as in the French translation (de trouver notre joie dans notre fidélité, "to find our joy in our fidelity"). If classical, however, it emphasises the divine-human exchange, whereby God's faithfulness is the reason for our rejoicing. Furthermore, God, the origin of all good things, gives us to rejoice, and enables us to serve in response, which produces a joy both lasting and full.

The official English evades the question by simplifying, whereas other translations negotiate exchange variously, for example, the English for the Liturgy of the Hours (give us grace to serve you always with joy), the Italian (Il tuo aiuto, Signore, ci renda sempre lieti nel tuo servizio, "may your help, Lord, make us ever happy in your service") and the German (Laß uns begreifen, daß wir frei werden, wenn wir uns deinem Willen unterwerfen, "Let us understand, that we become free, when we submit to your will").

The divine-human exchange is expressed by a chiasm of two correlations: the noun *devotione*, expressing God's faithfulness towards us, correlates with the verb *serviamus*, expressing our service of God, and the verb *gaudere*, expressing our inward joy, the result of God's faithfulness, correlates with the noun *felicitas*, expressing our happiness, the result of our cooperating with divine gift.

Furthermore, the adverb *semper* expresses our lasting joy due to God's eternal faithfulness; while the adverb *iugiter* may likewise mean "perpetually" but may also mean "instantly", expressing the immediacy of our service. ∎

Through veneration to redemption

The Corpus Christi celebration in England and Wales has moved from the Thursday after Trinity to the following Sunday. We examine the prayer for the feast, uncovering the depth of its appreciation of the mystery of the Eucharist

Long in the prayer, the phrase "and blood" was added to the title of the feast in 1970; ever on the table, his blood is once again offered in Communion.

Source. As Pope John Paul II assigned the latest name, "Divine Mercy Sunday", to the octave of Easter from St Faustina's devotion, wrapped in the colours of the Polish national flag, so too in 1262 Urban IV extended to the universal calendar Blessed Giuliana's eucharistic devotion that had been established since 1246 in his beloved Liège. There, it had been assigned to the Thursday after Trinity Sunday by Robert, Bishop of Liège. It is now transferred to the following Sunday in many dioceses. The liturgy was first attributed to Thomas Aquinas in the Ecclesiastical History of Fra Tolomeo of Lucca published in 1312-1317, although Aquinas' own papers do not indicate his authorship.

Analysis of the literary form

Invocation: One of few prayers in the *Missale* to invoke Jesus as *Deus*, "God", as is made clear in the concluding formula, "You who live and reign with God the Father…". This is clarified in the English invocation: "Lord Jesus Christ".

Amplification: The invocation is amplified by the relative clause, *qui nobis sub sacramento mirabili passionis tuae memoriam reliquisti* – "you who left to us a memorial of your Passion under the wondrous sacrament", which is rendered as, "you gave us the Eucharist as a memorial of your suffering and death". Celebrating the meal with his disciples before he died, Jesus left (*reliquisti*)

> ### the opening prayer
> ### The Body and Blood of Christ
>
> Lord Jesus Christ, you gave us the Eucharist as the memorial of your suffering and death. May our worship of this sacrament of your body and blood help us to experience the salvation you won for us and the peace of the kingdom where you live with the Father …
> (*The Roman Missal*, Collins, London, 1974)
>
> Deus, qui nobis sub sacramento mirabili passionis tuae memoriam reliquisti, tribue, quaesumus, ita nos Corporis et Sanguinis tui sacra mysteria venerari, ut redemptionis tuae fructum in nobis iugiter sentiamus. Qui vivis et regnas cum Deo Patre …
> (*Missale Romanum*, Città del Vaticano, 2002)

the Eucharist as a memorial of his Passion (*passionis tuae memoriam*), which we celebrate in his remembrance (*commemorationem*, NRS and Vulgate, throughout; Luke 22:9; 1 Corinthians 11:24-25).

The word *sacramentum*, referring to the soldier's oath of allegiance, was first used by Tertullian (c.155–c.220) to translate the Greek *musterion*, "mystery", as in the phrase "the mystery that has been hidden throughout the ages and generations but has now been revealed to his saints … this mystery [*sacramenti* (Vulgate); *mysterii* (New Vulgate)], which is Christ in you" (Colossians 1:26-27).

Petition: The imperative *tribue*, "grant", perhaps informed the word "help" in the English. The parenthetical *quaesumus*, "we ask; please", is typically expressed in the doxological formula concluding the prayer, "We ask this …", but is omitted due to the particular doxology of this prayer.

First purpose: The petitions *tribue*, *concede*, *da*, and *praesta*, all meaning "grant", and *fac* meaning "make", all may initiate a phrase that is either expressive of a concrete result or of the desired intention. Rendering this prayer as expressive of result, as in, "grant that we venerate in such a way that we perceive" produces a rather factual prayer, rather than one expressive of both intention and cooperation. The petition *tribue* is followed by the the accusative *nos* (us) and infinitive *venerari* (to adore), *ita nos Corporis et Sanguinis tui sacra mysteria venerari*, "that we may reverence the sacred mysteries of your Body and Blood in such a way …". This is reworked as an independent exhortative subjunctive, "May our worship of this sacrament of your body and blood."

The two purpose clauses expand upon the amplification. The first develops the phrase *sub sacramento mirabili … memoriam*, "memorial under the wondrous sacrament", in that the sacred mysteries (*sacra mysteria*) we venerate correspond to the memorial (*memoriam*) Christ left to us, and we receive the body and blood of Christ (*Corporis et Sanguinis tui*) under the sacramental (*sub sacramento*) signs of bread broken and wine poured out for us, that we might say "*Amen*" to the mystery we are (Augustine, Sermon 272).

Second purpose: The two purpose clauses build upon one another in that the adverb *ita*, "in such a way", beginning the first, coordinates with the *ut*, "that", beginning the second, which is expressed classically: *ut redemptionis tuae fructum in nobis iugiter sentiamus*, "that we may perceive continually the fruit of your redemption within us", reworked as an imperative petition, "help us to experience the salvation you won for us and the peace of the kingdom". The verb *sentiamus* literally refers to perceiving with the senses: "may we experience, undergo". The noun *fructum* refers to an enjoying: "the fruit, success".

The second purpose clause develops the phrase *passionis tuae memoriam*, "memorial of your Passion", in that Christ's Passion (*passionis tuae*) is his redemption (*redemptionis tuae*), which is enjoyed (*fructum*) within us in our celebrating the memorial (*memoriam*).

Summary. The prayer begins with Christ, who gives himself fully, but according to our ability to perceive. We pray that Christ then enable us to mature in our response to his self-gift by a series of steps. The first, presumed by the prayer, is the Eucharist we celebrate in remembrance of Christ. When we celebrate the sacred mysteries of Christ's body and blood by doing what Christ did at the Last Supper, taking, blessing, breaking/pouring out, giving and saying (Matthew 15:36, 26:6; Mark 8:6, 14:22; Luke 22:19, 24:13), whereby he prefigured what he was to do on the Cross, we pray that Christ might grant a further gift, *ut veneremur*, "that we may reverence with religious awe" the mysteries we celebrate. Thus, full conscious and active engagement leads to contemplative celebration. As we mature in giving ourselves in response to Christ's self-gift, we pray to venerate the sacred mysteries in such a way (*ita*) as leads to yet another stage of maturation; therein we experience (*fructum*) and so enjoy Christ's redemption within us. Yet, *fructum* is polyvalent, for once we are grafted into the vine we are called to bear much fruit, for Christ says: "I am the vine, you are the branches. Those who abide in me and I in them bear much fruit" (John 15:1-8, 16, 12:24; Luke 8:4-15, 13:6-9; Hebrews 13:15). ∎

Three into one is One

The mystery of the Trinity is at the heart of our faith and this Sunday's collect honours its central role. It recapitulates God's sending of the Word and the Spirit into the world, and our profession of faith and adoration

Trinity Sunday is a theme feast in that it does not celebrate any particular event of salvation history. Such feasts are late-comers to the Roman calendar. Although the Gelasian Sacramentary (seventh century) had a preface in honour of the Trinity, the feast was not added to the universal calendar until 1334 by Pope John XXII while in Avignon.

Source. The petition of the present prayer is a reworking of the amplification of the prayer found in the 1962 *Missale Romanum*. The Hadrianum was given by Pope Hadrian I to Charlemagne in 785-786. Because the Hadrianum was a papal sacramentary, it was supplemented during the reign of Louis the Pious with almost 800 prayers for parish use by Benedict of Aniane working between 810-815 in Septimania (roughly the Languedoc-Roussillon region of France).

Analysis of the literary form

Invocation: God is invoked by two titles given in apposition: *Deus Pater* literally means "God, Father", and is translated simply as "Father". This is the only Sunday of the liturgical year in which the opening prayer in Latin invokes God as "Father". Only one other opening prayer in the liturgical year does so, on the Saturday of the first week of Lent. God is invoked as "Father" in 13 other opening prayers, especially in Masses for various needs and occasions. We have seen, however, that the present English translation often renders the invocation as "Father", although this is not expressed in the Latin.

First amplification: This prayer has two amplification clauses, one tucked inside the other. First, the enclosing phrase is: *qui ...*

> ### the opening prayer
> ### Trinity Sunday
>
> Father, you sent your Word to bring us truth and your Spirit to make us holy. Through them we come to know the mystery of your life. Help us to worship you, one God in three Persons, by proclaiming and living our faith in you. (*The Roman Missal*, Collins, London, 1974)
>
> Deus Pater, qui, Verbum veritatis et Spiritum sanctificationis mittens in mundum, admirabile mysterium tuum hominibus declarasti, da nobis, in confessione verae fidei, aeternae gloriam Trinitatis agnoscere, et Unitatem adorare in potentia maiestatis. (*Missale Romanum*, Città del Vaticano, 2002)

admirabile mysterium tuum hominibus declarasti, which means "you who have manifested your wonderful mystery to human beings". This is rendered by an independent sentence in English: "Through them we come to know the mystery of your life." *Declarasti* means "you have shown, manifested, declared". The first definition given for *hominibus* is "to human beings", in contrast to *viris*, meaning "to males". Here, *mysterium* refers to the content of the second amplification.

Second amplification: Tucked inside the first amplification is the second, given in apposition to the implied "*tu*", the subject of *declarasti*: *Verbum veritatis et Spiritum sanctificationis mittens in mundum*, which means "sending into the world the Word of truth and Spirit of sanctification".

The subject is made explicit in the English translation, which renders the phrase as a separate sentence: "You sent your Word to bring us truth and your Spirit to make us holy." *Sanctificationis* refers not to the Spirit as holy, but to God's act of "making holy" through the Spirit. God has revealed the wonderful divine mystery in sending the Word and the Spirit to us.

Petition: The single petition *da nobis*, "grant to us", has as its compliment two infinitive phrases. The first infinitive phrase is *aeternae gloriam Trinitatis agnoscere*, meaning "to know the glory of the eternal Trinity". *Agnoscere* means "to recognise, know, acknowledge". The impossibility of our directly knowing in this life the eternal trinity is resolved by the glory of the eternal trinity revealed in the Word, who became flesh and lived among us, whose glory, *gloriam*, we have beheld, full of grace and of truth, *veritatis* (John 1:14). Thus, the first infinitive phrase corresponds to the *Verbum veritatis* mentioned above. We come to this knowing, *in confessione verae fidei*, "in confessing the true faith". This is translated into English as "by proclaiming and living our faith in you". Two meanings of *confessione* are at play here, as it means both "by confessing the glory of God", thus "by praising" as well as "by confessing faith", which is another form of acknowledging, *agnoscere*.

The second infinitive clause is *et Unitatem adorare in potentia maiestatis*, meaning "and to adore the Unity in the power of majesty". Expressing the highest degree of reverence, *adorare* means "to adore, worship". *Maiestatis* can mean "splendour", thus echoing the word *gloriam*. The two infinitive clauses form a chiasm, whose symmetry is broken so as to emphasise the last three words. The first phrase of the Chiasm begins with *in confessione* … , followed by the infinitive clause, … *agnoscere*, whereas the second phrase switches the two, beginning with the infinitive clause … *adorare*, and ending with *in*

potentia maiestatis. The break in symmetry is that the phrase *in confessione verae fidei* refers to our confessing the true faith, and thus one would expect *in potentia maiestatis* to refer to us as well, although the prayer actually ends by highlighting this reference to the sovereignty of God's majesty. The petition is translated as an independent sentence with an imperative petition: "Help us to worship you, one God in three Persons."

Much of the prayer echoes the letter of Paul to the Ephesians 1:13-14 (New Revised Standard): "In him you also, when you had heard the word of truth, the gospel of your salvation, and had believed in him, were marked with the seal of the promised Holy Spirit".

The construction of the petition *da*, "grant", followed by both *nobis*, "to us", and the two infinitives, *agnoscere*, "to know", and *adorare*, "to adore", is a medieval construction that could have been expressed classically by *da*, "grant", followed by a compound purpose clause, *ut… agnoscamus et adorare*, "[grant] that we may know and adore". I see this as expressive of God's intention in granting rather than a statement of the result of our cooperation with divine gift, because it is only in the act of confession of the true faith that we come to know and adore.

Summary. Because one amplification is tucked into the beginning of the other, the prayer mentions the Father, the Word and the Spirit within the first seven words, establishing its Trinitarian content. The prayer emphasises not only the inner life of the Trinity as we know the glory of the Trinity and adore the Unity, but also the Trinity for us, as God is manifested by revealing the Word and Spirit. The prayer juxtaposes the Trinity and Unity, our knowing God's inner life by means of the revelation. The admirable divine mystery is both the Trinity's inner life and Unity, and its self-revelation to human beings, and our response in the profession of faith and praise of God's glory. ∎

Show us the splendour

The Feast of the Transfiguration may have had martial origins, but in the opening prayer this week, the language of royal glory has been replaced by a hope that God will make us worthy to share in Christ's eternal life

---

the opening prayer
Transfiguration of the Lord

God our Father in the transfigured glory of Christ your Son, you strengthen our faith by confirming the witness of your prophets, and show us the splendour of your beloved sons and daughters.
As we listen to the voice of your Son, help us to become heirs to eternal life with him.
(*The Roman Missal*,
Collins, London, 1974)

Deus, qui fidei sacramenta
in Unigeniti tui gloriosa Transfiguratione
patrum testimonio roborasti,
et adoptionem filiorum perfectam
mirabiliter praesignasti, concede nobis
famulis tuis, ut, ipsius dilecti Filii tui
vocem audientes,eiusdem coheredes
effici mereamur.
(*Missale Romanum*,
Città del Vaticano, 2002)

Several millennia of religious tradition afford multiple layers of meaning and the juxtaposition of diverse realities in the feast of the Transfiguration.

Source. The scriptural nucleus of the feast comes from Psalm 2:7: "[The Lord] said to me, 'You are my son; today I have begotten you [*Filius meus es tu*; *ego hodie genui te*]'" (New Revised Standard Version, Vulgate throughout). At the baptism of Jesus, when the Spirit of God descended upon him, this phrase is spoken by the voice from the heavens, and again from the cloud in his Transfiguration: *hic est Filius meus dilectus in quo mihi bene conplacuit ipsum audite*, "this is my Son, the Beloved; with him I am well pleased; listen to him!" (Matthew 17:5; cf. Matthew 3:17; Mark 1:11, 9:7; Luke 3:22, 9:35; 2 Peter 1:17-18). The Spirit-baptism of Jesus characterises his ministry, so that Jesus is aware of fulfilling what the prophet Isaiah said: "Here is my servant, whom I have chosen, my beloved [*dilectus*], with whom my soul is well pleased [*in quo bene placuit*]. I will put my Spirit upon

him, and he will proclaim justice to the Gentiles" (Matthew 12:18, cf. Isaiah 42:1).

Furthermore, the command to listen to *Jesus, ipsum audite*, refers to the promise of the Lord through Moses, who spoke to the Israelites about to cross the river Jordan and inherit the promised land: "the LORD your God will raise up for you a prophet like me from among your own people; you shall heed such a prophet [*ipsum audietis*]" (Deuteronomy 18:15). Because God has fulfilled this promise in Jesus, as Peter tells the crowd, so are we to listen to Jesus (Acts 3:22).

The feast of the Transfiguration originated in the fourth century in the Christian East to commemorate the dedication of the Church of the Transfiguration on Mount Tabor in the Galilee. By the end of the fifth century the feast had spread to the East Syrian Church, in current Iraq, and in the seventh to West Syria before its introduction into the Christian West in the ninth century. In honour of the military victory of Hunyady over the Ottoman Turks at Belgrade on this day,

6 August 1456, Calixtus III (pope from 1378 to 1458) declared the Transfiguration a universal feast for the Roman rite to help rouse Catholics to the armed conflict. The opening prayer for the feast, then, appears in the first edition of the *Missale Romanum* of 1474.

Analysis of the literary form

Invocation: The simple invocation *Deus*, "God", is rephrased as "God our Father".

First amplification: Two relative clauses provide two amplifications. First, *qui fidei sacramenta in Unigeniti tui gloriosa Transfiguratione patrum testimonio roborasti*, means, "you who have strengthened the mysteries of faith in the glorious Transfiguration of your Only-begotten by the witness of ancestors [Moses and Elijah]", and in translation, "in the transfigured glory of Christ your Son, you strengthen our faith by confirming the witness of your prophets".

Second amplification: Second, *et adoptionem filiorum perfectam mirabiliter praesignasti*", means, "and you have wonderfully foreshadowed the perfect adoption of daughters and sons", rendered in English as "and show us the splendour of your beloved sons and daughters".

Petition: The imperative petition, *concede nobis famulis tuis*, meaning "grant to us your servants", is absent from the English.

Purpose: Expressed classically by *ut* followed by the subjunctive *mereamur*, the purpose clause, *ut ... eiusdem coheredes effici mereamur*, means "that we may merit to be made co-heirs of the same one [the only-begotten]", expressed by an imperative petition: "help us to become heirs to eternal life with him". Its source is the preface of a Mass for the king to be said during a synod, found in the supplement to the Hadrianum, composed by Benedict of Aniane c. 810-815: *beatorumque spirituum coheredes effici mereantur*,

"may they be worthy to be made co-heirs of the blessed souls".

Motive: God's motive for making us worthy co-heirs is expressed in apposition, *ipsius dilecti Filii tui vocem audientes*, meaning, "[we] listening to the voice of your very own beloved Son", and translated as, "as we listen to the voice of your Son". The phrase parallels the preface of St Andrew found in the Paduense, a sacramentary redacted c. 670-680 for presbyteral use at St Peter's: *qui mox ut uocem domini saluatoris audiuit, unigeniti tui divina uestigia comitatus*, "who as soon as he heard the voice of the Saviour Lord, having followed along the sacred footsteps of your only-begotten".

Summary. The former purpose clause was double – first, *ut ipsius Regis gloriae nos coheredes efficias*, "that you may make us co-heirs to the glory of the very king", which shares some of the vocabulary and structure of the current prayer, then, *et ejusdem gloriae tribuas esse consortes*, "and you may grant that we be sharers of the glory of the same one". In changing the purpose clause, the language of royal glory is removed with its militaristic connotations. The new prayer concurs with Jesus' spirit-filled ministry to "proclaim justice to the Gentiles".

The voice commands us *ipsum audite*, "listen to him!" In the prayer, our listening, *audientes*, becomes God's motive for making us worthy co-heirs. Jesus is manifested both in his baptism and transfiguration as God's beloved Son, whereas in the prayer the word "son" is used only of us. As the Psalmist and prophet prefigure the Transfiguration, so Moses and Elijah witness to the Gospel revelation; as the Transfiguration prefigures the Resurrection, it also prefigures our full adoption as daughters and sons in the Son. ∎

Taken up in glory

We petition God to grant that we may be worthy to have an equal share in the heavenly glory of the Virgin

The wondrous exchange between the humanity and divinity of Christ involves the Church, as we, like Mary, host the divine indwelling, that we may be welcomed into the divine dwelling.

Source. Although prayers have been assigned to the Feast of the Assumption on 15 August at least since the Verona collection of Mass booklets compiled between 561-574, this newly composed opening prayer was promulgated with its revised Mass formulary by the Sacred Congregation of Rites on 31 October 1950, in anticipation of the Apostolic Constitution *Munificentissimus Deus* promulgated on the following day by Pius XII. Prior to the decree the opening prayer expressed quite a different sentiment: "Forgive the sins of your servants, we ask, O Lord, that we, who are not capable [*non valeamus*] of pleasing you on account of our actions, may be saved [*salvemur*] by the intercession of the Mother of your Son our Lord".

Analysis of the literary form
Invocation: The complex invocation *Omnipotens sempiterne Deus* is translated literally as "All-powerful and ever-living God".

Amplification: The invocation is further amplified by the relative clause, *qui immaculatam Virginem Mariam, Filii tui Genetricem, corpore et anima ad caelestem gloriam assumpsisti*, "you who took up in body and soul the immaculate Virgin Mary, Mother of your Son into heavenly glory", which is recast as a declarative sentence: "you raised the sinless virgin Mary, mother of your Son, body and soul to the glory of heaven". The phrase is reworked from

> *the opening prayer*
> **Assumption of the Blessed Virgin Mary**
>
> All-powerful and ever-living God, you raised the sinless virgin Mary, mother of your Son, body and soul to the glory of heaven. May we see heaven as our final goal and come to share her glory.
> (*The Roman Missal*, Collins, London, 1974)
>
> Omnipotens sempiterne Deus, qui immaculatam Virginem Mariam, Filii tui Genetricem, corpore et anima ad caelestem gloriam assumpsisti, concede, quaesumus, ut, ad superna semper intenti, ipsius gloriae mereamur esse consortes.
> (*Missale Romanum*, Città del Vaticano, 2002)

Munificentissimus Deus, which says: "Immaculatam Deiparam semper Virginem Mariam, expleto terrestris vitae cursu, fuisse corpore et anima ad caelestem gloriam assumptam", "that the Immaculate Mother of God, the ever Virgin Mary, when the course of earthly life had been completed, was taken up body and soul into heavenly glory". The mystery into which Mary was assumed is our future glory; thus, the amplification combines the historical tense, *assumpsisti*, "you took to your self; you took up, received, accepted", with the eschatological *ad caelestem gloriam*, "into heavenly glory".

Double petition: The imperative petition *concede*, "grant", is omitted in translation, which restructures the prayer as a declarative sentence and two exhortative clauses. The parenthetical petition *quaesumus*, "we ask, please" is rendered in the doxology as, "we ask this". God's granting is mentioned before our asking.

Purpose: What we ask God to grant is expressed by the entire purpose clause composed classically by *ut* followed by the first subjunctive: *ut ... ipsius gloriae mereamur esse consortes*, "that we ... may be worthy to be partners of the glory of the very one [Mary]", which is rephrased in the second exhortative clause, "and come to share her glory". The noun *consortes*, "colleagues", refers to dividing something with someone, having an equal share. Thus, we ask God to bring us to an equal share of the heavenly glory to which Mary was assumed.

The word *consortes* alludes to the phrase, "that through these things you may be made sharers [*consortes*] of the divine nature" (2 Peter 1:4; Vulgate, translation by author throughout), and to Moses' fellowship with God that caused his face to shine (Exodus 34:29).

The words *mereamur* and *consortes* appear frequently together in ancient Christian authors, as in Chromatius of Aquilea (d. c. 407), who said: "that in the heavenly reign, we may merit to be made sharers [*consortes*] of the body of the Lord" (Sermon 8), and "that we may merit to be made partakers of the glory of the prophets and apostles" (Sermon 17). Ambrose of Milan (340-397) says: "that we may be worthy of the fellowship of the resurrection". Leo the Great (440-461) said: "that we may be worthy of being sharers of his Resurrection" (Sermon 53) and, "that we may merit to be sharers of promised joys"(Sermon 32) and, "he will acquire the fellowship of eternal glorification".

Motive: Nestled within the purpose clause is the participial-adjectival phrase

ad superna semper intenti, "we, always directed unto heavenly realities", which is rendered as the first exhortative clause, "May we see heaven as our final goal". As an adjective *intenti* means simply "attentive, intent upon", but such can always also express its origin as an antecedent, passive participle, meaning, "ones having been directed", which corresponds to *ad superna*, "unto heavenly realities".

Summary. The times of the verbal forms give the developmental stages of Christian maturation. The eternal God acted in our history (*assumpsisti*). We petition (*concede, quaesumus*) God to act now by granting. What God grants, however, involves our cooperation, because our having been directed (*intenti*) unto heavenly realities is prior to and a motive for our being worthy (*mereamur*). Because, relative to God's granting (*concede*), the first subjunctive *mereamur* "may we merit, earn, obtain" is contemporaneous, ongoing, unfinished, future, eternal; the prayer may be understood to include each and all of these time frames. Thus, a future interpretation would be that we now petition God to grant that at the end of our lives, during which we have been directed towards heavenly realities, we may be worthy of being sharers of heavenly glory. But a contemporaneous interpretation is just as warranted grammatically and theologically in that we petition God to grant now that, we, already having been directed towards heavenly realities, may now be worthy to have an equal share of the glory of Mary: the glory Mary shares is our future, breaking into our present.

In the Incarnation, Christ, by a divine-human exchange, assumed our humanity to bring us to share in his divinity. Thus, Mary, ever an image of the Church, who had borne Christ within, was taken up in her humanity into heavenly glory, which we hope to share. ∎

Delivered and brought to redemption

We examine the collect for the Feast of the Triumph of the Cross, celebrated on 14 September

This feast day commemorates the anniversary of the two-day dedication of the church of the Holy Sepulchre in Jerusalem, 13-14 September, c. 334, to house the true cross found on the site nine years previously by Helena, mother of the Emperor Constantine. It is said that on the second day the relic was brought outside the church for public veneration, the feast day thus being set as 14 September. It also corresponds to a celebration of Good Friday outside the Easter *Triduum*, as the feast of the Body and Blood of Christ corresponds to Holy Thursday. In our day, the opening prayer for the feast of the Triumph of the Cross is a redaction of the one found in the 1962 *Missale Romanum*, and thus offers a point of comparison between the two missals.

Source. The prayer in the 1962 *Missale* first appears in the Gelasian Sacramentary, composed between 628 and 715 for presbyteral celebrations in the titular churches of Rome, where it was assigned to this feast on this day. For the 1970 *Missale* the amplification clause was redacted from two ancient prayers.

Analysis of the literary form

Invocation: The invocation *Deus*, "God", is elaborated in translation as, "God our Father".

Amplification: The invocation is amplified by the relative clause, *qui Unigenitum tuum crucem subire voluisti*, "you who willed that your Only-begotten endure the cross". The translation changes the subject to the son in the declarative sentence: "in obedience to you your only son accepted death on the cross". The verb *voluisti* also

> *the opening prayer*
> **Triumph of the Cross**
>
> God our Father, in obedience to you your only son accepted death on the Cross for the salvation of mankind. We acknowledge the mystery of the Cross on earth. May we receive the gift of redemption in heaven.
> (*The Roman Missal*, Collins, London, 1974)
>
> Deus, qui Unigenitum tuum crucem subire voluisti, ut salvum faceret genus humanum, praesta, quaesumus, ut, cuius mysterium in terra cognovimus, eius redemptionis praemia in caelo consequi mereamur.
> (*Missale Romanum*, Città del Vaticano, 2002)

means, "you wished, ordered, consented". It alludes to Christ saying in Gethsemane "your will be done" (Matthew 26:42). What God willed is expressed by the entire object sentence in the accusative, *Unigenitum tuum*, "your Only-begotten", and the infinitive *subire*, "to undergo, submit one's self to, suffer". Thus, God willed "that the Only-begotten suffer the cross".

First purpose: The amplification has its own purpose clause expressed classically by *ut* and the second subjunctive *faceret*, all of which expresses the intent in suffering the cross, *ut salvum faceret genus humanum*, "that he would save the human race", which is expressed by the prepositional phrase, "for the salvation of mankind".

The new amplification was redacted from two ancient prayers both found in the Hadrianum, a Papal sacramentary given by Pope Hadrian I to Charlemagne in 785-786, one assigned to Wednesday of the sixth week of Lent, the other to Palm Sunday, where it is also found in the Gelasian. From the first of these two source prayers comes the basic structure of the relative clause with its object sentence and purpose clause: *qui ... filium tuum crucis patibulum subire voluisti, ut ... expelleres ...* "you who wished that your son undergo the yoke of the cross, that you would cast out ...". From the other prayer come the phrases *crucem subire, humano generi* and *salvatorem*, which, perhaps, inspired the phrase *salvum faceret*, "he would deliver, bring to salvation" (1 Corinthians 7:16, Acts 16:30).

Petition: The imperative petition, *praesta*, "grant", is omitted in translation. The parenthetical, *quaesumus*, "we ask, please" is rendered in the doxology as, "we ask this". The English has two declarative sentences and an exhortation.

Second purpose: The petition has a second purpose clause expressed classically by *ut* and the first subjunctive *mereamur*, all of which expresses the purpose for which God grants: *ut ... eius redemptionis praemia in caelo consequi mereamur*: "that we may deserve to attain the rewards of his redemption in heaven", translated by an exhortative subjunctive, "May we receive the gift of redemption in heaven".

Motive: Nestled within the second purpose is the relative clause, *cuius mysterium in terra cognovimus*, "whose mystery we have come to know on earth", which is translated by the declarative sentence, "We acknowledge the mystery of the cross on earth". The motive and second purpose exhibit a parallelism between *cuius mysterium*, "of whose mystery", and *eius redemptionis*, "of his redemption", and between *in terra*, "on

earth", and *in caelo*, "in heaven", where the *mysterium*, "mystery", yields to the *praemia*, "rewards".

Summary. The two halves of the prayer correspond to one another, in that the first follows an historical sequence expressing the will of God (*voluisti*) not only that the Only-begotten would endure (*subire*) the cross, but also that the intent was to save (*salvum faceret*) the human race. Correspondingly, the second half of the prayer follows a present sequence whereby we express God's intent in granting (*concede*) that, as we cooperate with the divine initiative by coming to know (*cognovimus*), we may be worthy (*mereamur*). Furthermore, just as the object clause states how the Only-begotten cooperated with the will of God, by undergoing the cross, so the motive states how we cooperate with God's granting, by coming to know (*cognovimus*). But the motive also springs from the entire first half of the prayer, for the mystery we know is the Only-begotten's undergoing the cross with the intention of saving the human race. Moreover, the desire of God and of the Only-begotten expressed in the amplification and first purpose, namely that the Only-begotten endure the cross with the intent of saving the human race, finds its fulfilment in the second purpose clause expressing God's intention that we may merit to attain the rewards of redemption. This redemption to which both purpose clauses refer (*salvum faceret, redemptionis*) is described in the object clause as the Only-begotten's suffering the cross (*crucem subire*).

The clausal structure of the prayer in the 1962 *Missale* is simpler than that of the current prayer in that the amplification is a stock relative clause, "you who gladden us on today's day, the annual solemnity of the Exaltation of the Holy Cross", which has no accompanying object or purpose clause. ∎

True kingship, truly shared

For the feast of Christ the King, the opening prayer draws on two constitutions of the Second Vatican Council, as well as earlier sources. We examine the complexity of the concept of King in the prayer, and what we can discern from it about our place in the Kingdom

As an idea feast, Christ the King draws from several sources, but is not identified with any single mystery in the life of Christ. This means that the idea tends to be objectified by our positing the king as if an object and then negotiating our relationship to "it" as either subject or vassal. The opening prayer this Sunday shatters this tendency to objectify, because the difference with Christ as King is that by baptism we are not separate from, but in Christ, thus a royal people, who devotes itself not to serving Christ, as if an object, but in Christ to serving God, which always involves serving our neighbour as well. Furthermore, in John's Gospel, Christ reigns from the throne of the Cross revealing the majesty of God's self-emptying love, whereby our humanity is divinised in Christ's very act of self-emptying; our resulting royalty, then, is first proclaimed in baptism when we die and rise with Christ and then in our daily service of God and neighbour.

Source. When Pope Pius XI realised the fervour of the crowds cheering Mussolini, he knew that the Church had a better idea, and thus in 1925 he established the solemnity of Christ the King to be celebrated on the last Sunday of October. After the Second Vatican Council, when the feast was transferred to the last Sunday in Ordinary Time, its original opening prayer was given a new purpose clause drawn from two Conciliar constitutions: *Lumen Gentium* 36 and *Gaudium et Spes* 39.

Analysis of the literary form

Invocation: The complex invocation *Omnipotens sempiterne Deus*, "All-powerful ever-living God", is translated as, "Almighty and merciful God".

---

the opening prayer
Christ the King

Almighty and merciful God, you break the power of evil and make all things new in your son Jesus Christ, the King of the universe. May all in heaven and earth acclaim your glory and never cease to praise you.
(*The Roman Missal*,
Collins, London, 1974)

Omnipotens sempiterne Deus, qui in dilecto Filio tuo, universorum Rege, omnia instaurare voluisti, concede propitius, ut tota creatura, a servitute liberata, tuae maiestati deserviat ac te sine fine collaudet.
(*Missale Romanum*,
Città del Vaticano, 2002)

Amplification: The invocation is amplified by the relative clause *qui in dilecto Filio tuo, universorum Rege, omnia instaurare voluisti*, "you who have desired to restore all things in your beloved Son, King of all", translated as a second amplification, "you ... make all things new in your Son Jesus Christ, the King of the universe". The Latin construction *instaurare voluisti* expresses the intention of God, and so is expressive of purpose.

One allusion is to the baptism of Jesus when "a voice from heaven said, 'This is my Son, the Beloved [*Filius meus dilectus*]'" (Matthew 3:13; cf. Mark 1:9, Luke 3:22; NRSV, Vulgate throughout) and to the transfiguration of Jesus when the voice repeated the affirmation (Matthew 17:5; cf. Mark 9:7). A second allusion is to the plan of God "for the fullness of time, to gather up all things in him [*instaurare omnia in Christo*]" (Ephesians 1:10). That all of creation is in Christ the King is emphasised by the phrase *in dilecto Filio tuo*, "in your beloved Son" and *in … universorum Rege*, "in [your Son as] King of all things".

Petition: The imperative petition concede, "grant" is not translated.

First motive: The petition is modified by the adjective *propitius*, "merciful", used as an adverb meaning "mercifully". God's reason for granting our petition is God's mercy, as expressed in the English invocation, "merciful God".

Double purpose: Expressed classically by *ut* followed by two subjunctive verbs *deserviat* and *collaudet*, God's purpose for granting is, *ut tota creatura … tuae maiestati deserviat ac te sine fine collaudet*, "that all creation may serve your majesty and praise you without end", which is |rendered by an exhortative subjunctive petition in an independent sentence: "May all in heaven and earth acclaim your glory and never cease to praise you". God's reign is universal (*universale regnum*; from this feast's preface) for it involves all creation (*tota creatura*). Although in classical Latin deserviat refers to eager service, in the Vulgate New Testament the verb refers to worshipping God.

Moreover, the double purpose clause of serving and praising God finds its parallel in *Lumen Gentium*, for not only is the intimate nature of creation ordered unto the praise of God (*in laudem Dei*), but we also come to a more holy life when our actions imbue the world with the Spirit of God and bring the world to its proper end in justice, love and peace (36), for God's is a reign of truth, and life, of holiness and grace, of justice, love and peace (from the preface; cf. *Gaudium et Spes* 39).

Second motive: A further motive for God's granting that creation may serve and praise is expressed in the participial phrase *a servitute liberata*: "[creation] having been freed from slavery", which is rendered by the first of two amplifications, "you break the power of evil". The phrase is an allusion to Romans 8:21: "that the creation itself will be set free from its bondage to decay and will obtain the freedom of the glory of the children of God [*quia et ipsa creatura liberabitur a servitute corruptionis in libertatem gloriae filiorum Dei*]" (cf. *Lumen Gentium* 36, *Gaudium et Spes* 39).

Summary. God's omnipotence (*omnipotens*) is expressed first in creation (*creatura*), then by mercifully (*propitius*) setting fallen creation free (*liberata*) to cooperate with the divine favour by serving (*deserviat*) God and neighbour and by praising (*collaudet*) God. The ever-living God (*sempiterne*), who was before creation, desired (*voluisti*) to establish (*instaurare*) all creation (*creatura*) in God's eternity (*sine fine*).

The transfiguration is the inbreaking before the passion of Christ's resurrected glory revealing both the human face of divinity and the divinised face of humanity, the divine-human exchange by which we, who have been baptised into Christ's dying and rising, are brought to serve God's majesty, as we humbly serve others, and to praise God for ever. Christ the King, then, is the mystery of the Church and of the baptised, a royal nation in the Son, who then subjects all things to God (*Ipse se cunctaque creatura Patri subiiciat*; *Lumen Gentium* 36) "so that God may be all in all" (1 Corinthians 15:28). ∎

Five Hermeneutic Exercises

The following five homilies are offered as a guide to the reader who wishes to preach on the prayers of the Roman Missal. To the literary-critical analysis of the opening prayers of their respective Sundays, as presented in this little work, the homilists posed the hermeneutical question:

"How does this prayer help me to live more deeply the mystery of God's love among us".

In preparation for developing the homily, the analysis of the respective prayers was first written in full article-length comparable to the articles that appear in the body of this book. Then, each homily was edited and prepared for oral delivery. Four of the homilies were delivered in Italian during the conventual mass, Sant'Anselmo, Roma, on their respective Sundays in 2007 and 2008. One homily was delivered in 2007 in English at the conventual mass of the sisters of Mount St. Scholastica Monastery, Atchison, Kansas.

Recovering what was lost

Homily on the opening prayer of the Fifth Sunday of Easter by James G. Leachman OSB

The heart of today's opening prayer, for me, is, "that both true freedom and eternal inheritance be given to people trusting in Christ." That is what I want, God's gifts of true freedom and an eternal inheritance.

Occasionally, we may find ourselves immersed in such an experience of "true freedom" and "eternal inheritance" for which God has made us. It may be a moment of peace and intimacy with God, family or friends. On other occasions, however, alien feelings, very different from those which bring peace and intimate union, can sweep over us. When these occur, we need to pause for reflection and then plan our action. For example, when I become suspicious, jealous or selfish, I can realize that I have been robbed of my freedom and of my sense of intimacy with God. Then I can decide to do something about this "robbery", and to recover what has been stolen from me.

This prayer-collect tells me what I can do to recover that intimacy. It can teach me to become ever more responsible for what I shall become. It can show me how to yield myself once again to be possessed by divine love, thereby restoring and deepening my way of living in "true freedom". Let us see what our prayer teaches.

The prayer leads us through the various moments marking the recovery of our eternal inheritance, whereby, as we are transformed by stages of participation and maturation, we are led by a gentle God into an intimate participation in God's own life.

The first moment presents God as

---

the opening prayer
Fifth Sunday of Easter

God our Father, you redeem us and make us your children in Christ. Look upon us, give us true freedom and bring us to the inheritance you promised.
(*The Roman Missal*,
Collins, London, 1974)

Deus, per quem nobis et redemptio venit et praestatur adoptio, filios dilectionis tuae benignus intende, ut in Christo credentibus et vera tribuatur libertas, et hereditas aeterna.
(*Missale Romanum*,
Città del Vaticano, 1970)

Translation by author
for study purposes:
O God, through whom both redemption comes and adoption is granted to us, gently look upon the daughters and sons of your love, that both true freedom and eternal inheritance be given to people trusting in Christ.

---

benignus, which means more than just benign or indifferent, but kind and gentle with the welfare of all at heart.

The second moment is expressed in the phrase, "through whom redemption comes to us". Redemption refers to "releasing the debtor by paying the creditor" and "releasing from sin or rescuing from death". The phrase is an allusion to Galatians 4:5: "in order to redeem those who were under the law, so that we might receive adoption as children" (*NRSV* throughout).

The third moment is the phrase, "through whom adoption is granted to us", referring to our baptism, our rebirth as God's children. The verbs indicate both that God is working out our redemption within us and adopting us, and that we are being transformed at God's hand. Our active passivity, however, has not yet given way to the full force of our acting.

The fourth moment is that we are made not simply children, but the daughters and sons of God's love. The allusion is to the baptism and transfiguration of Christ, when the voice said, "This is my Son, the Beloved" (Matthew 3:17, 17:5 and parallels; 2 Peter 1:17). "Love" reminds us of today's Gospel: "Love one another as I have loved you". Throughout salvation history God's teaching on love and our understanding of it have developed. Moses once taught, "You shall love the Lord your God with all your heart, and with all your soul, and with all your might" (Deuteronomy 6:5), and "you shall love your neighbour as yourself" (Leviticus 19:18). Jesus established these as the first two commandments (Matthew 22:37, 39). Now the measure of our love is revealed in God's love for us in Christ. Thus does our gradually yielding to God's possession of our hearts and minds bring us to self-transcending love, our participation in the divine life; precisely this loving with Christ's love constitutes our witness to the world (John 13:35).

The fifth moment is when we ask God, kindly to stretch out (*intende*) to us – to be "God-with-us," (Revelation 21:3-4).

The answer to our question of how I can recover what has been stolen from me and deepen my experience of intimacy with God, finally comes in the sixth moment, in the phrase, "to people trusting in Christ". In response to God's self-gift as intimate presence and kindness, our response is now to place our "trust in Christ" (Galatians 2:16). Trusting is the active work we are called to do (*vide* John 6:29).

God's response to our trusting is given in the seventh moment, for, as we cooperate by coming to trust in Christ, we pray that the further gifts of true freedom and an eternal inheritance be given, that we may come to share more fully on earth in divine life and love.

The gift of our yielding to God's acting on us is given over and over again. Not only does this cycle of love, adoption, and coming to intimate union really happen to us, but even when diminished by our clumsiness and childishness, the intimacy between us and God can be recovered. It does not happen just once in our lives – that would be merely a magical transformation. Rather, the cycle of love, its diminishment and the recovery of ever deepening intimacy is repeated and built upon over and over again as we grow into Christian maturity (see my article, *The Tablet*, Christmas 2008). Here we find layer upon layer of transformation at God's hand.

When we cooperate with God's gentle intimacy and the gift of redemption and adoption, according to this prayer, we, God's children by baptism, gradually mature into adult daughters and sons of God, until by further steps, we come into our full dignity as spouse, like a bride prepared for her groom (cf. Revelation 21:2).

Today's prayer reveals the exchange of life and love between God and humanity, which alone can satisfy the human heart, whereby God's self-revealing love and our response in love and trust, this divine-human mutual self-gift or nuptial union, brings us to a new state of existence, true freedom and our eternal heritage. ∎

This homily was given in Italian during the conventual Mass at Sant'Anselmo

By Mutual Participation

*Homily on the opening prayer
of the Sixth Sunday of Easter
by Daniel P. McCarthy OSB*

Our mutual participation in the divine-human exchange both ever informs our daily lives and develops as we mature in the faith. St. Augustine said, "Christ conducts a wondrous exchange with us by mutual participation". When I saw this quote of St. Augustine, I was struck, as if for the first time, that we should share in the divine-human exchange by mutual participation with God. But, how could our participation in this wondrous exchange with God be mutual, when God is so fully other and we God's image and likeness but not equal. Augustine continues: "from our part, Christ died, from his part, we live". Yet how can this exchange be mutual: our death for his life. The opening prayer of the Eucharist this Sunday tells us how and what we can do.

The prayer begins with God's enabling. In fact, the only action ascribed to God in this prayer is to enable us to act, which God does at every step of our growth in Christian maturity. The rest of the prayer, then, is about what we want to be able to do.

We cooperate, first of all, with God's enabling by our fulfilling "these days of joy unto the honour of the rising (appearing) Lord". Throughout these fifty days of Easter until the feast of Pentecost, we prolong the proclamation of the good news of Lord's rising and appearing, not as a past event, but as an ever present reality, for the Lord continues to manifest himself in the assembly, in the word proclaimed, in the breaking the bread, in our common life and in commissioning us to serve others in their need in the power of the Spirit. By our ongoing proclamation of the good

> *the opening prayer*
> **Sixfth Sunday of Easter**
>
> Ever-living God,
> Help us to celebrate our joy
> in the resurrection of the Lord
> and to express in our lives
> the love we celebrate.
> (*The Roman Missal*,
> Collins, London, 1974)
>
> Fac nos, omnipotens Deus, hos laetitiae dies, quos in honorem Domini resurgentis exsequimur, affectu sedulo celebrare, ut quod recordatione percurrimus semper in opere teneamus.
> (*Missale Romanum*,
> Città del Vaticano, 2002)
>
> *Translation by author
> for study purposes:*
> Enable us, almighty God, to celebrate with steadfast zeal these days of great joy, which we fulfil unto the honour of the rising (appearing) Lord, Make holy these gifts of our service, that we may ever hold in action that which we experience by meditation.

news in rite and word, liturgical service and service of others, we cooperate with God's enabling power.

By our sustaining the Easter celebration throughout these fifty days until the feast of Pentecost, we are given a greater gift by God, who enables us to "celebrate these days with steadfast zeal". We celebrate by frequently gathering as an assembly to narrate the Lord's glorious deeds in word and sacrament. Our celebrating with zeal is itself the gifted fruit of our cooperating with God's enabling by steadfastly carrying out these days of joy unto their full.

The prayer, however, does not stop there, as if celebrating with steadfast zeal were sufficient, for our celebrating has quite a different purpose. To arrive at this further goal, however, we are called to cooperate in a new way with God's enabling power by meditating upon our celebration, for our meditative proclamation of the good news and reflective celebration of these days of joy bring us to a new experience of Christian maturity. When we penetrate the sacred mysteries by our recollected celebration of them, we are then given an even greater gift of God, who enables us to bring our meditative celebration to active fruition in our daily lives. The final goal of this prayer, then, is our putting into action in our daily lives what we celebrate in the liturgy: the fruit of liturgy is our daily work.

Our daily work is the basis for our heavenly reward, according to the judgement scene in the book of Revelation, where Christ says to John, "See, I am coming soon; my reward is with me, to repay according to everyone's work" (22:12-14, 16-17, 20; *NRSV* throughout). Again, whatsoever we do to the least among us is the criteria for our judgment in the gospel of Matthew (25:31-46). Thus, our heavenly reward is based on the works we do, which are themselves the fruition of our reflective celebration of these days of joy.

In Christ we are drawn into the divine life of the Trinity. In the gospel Jesus prays to God for the church: "As you, Father, are in me and I am in you, may they also be one in us, so that the world may believe that you have sent me" (John 17:21), and again, "I in them and you in me, that they may become completely one, so that the world may know that you have sent me and have loved them even as you have loved me" (John 17:23). We already share the beatific vision of God, as we mature in our mutual participation in God's self-gift in love to us by offering ourselves in love to God. By our full, conscious and active celebration of the liturgy, then, we come by stages of cooperation with God's enabling, and thus by stages of Christian maturation to share in this wondrous exchange, not only, as St. Augustine said, an exchange of our death for his life, but a mutual participation in God's self-gift in love to us by offering ourselves in love to God, that the world may believe.

We pray to God *omnipotens*, "almighty", a translation of *pantocrator*, creator of all and goal, genitor and nurturer, lawgiver and judge, companion and spouse. In our human life we pass from being nurtured at our mother's breast through various stages of human maturation to adult spousal love, which in turn leads to life-giving nurturing. In our reflective celebration of the liturgy with steadfast zeal throughout these fifty days, God enables us to mature in our participation in the divine life, that, as God ever remains genitor and nurturer at this eucharistic table, we may come to mutual participation in the Trinitarian self-gift by coming to know God as spouse, that we may be Christ for the world.

In Christ's ascension, within the week, our humanity comes to full participation in the triune life of mutual self-gift. ∎

This homily assumes that the second reading and the Gospel for the seventh Sunday of Easter are proclaimed on the sixth Sunday, which is permitted when the feast of the Ascension is transferred to the seventh Sunday.
I have done this for greater coherence with the opening prayer.

How to serve better –

Homily on the Prayer over the Gifts of the ninth Sunday in Ordinary Time by James G. Leachman OSB

Today I comment on the prayer over the gifts that we shall pray shortly. Its goal for me is "that we may be enlightened by the mysteries which we serve"; I do not want to be stuck in demanding that others serve me. I want my service to bring me enlightenment for better service of others.

The prayer first states what we are doing; trusting God's kindness we assemble, and our intention is that we may venerate. But there is a further purpose to all of this; that, grace ever enlightening, through our serving at the Eucharist our whole lives may be enlightened by God.

Source. This prayer shows the Church's creativity and innovativity; first the prayer is a new composition for the *Missale Romanum* 1970, formed by editing three phrases from different prayers in the *Veronense Sacramentary*, dated 600-625; second, each time a prayer is proclaimed it is a new revelation of the Church's response to God in the power of the Spirit.

Step 1 Motive 1: The foundation of our celebration of the Eucharist and of our Christian lives is God's loyalty and mercy. The prayer begins with the participial phrase, *In tua pietate confitentes*: "Trusting in your loyalty". *'Pietas'* refers to the dutiful respect reciprocated between those bound by social ties – as commander and troops, parents and children, spouses, God and the faithful. Thus there is already at the beginning of the prayer an act of cooperation with God by our trusting in the loyalty of God already shown towards us.

Step 2 (Premise 1): The context or setting

---

prayer over the gifts
Ninth Sunday in Ordinary Time

God our Father,
teach us to cherish the gifts
that surround us.
Increase our faith in you
and bring our trust to its
promised fulfilment
in the joy of your kingdom.
(*The Roman Missal*,
Collins, London, 1974)

In tua pietate confitentes, Domine,
cum muneribus ad altaria veneranda
concurrimus, ut, tua purificante nos
gratia, iisdem quibus famulamur
mysteriis emundemur.
(*Missale Romanum*,
Città del Vaticano, 2002)

*Translation by author
for study purposes:*
Trusting in your loyalty, O Lord,
we assemble with gift-offices for
venerating the altars, in order that, as
your grace purifies us, we may be
cleansed by the same mysteries,
which we serve

---

of our trusting in God's loyalty is the statement of what we are doing in this liturgy, that, *cum muneribus… concurrimus*, "we assemble with gift-offices". The *munera*, gift-offices consist in our gifts for the poor, the bread and wine for the Eucharist and also our offices or ministries, liturgical in the assembly and diaconal in the world.

Step 3 (Purpose 1): Why do we gather with gifts? Our intent is expressed by the gerundive *ad altaria veneranda*, literally "for venerating the altars", that we may venerate the altars.

Here *altaria* refers to the "altars", or the locations where gifts are exchanged between God and humanity. These *altaria*

not how better to be served

are many. The primary altar is the *christological* altar of Jesus' body, for the Word "assumed our mortal humanity that we might share divine life". Second: we are Christ's body and so we exercise our baptismal priesthood as the "altar of Christ's body", Third: during the Eucharist the church gathers at the *architectural* altar, Fourth: our lives of witness and service in the world constitute the *cosmological* altar. Fifth: the *axiological* altar at which our status is changed and we are counted worthy to stand here (Eucharistic Prayer II), and finally sixth: at the *maturational* altar where we are changed from child to adult, to spouse of God.

Summary: This is what we are invited to do in this liturgical celebration: to assemble with gifts for venerating at the many altars.

Transition: We do all this first part trusting that God in his kindness will bring about a further gift, a further invitation to cooperate with God's enabling gift of self, leading to our further maturation in the faith.

Step 4 (Premise 2): The second half of the prayer is one big purpose clause; but nestled within it is an ablative absolute *tua purificante nos gratia*: "as your grace purifies us". God's grace purifying us is the setting for this further gift that leads us beyond the mechanics of this celebration.

The phrase *tua purificante nos gratia*: "as your grace purifies us" does not detail what sort of purification is intended: scouring, bleaching, dry cleaning, washing or flushing, but I prefer the latter. When a heavy shower of rain cleanses a stream, – then we are able to clearly see every fish, ripple and stone in it. When God purifies all that we are and do and bring – we too are made more transparent: more self-

aware of inappropriate behaviour to be changed, of the seeds of good behaviour to be nurtured and of obstacles to overcome.

So, we come to see the presence of God – not only in the sacraments, but in our ministries, not only the exercising of our baptismal priesthood at the "altars", but in our whole lives of service.

We are helped to mature psychologically (see my article, *The Tablet*, Christmas 2008), and to create a new identity through every good action we are accomplishing, for every good action is open and transparent to myself, to others and to God who is their origin and completion.

Step 5 (Motive 2): (*quibus famulamur* – the mysteries which we are serving). A second phrase nestled within the purpose clause is the relative phrase *quibus famulamur*: "which we serve". As we said, our serving the mysteries is our cooperation with purifying grace, our maturational step ahead, our axiological change from served to servant. Thus, it is our serving which becomes God's motive for cleansing us. It is through our serving at the several altars of life, through our bringing gifts for the poor and for the Eucharist, through our exercising our baptismal priesthood in the assembly and in our daily lives that God is able to purify the vision of each one of us.

Serving the mysteries being celebrated is the motive for God's purifying us. Yet this serving, "*famulamur*", one of the very gift-offices, which we bring to the altar to be transformed – is to be transformed. Not only is our moral behaviour, but also the way we minister liturgically, and the way we see ministry to be transformed, clarified and enlightened as we mature – from being served to serving others; from seeing the full, conscious and active participation of the whole assembly as being primarily visual and auditory to being fully ministerial.

Step 6 (Purpose 2): *ut, … iisdem … mysteriis emundemur*: literally "in order that … we may be cleansed by the same mysteries".

From trust in God's loyalty we are brought first to assemble with our gifts-ministries at the altars – with the goal that our vision will be further purified. God's intent is that we be enlightened by the mysteries at which we serve.

Summary. The prayer presents stages of maturation for those celebrating the liturgy. First we trust, then we assemble and then we venerate the exchanges between God and humanity. Though our cooperation with divine self-revelation and self-gift, we are changed by serving the mysteries. As the intentions of our self-gift (*munus* as gift and ministry) are clarified, we mature in our capacity to receive the gift of God and to give ourselves even more fully in response.

We find links between the words *purificante* and *emundemur* with early theological strands in the third and fourth centuries, frequently overlooked. Let me give one example.

In the writings of St Ephrem the Syrian, Doctor of the Church, we find a similar hermeneutic of luminosity and enlightenment to that which we find in our prayer. Ephrem uses the word *shaphya* (bright, clear, limpid lucid, luminous) to describe the mind or heart of Christians united with God through transformation and the imagery of the "luminous eye" to describe how the inner eyes of the mind function by means of faith.

The presence of sin darkens this inner eye by keeping out the light of faith, and so, in order that this inner eye may see properly it needs to be kept clear and clean. The eyes of Mary were clean and clear and the Syriac word "*shaphya*" includes clear,

pure, limpid and lucid, as with a pure stream of water, or luminous and bright as was Jesus to his disciples at his Transfiguration.

This luminosity, clarity, enlightenment is given to us too in our prayer as we cooperate with the working of God's grace, trusting, assembling honouring and serving.

We touch here too on a presupposition of catholic theology consciously recovered by Anglicans, later by Cardinal John Henry Newman, and earlier in the 17th C. renaissance of Christian Platonism, itself successor to the "long reign of Nominalism through the reformation", that we have access to the divine by considering the facts of this world. The Anglican pastor, George Herbert's hymn "teach me my God and King" has a verse reflecting this theology, that bypasses Scholastic terminology of causality.

A man that looks on glass
on it may stay his eye
or if he pleaseth through it pass
and then the heaven espy.

The prayer presents stages of maturation for those celebrating the liturgy, praying and offering the sacrifices of our daily lives lived "in the Spirit" (*Lumen gentium* 34). As the intentions of our self-gift (*munus* as gift-ministry) are clarified, we mature in our capacity to receive the gift of God's self and to give ourselves more fully in response.

Thus, God's loyalty (*pietas*) clarifies, illuminates and enlightens our intentions that we may be prepared to see God not only in the celebration of the mysteries, but also in the manner in which we celebrate, in those we serve and in our manner of serving others day by day. ∎

This homily was given in Italian at the conventual Mass at Sant'Anselmo, Rome

Liturgy – our offering

Homily on the Prayer over the Gifts of the fourth Sunday of Advent by Daniel P. McCarthy OSB

prayer over the gifts
Fourth Sunday of Advent

Lord, fill our hearts with your love, and as you revealed to us by an angel the coming of your Son as man, so lead us through his suffering and death to the glory of his resurrection.
(*The Roman Missal*, Collins, London, 1974)

Altari tuo, Domine, superposita munera Spiritus ille sanctificet, qui beatae Mariae viscera sua virtute replevit.
(*Missale Romanum*, Città del Vaticano, 2002)

Translation by author for study purposes:
May that Spirit, Lord, which filled the womb of blessed Mary with its power, sanctify the gifts placed on your altar.

The prayer over the gifts assigned to the Mass today says, and I translate:

May that Spirit, Lord,
which filled the womb of blessed Mary
with its power,
sanctify the gifts placed on your altar.

This prayer is astounding for linking the annunciation of the Angel to Mary, and thus the incarnation of the Word made flesh, with the gifts we are soon to place on the altar. The annunciation is linked with the presentation of the gifts by the Spirit's action in each.

The prayer refers to gifts having been placed upon God's altar. These gifts of bread and wine are the fruit of divine and human cooperation for God gives life to the grain and vine, and, with the help of human cultivation, the plants mature until they ripen in abundance. Upon harvest, the grain and grape are worked by human hands and feet, and then the gift of fermentation and leaven bring about a further change in the loaf and in the wine, and these products of human manufacture take on their own life of maturation.

In offering bread and wine to God, we offer this product of our human cooperation with divine gift. Thus, these gifts express the human response of self-gift to God and neighbour, which, in turn, becomes the motive for the Spirit's sanctifying action.

The reference to the sanctifying action of the Spirit is new to the post-Vatican II text of this prayer. Previously the prayer had the verb *assumat*, "may the Spirit assume", corresponding to the use of this

prayer on the feast of the Annunciation, when the eternal Word assumed our mortal flesh, but now the prayer has the verb *sanctificet*, "may the Spirit sanctify". This shift from "may the Spirit assume" to "may the Spirit sanctify" corresponds to the introduction of an explicit reference to the sanctifying work of the Spirit in the new Eucharistic Prayers composed after the Second Vatican Council, a reference never introduced into the Roman Canon, now Eucharistic Prayer I.

Thus, in a few moments we shall pray, and I translate literally:

May that Spirit, Lord,
which filled the womb of blessed Mary
with its power,
sanctify the gifts placed on your altar.

The same sentiment as is expressed in this prayer is also expressed in the architecture of both the St. Scholastica Chapel just down the corridor from here, and of this choir chapel.

In the St. Scholastica Chapel, at the four corners of the altar there arise four monoliths that support four arches spanning from one pillar to the other, all of which is surmounted by a spherical dome. This structure over the altar is called a *ciborium*. As an aside, what we commonly call a *ciborium*, the lidded container for conserving consecrated hosts in the tabernacle, is properly called a *pyx*.

The *ciborium* over the altar in the St. Scholastica chapel is surmounted by a dome, that is part of a sphere. The sphere expresses architecturally the infinity and perfection of God. The sphere is cut-off on all four sides, forming four arches that connect the four pillars, each arch is in turn part of a circle, again an architectural way of expressing the eternity of God. Taken together, the image is of the heavens inbreaking above the altar. To reinforce this, at the highest point of each arch is a medallion of the victorious lamb that was slain.

In the ceiling of the dome, at the highest point underneath, an image of the Holy Spirit is traditionally located, as if the Spirit were inbreaking from the arching heavens and descending upon the altar. The *ciborium*, then, with this image of the Spirit is the architectural projection of the descent of the Holy Spirit proper to all sacramental action. This is expressed in the prayer over the gifts which says: "May that Spirit sanctify the gifts placed upon your altar".

That full *ciborium* structure in St. Scholastica's chapel is echoed in this choir chapel in the conch of the apse. The ribs of the conch express the inbreaking and descent of the Spirit in the sacramental action that was once celebrated on the old altar still against the wall immediately below the conch.

As the dome and the arch are the architectural projection of the eternity and perfection of God and of the holy Spirit's action during the liturgy, so too the architectural projection of humanity is an altar in the shape of a cube. A cube is formed by taking a sphere and breaking its unlimited curve to form right angles and straight lines of equal length. As such, the cube is derived from the sphere, yet limited and broken. The cube, furthermore, offers access from the four corners of creation.

Many ancient altars were once in the shape of a cube, as was that of Hagia Sophia in Constantinople and in Rome at St. Paul's outside the walls, which was subsequently augmented to sarcophagal shape to express the death of the Lord.

The altar in the St. Scholastica chapel is sarcophagal in shape, and is part of an ensemble that begins with the crucified one, then continues with the sepulchre shaped altar, from which rises on the height of each arch the victorious lamb that was slain, and the descent of the Spirit expressed in the image and geometry of the *ciborium*.

The new altar in this choir chapel, however, is cubic in its outer dimensions, not only offering access from all four sides, but also expressing the finite and broken human form derived from the divine perfection.

Thus, in the prayer over the gifts we ask the Spirit to make holy the gifts placed upon the Lord's altar. The gifts, already the product of divine and human cooperation expressing the offering of ourselves to God and neighbour, are placed on the altar. This simple gesture is expressive of finite humanity, formed in the image of divine perfection, offering itself back to God as self-gift. Having placed the gifts on the altar, we pray that the Spirit sanctify the gifts, which is architecturally expressed by the *ciborium* surmounting the altar with its gifts.

Just as the ritual of offering gifts is projected architecturally in the cubic altar, and just as the ritual of extending our hands over the gifts or over one another when invoking the Spirit is projected architecturally by the *ciborium*, so too the prayer this Sunday gives voice first to the offering of gifts and then to the invocation of the Spirit. Moreover, the concurrence between the prayer and the architecture renders the altar and ciborium as the reverberation of the Word; they are expressive of the word and rite even while the liturgy is not being celebrated.

We have said, however, that this prayer links the annunciation with the preparation of the gifts, for just as the Spirit filled the womb of blessed Mary with its power, so too we pray that the Spirit sanctify the gifts placed upon this altar. Thus, the void between a cubic altar and its *ciborium* evokes the womb of blessed Mary filled by the power of the same Spirit as sanctifies our gifts. To enter into this space, to gather at the altar, is to pray that we too, not merely as men and women, but our full humanity in all its diversity may be transformed by the power of this same Spirit.

Furthermore, there is a tradition, represented by Ephrem the Syrian (c. 306-373), that blessed Mary conceived the Word through her ear. Thus, we have the Word and the Spirit, the rite and their architectural reverberation.

The transformation of the entire assembly in the power of the Spirit is further projected architecturally by the *ciborium* over the entire assembly, that is by the dome of the church, which, like the *ciborium* over the altar, traditionally has an image of the Spirit at the highest point of its ceiling, with rays coming down upon the entire liturgical assembly. Like the emptiness between the altar and *ciborium*, the emptiness of this hall is filled by the proclamation of the Word, the self-manifestation

of Christ as gift, and the Spirit helps us to respond by offering ourselves as gift to God and neighbour.

This prayer also implies a developmental process of maturation in the faith. To be sure, there is a sequential process whereby first the gifts are offered then the Spirit sanctifies the gifts. Yet, because this process happens time and again in our lives, the developmental process of Christian maturation presented in this prayer is less one of sequential steps as the maturation of we who celebrate the rite, for the prayer links our placing the gifts on the altar with the Annunciation of our Lord in the nuptial chamber of blessed Mary where the Word put on our flesh that we may put on the Spirit, and in that Word the fullness of divinity wed the fullness of our humanity. As Cyril of Jerusalem (c. 315-386) says, we are the offspring of that nuptial chamber, who come to feast first as infants at the breast on the body and blood of Christ (*Patrologia Graeca*, ed. J.P. Migne, Paris 32,1100). But then, as we mature in the faith and become adult daughters and sons; we are called to enter the same bridal chamber as spouse. This we do ritually in the rite of monastic profession when the sister comes under the *ciborium* and, placing her vows formula on the book of the Gospels, that is on the word, signs her name to her vows formula, thereby offering herself in the power of God's transforming Spirit upon this altar to God. This happens every Eucharist when we approach the altar to feast on the body and blood of Christ who put on our flesh that we might put on the Spirit.

Let us enter, therefore in reverence before this mystery of our salvation. ∎

This homily was given on the Fourth Sunday of Advent during the conventual liturgy of the sisters of Mount St. Scholastica Monastery, Atchison, Kansas, by Daniel McCarthy, O.S.B. The homily was given in the choir chapel, but refers to the ciborium and sarcophagal altar in the large chapel of St. Scholastica, and was first published as: "Liturgy – Our Offering" Monastic Liturgy Forum Newsletter 19: 3 (Spring 2008) 1-4.

To mutual self-gift through service

Homily on the Prayer over the Gifts of the feast of the Most Holy Trinity by Daniel P. McCarthy OSB

As we celebrate the mutual self-gift in love of the Triune Unity, we pray that through our ministries of service, we may be fully formed as gifts to God.

Such is the vision of the prayer over the gifts assigned to the liturgy today. This prayer begins with the ministries of our service, and these ministries of our service, in turn, become the means through which God brings us to mature self-gift.

The text of this prayer over the gifts from antiquity until the *Missale Romanum* of 1970 had a variant of this phrase in Latin:

Sanctifica... huius oblationis hostiam,

"Sanctify the sacrifice of this oblation".

This sentence was changed in the *Missale Romanum* of 1970 to read in Latin:

Sanctifica... haec munera nostrae servitutis,

"Sanctify... these ministries of our service".

With the substitution of the phrase "the sacrifice of this oblation" with "these ministries of our service", the cultic emphasis of the prayer changed to one of diaconal service.

What is it to serve, then? The apostle exhorts us saying: "Let the same mind be in you that was in Christ Jesus, who, though he was in the form of God, did not regard equality with God as something to be exploited, but emptied himself, taking the form of a slave, being born in human likeness" (Philippians 2:5-7).

---

prayer over the gifts
Most Holy Trinity

Lord our God, make these gifts holy, and through them make us a perfect offering to you.
(*The Roman Missal*, Collins, London, 1974)

Sanctifica, quaesumus, Domine Deus noster, per tui nominis invocationem, haec munera nostrae servitutis, et per ea nosmetipsos tibi perfice munus aeternum.
(*Missale Romanum*, Città del Vaticano, 2002)

Translation by author for study purposes:
Make holy these gifts of our service, we ask, O Lord our God, through the invocation of your name, and through them bring our very selves to perfection as an eternal gift to you.

Christ who came as a servant will return again at the end of time as a servant, for in the Gospel of Luke we find the passage: "Blessed are those slaves whom the master finds alert when he comes; truly I tell you, he will fasten his belt and have them sit down to eat, and he will come and serve them" (Luke 12:37). In the heavenly banquet, Christ will serve us.

In his first coming Christ came as a servant, revealing the self-emptying love of God who gives himself to us as a servant, that we might mature to such self-transcending love as to serve our neighbour. In his second coming Christ will come to serve, and so our hopes our longings for the heavenly banquet find their fulfilment now in our ministries of service.

Our memories and hopes, anamnesis and eschatology, revelation and its fulfilment, all impinge upon serving others not upon our being served by others.

Our Omnipotent God serves us through self-emptying love, we creatures serve God and neighbour as we mature to self-transcending love.

How, then, do we mature in the ministries of our service, that we may become gifts to God? According to the prayer over the gifts today the beginning of our maturation to the full stature of gift to God, the first step is to perform ministries of service. These become the means through which God brings us to perfection as gifts to God. Our beginning to serve is not the end product of our formation, as if paying attention exclusively to ourselves could somehow bring us to the point, once our formation is perfected, when we might begin to serve others. Rather, we are formed by serving others. We come to Christian maturity through the school of service. God uses our ministries of service to bring us to mature formation.

How do we mature, then, to become eternal gifts to God? I believe that through acts of service we learn to discern within

ourselves the difference between true self-gift from its many imitations and imposters.

By serving, we come to see ourselves more clearly, to discern our own competing intentions. By our serving others, we are purified of what poses within us as if it were self-gift so that we may come to the maturity of self-gift that we celebrate today.

For, what is the Circumincession (*perichoresis*) of the Triune God other than pure and mutual self-gift of the triune unity. We are drawn into this mutual self-gift through the ministries of our service. It seems to me that God's self-gift to us and our response in self-gift to God, while incomparable in their difference, are made in a certain way "mutual" by the Word's self-emptying to become a servant that we, purified of intention through ministries of our service, might learn self-transcending love and so come to share in the divine life through Christ who comes among us as one who serves. ∎

Patrologia Graeca, ed. J.P. Migne, Paris 32,1100.

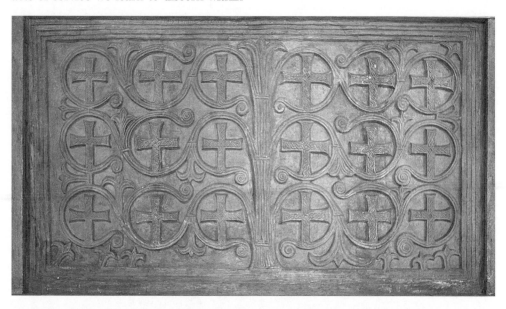

Scriptural index

Names index

About the authors

Fr Daniel P. McCarthy OSB

is a monk of St Benedict's Abbey, Atchison, Kansas. At the Pontifical Institute of Liturgy, recently, he successfully defended his doctoral thesis, which presents a theology of presiding in the liturgical assembly from an analysis of the history and models of the presidential chair. He now teaches liturgy at the Pontifical Beda College and writes while living in Rome. He has also published on the celebration of evening prayer for the dead in the parish. He has recently completed a series of commentaries on the prayers over the gifts. His commentaries on the prayers after communion currently appear in *The Tablet*. He is co-director of *Appreciating the Liturgy* and DREI publishing and co-editor of the series *Liturgiam Aestimare*: *Appreciating the Liturgy*.

Fr James G. Leachman OSB

is a monk of St Benedict's Abbey, Ealing, London, who teaches and writes in Rome and is also principal of The Benedictine Study and Arts Centre, Ealing Abbey in London. He is co-director of *Appreciating the Liturgy* and DREI publishing for the study of the liturgical books mandated by the Second Vatican Council and co-editor of the series *Liturgiam Aestimare*: *Appreciating the Liturgy*, one of the goals of the same project. He writes in *Ecclesia Orans* on the liturgy of the Church of England and elsewhere on of Rite of Christian Initiation of Adults. He edited the volume *The Liturgical Subject*: *Subject, Subjectivity and the Human Person in Contemporary Liturgical Discussion and Critique*, SCM Press, London 2008

The authors jointly edited the book:
Appreciating the Collect: *An Irenic Methodology*,
ed. J.G. Leachman – D.P. McCarthy
(Documenta rerum ecclesiasticarum instaurata),
St. Michael's Abbey Press, Farnborough, England 2008:

Information on DREI publishing is available on-line both at:
http://web.mac.com/danielmccarthyosb/iWeb/DREI/Welcome.html
and at: http://www.bsac.ac.uk/DREIseries/DREIindex.htm

Bibliography

A. Holy Scripture

Biblia Sacra: *Iuxta vulgatam versionem*, ed. R. Gryson, Deutsche Bibelgesellschaft, Stuttgart ⁴1994.

The Holy Bible Containing the Old and New Testaments with the Apocryphal / Deuterocanonical Books, New Revised Standard Version, Oxford UP, New York – Oxford 1989.

B. Research tools

BRUYLANTS, P., *Les oraisons du Missel Romain, texte et histoire* (Études liturgiques 2 vol.), Mont César, Louvain 1952.

Corpus orationum, 14 vol., ed. E. Moeller – J.-M. Clément – B.C. 't Wallant (Corpus christianorum series latina 160-160 M), Brepols, Turnhout 1992-2004.

DESHUSSES, J., – B. DARRAGON, *Concordances et Tableaux pour l'étude des grands Sacramentaires*, 3 vol., Editions Universitaires, Fribourg 1982-83.

GILDERSLEEVE, B.L, - G. LODGE, *Gildersleeve's Latin Grammar*, Bolchazy-Carducci, Wauconda IL 2003, reprint of ³1985.

LEWIS, C.T., – C. SHORT, *A Latin Dictionary*, Oxford UP, Oxford – New York 1879, reprinted 1995.

C. Liturgical sources

The Eucharistic Prayer of Addai and Mari, ed. A. Gelston, Clarendon Press, Oxford 1992.

"Hadrianum ex authentico", *Le Sacramentaire Grégorien*, 3 vol., ed. J. Deshusses (Spicilegium Friburgense 16), Éditions universitaires, Fribourg ³1992, 1, 83-348.

Liber sacramentorum gellonensis, textus, ed. A. Dumas (Corpus christianorum series latina 159), Brepols, Turnhout 1981.

Liber sacramentorum paduensis, ed. A. Catella – F. dell'Oro – A. Martini (Bibliotheca Ephemerides Liturgicae, Subsidia 131. Monumenta italiae liturgica 3), Centro Liturgico Vincenziano edizioni liturgiche, Rome 2005.

Liber sacramentorum romanae aeclesiae ordinis anni circuli (*Sacramentarium Gelasianum*), ed. L.C. Mohlberg – L. Eizenhöfer – P. Siffrin (Rerum ecclesiasticarum documenta. Series maior, Fontes 4), Herder, Rome ¹1960, ³1980.

Missale Ambrosianum iuxta ritum Sanctae Ecclesiae Mediolanensis ex decreto sacrosancti Oecumenici Concilii Vaticani II instauratum auctoritate Ioannis Colombo Sanctae Romanae Ecclesiae Presbyteri Cardinalis Archiepiscopi Mediolanensis promulgatum, Centro Ambrosiano di Documentazione e di Studi Religiosi, Milan 1981.

Missale Gothicum, ed. L.C. Mohlberg (Rerum ecclesiasticarum documenta. Series maior, Fontes 5), Herder, Rome 1961.

Missalis Romani, editio princeps Mediolani anno 1474 prelis mandata, ed. A. Ward – C. Johnson (Bibliotheca Ephemerides Liturgicae, Subsidia 78, Instrumenta Liturgica Quarreriensia, Supplementa 3), Centro Liturgico Vincenziano edizioni liturgiche, Rome 1996.

Missale Romanum, editio princeps (1570), ed. M. Sodi – A.M. Triacca (Monumenta liturgica Concilii Tridentini 2), Libreria editrice Vaticana, Città del Vaticano 1998.

Missale Romanum ex decreto SS. Concilii Tridentini restitutum summorum pontificum cura recognitum, editio typica, Typis polyglottis Vaticanis, Città del Vaticano 1962.

Missale Romanum ex decreto sacrosancti Oecumenici Concilii Vaticani II instauratum auctoritate Pauli PP. IV promulgatum, editio typica, Typis polyglottis Vaticanis, Città del Vaticano ¹1970.

Missale Romanum ex decreto Sacrosanti Oecumenici Concilii Vaticani II instauratum auctoritate Pauli PP. VI promulgatum Ioannis Pauli PP. II cura recognitum, editio typica tertia, Typis Vaticanis, Città del Vaticano ³2002.

Rituale Romanum ex decreto Sacrosancti Oecumenici Concilii Vaticani II instauratum auctoritate Pauli PP. VI promulgatum, Ordo Initiationis Christianae Adultorum, Typis polyglottis Vaticanis, Città del Vaticano 1972.

"Le Rotulus de Ravenne", in *Corpus orationum 11. Addenda et corrigenda; indices; initia et clausulae orationum*, ed. E. Moeller – J.-M. Clément – B.C. 't Wallant (Corpus christianorum series latina 160 J), Brepols, Turnhout 1999, 17-26.

Sacramentarium Bergomense: Manoscritto del secolo IX della Biblioteca di S. Alessandro in Colonna in Bergamo, ed. A. Paredi (Monumenta Bergomensia 6), Fondazione Amministrazione Provinciale, Bergamo 1962.

Sacramentarium Veronense, ed. L.C. Mohlberg – L. Eizenhöfer – P. Siffrin (Rerum ecclesiasticarum documenta. Series maior, Fontes 1), Herder, Rome³ 31978.

D. **Translation of Liturgical Sources**

The Roman Missal, revised by decree of the Second Vatican Council and published by the authority of Paul VI, official English texts, Collins, London 1974.

The Roman Ritual, revised by decree of the Second Vatican Council and published by the authority of Paul VI: Rite of Christian Initiation of Adults, approved for use in England and Wales, Scotland, International Commission on English in the Liturgy, Geoffrey Chapman, London 1987.

E. **Magisterial Sources**

Decrees of the Ecumenical Councils, 2 vol., ed. N. Tanner, Sheed & Ward – Georgetown UP, London-Washington 1990.

F. **Studies**

TALLEY, T., *The Origins of the Liturgical Year*, Liturgical Press (Pueblo Book), Collegeville MN ²1991.

G. *Liturgiam aestimare* : Appreciating the Liturgy

Appreciating the Collect.
An Irenic Methodology,
ed. J.G. Leachman – D.P. McCarthy
(Documenta rerum ecclesiasticarum
instaurata. Liturgiam aestimare:
Appreciating the Liturgy 1) St. Michael's
Abbey Press, Farnborough, England 2008.

LEACHMAN, J.G., "A new Liturgical
Hermeneutic: Christian Maturation by
Developmental Steps", Paper given at
Catholic Theological Association of Great
Britain, 11 September 2008, *New
Blackfriars* (2009) in press.

LEACHMAN, J.G., – D.P. McCARTHY, "The
Formation of the Ecclesial Person
through Baptismal Preparation and the
Celebrations in the OICA:
The Collects for the Scrutinies", in *The
Liturgical Subject: Subject, Subjectivity,
and the Human Person in Contemporary
Liturgical Discussion and Critique* (Faith
in Reason 7), ed. J. Leachman, SCM,
London 2008, 172-200.

LEACHMAN, J.G., – D.P. McCARTHY,
"Preparation for the Piazza:
The Preface of the Second Scrutiny (the
Fourth Sunday of Lent):
The Mystagogical Formation of the
Neophytes and the Assembly",
Studia Liturgica 38. (2008) 114-33.

McCARTHY, D.P., *Listen to the Word*:
*Commentaries on Selected Prayers
Opening Prayers of Sundays and Feasts*, a
weekly series, *The Tablet*
(18 March 2006 – 4 March 2007,
thereafter occasionally).

McCARTHY, D.P., *Listen to the Word*:
*Commentaries on Selected Prayers over
the Gifts of Sundays and Feasts*, a weekly
series, *The Tablet* (1 December 2007 –
22 November 2008).

McCARTHY, D.P., *Listen to the Word*:
*Commentaries on Selected Prayers after
Communion of Sundays and Feasts*, a
weekly series, *The Tablet*
(29 November 2008 – present).

McCARTHY, D.P., *Listen to the Word*:
*Commentaries on Selected Opening
Prayers of Sundays and Feasts* as they
appeared in *The Tablet*, 18 March 2006 –
19 May 2007, and published privately,
Rome 2007. ∎